CAREER OPPORTUNITIES FOR WRITERS

THIRD EDITION

R<small>OSEMARY</small> E<small>LLEN</small> G<small>UILEY</small>

Facts On File®

AN INFOBASE HOLDINGS COMPANY

Career Opportunities for Writers: Third Edition

Facts On File, Inc.
460 Park Avenue South
New York NY 10016

Library of Congress Cataloging-in-Publication Data

Guiley, Rosemary.
    Career opportunities for writers / Rosemary Ellen Guiley.—3rd
ed.
       p. cm.
    Includes bibliographical references and index.
    ISBN 0-8160-3203-3.—ISBN 0-8160-3204-1 (pbk.)
    1. Authorship—Vocational guidance. I. Title.
PN151.G84 1995
808'.02—dc20   94-41095

Facts On File books are available at special discounts when purchased in bulk quantities for businesses, associations, institutions or sales promotions. Please call our Special Sales Department in New York at 212/683-2244 or 800/322-8755.

Jacket design by Amy Beth Gonzalez

This book is printed on acid-free paper.

Printed in the United States of America

VB FOF 10 9 8 7 6 5 4 3 2 1

CONTENTS

PREFACE
How to Use This Book

Purpose

Career Opportunities for Writers presents one of the most comprehensive catalogs of writing jobs available in a single volume. It does not focus on a single field of writing, but covers numerous jobs in eight major fields. Jobs are not merely summarized in a paragraph or two but described in detail, including duties, salaries, prerequisites, employment and advancement opportunities, organizations to join, and opportunities for women and minorities. It is intended to help both aspiring writers who are seeking entry-level jobs as well as experienced writers who are interested in making career changes.

Generally the jobs included in this book are open to persons with appropriate educational credentials (usually a bachelor's degree) and up to five or so years of experience. These are predominantly entry- and middle-level positions, those that are available to the largest number of candidates.

Sources of Information

Research for this book included the author's own experience, interviews with numerous professionals in various fields, and surveys, reports, facts, and other information obtained from professional associations, trade unions, the federal government, and universities. The author has worked as a writer, journalist, or editor, either on staff or on a freelance basis, in newspaper and magazine journalism, advertising trade news and sales promotion, corporate communications, ghostwriting and collaboration, and scriptwriting.

The job descriptions are based on representative samples of actual job positions. In general, writing jobs are broad in their responsibilities, and they can vary greatly from one employer to another. In many cases, a writing job is what the employee makes of it. Jobs at small firms tend to be broader in scope than those in large, structured companies and organizations. The descriptions in this book note some of the wide ranges of duties and responsibilities for various types of jobs.

Organization of Material

This book has nine parts: eight cover different fields and industries that employ many writers; the last section consists of appendices listing educational institutions and scholarships, associations and unions, periodicals, and a bibliography of additional sources, all pertinent to writing careers. While most of the jobs listed are based solely on writing and editing skills, a few are writing-related; that is, in addition to substantial writing and editing skills, they require other skills or education. Some of the jobs that fall into this category are sales-oriented positions, research positions, and jobs requiring technical, legal, academic, or foreign-language training. The Introduction gives an overview of job opportunities for writers, as well as explaining employment trends for the next decade or so.

Section 8, which covers freelance opportunities, has been expanded in the third edition. This edition also includes more jobs directly related to computerized databases—some requiring computer-aided research skills, others in writing for or promoting databases. As more information is transmitted electronically, the ability to conduct research using computers and distribute information to specialized audiences via the information superhighway will become increasingly important to writers. Advances in technology also make it possible for freelancers to provide more sophisticated services.

Explanation of Job Descriptions

Each job description follows a basic format and is complete unto itself; the reader does not have to consult another section of the book to get a complete picture of a particular job. Therefore, readers may encounter some repetition from job to job within a given industry.

Jobs are listed by their predominant title, followed by a Career Profile, which summarizes main duties, alternate titles, salary ranges, employment prospects, advancement prospects, and prerequisites of education, experience, and special skills. A Career Ladder diagram shows a typical career path, including the positions above and below each job. If a job is entry level, school or other related positions are listed as preceding it.

The Position Description is a narrative that describes typical job duties and responsibilities, working hours and conditions, and optional duties that may or may not be part of an individual job. It covers peers and superiors, and it indicates the frequency of overtime or travel, wherever pertinent.

Salaries explains income ranges and the factors, such as individual skills, size of employer, or geographic location, that affect how much a particular job may pay. Salary ranges are based on averages, and readers may find positions that pay less or more than the figures cited in this book.

Readers will find particularly helpful the sections on Employment Prospects and Advancement Prospects. Some jobs may sound terrific or be very glamorous, but they also may be extremely difficult to obtain. Others may prove to be dead ends, with advancement difficult or impossible. These are important factors to weigh in any job search.

Education describes academic requirements for various jobs. In most cases, writers who have earned undergraduate degrees in liberal arts or communications will qualify; some jobs require other educational backgrounds. Graduate degrees are not often required but are increasingly advantageous for many jobs. At the opposite end of the spectrum, some writing jobs require only high school diplomas.

In addition to education, many jobs require prior experience. The Experience/Skills section describes what background is essential or helpful in competing for a job. Previous experience may not be required for many entry-level positions, but candidates who have had some kind of related experience—even on collegiate, volunteer, or community levels—often have significant competitive advantages. In addition, this section spells out the skills and qualities employers look for, attributes which enhance prospects for success in particular fields.

Most communicators—a generic term that includes writers, editors, and others in various communications jobs—do not belong to a union. Those who do, work for organized fields such as print and broadcast journalism, film and television entertainment, schools, and government. Even in those areas, unionization is not uniform throughout. Many do, however, belong to one or more professional associations, where they meet others who have similar jobs, exchange information and ideas, and make contacts. The Unions/Associations section, which ends each job description, lists the major associations of interest to professionals in a particular field, as well as the most likely unions, if any, that would represent them in wage negotiations.

Appendices

Appendix I, "Educational Institutions," lists colleges, universities, and educational institutions, in every state and the District of Columbia, which offer undergraduate degrees in major areas of communications—broadcasting, advertising, public relations, education, technical and specialized journalism, newspaper and magazine journalism, as well as courses in publishing. The list does not include every institution which offers courses or degrees in communications. The list also does not include two-year colleges, since most jobs require or give preference to degree-holders from four-year institutions.

The list gives each institution's address and telephone number, as well as the major programs, sequences, and courses of interest to writers.

Appendix II, "Professional, Industry, and Trade Associations and Unions," lists major organizations for writers, editors, and those in the writing-related fields included in this book.

Appendix III, "Major Trade Periodicals," groups such periodicals according to field or industry.

Finally, Appendix IV is a Bibliography of sources that give additional career and salary information.

ACKNOWLEDGMENTS

I would like to thank the Newspaper Association of America, which granted me generous access to its library at the Newspaper Center and supplied several helpful salary surveys. The Newspaper Guild also provided me with salary information; Professor Lee B. Becker of the School of Journalism at Ohio State University provided a copy of his 1992 survey of journalism school graduates, done with Gerald M. Kosicki.

Thanks also to Joe Pinder, press secretary to Rep. Jim Leach of Iowa; Elizabeth Stoloff Vehse of the University of Chicago alumni office; Anne Hinman Diffily, editor of the *Brown Alumni Monthly*; Helene Redmond, a graphic artist and freelance desktop publisher; Gary Craig, manager of Thomas Online at the Thomas Publishing Company; and Kathy Christensen of the Cable News Network library.

Thanks also to Jewel Bradstreet Heldman, who researched part of this book.

INTRODUCTION
The Job Outlook for Writers and Other Communicators

So you want to be a writer. Or maybe you write already, but want to try something new.

Perhaps you want to crouch in a musty newsroom, inkstains on your hands, ear tuned to a police scanner. Or maybe you want to speak indirectly to voters, telling them why the country should pass a bill, or wage a war, or vote for your boss.

You can extol the virtues of consumer goods. Or write a screenplay someone else will rewrite and someone else will change again, until finally an actor mouths words something like yours on the big screen.

Or maybe your prose will be little dots of light transmitted on the small screen of the computer.

Whatever it is you want to do, can afford to do, or have the talent to do, the jobs are there. You can probably make a better-than-average living, but unless you write that best-seller or Oscar-winning screenplay, don't plan on a fortune. And the more familiar you are with finance, economics, computers, or technical subjects, the better you will do. During the next 10 years, job prospects for writers and communicators should continue to grow in the service sector. Health, environmental-related areas, leisure, travel, and international trade should all grow.

Since the first edition of this book was published in 1983, many of the fields covered here have been transformed by computer technology and the ability to transmit information quickly via modem, fax, or electronic mail.

Traditional forms of the printed word—books, newspapers, and magazines—are scrambling to keep up with the new technology and assess how it helps or hurts them.

Increasingly specialized information can now be made available to smaller audiences at low cost. This has spawned thousands of specialized magazines; small publishing houses that, through desktop publishing, can produce titles for a small segment of the market; and computerized databases targeting financial investors or other small but sophisticated audiences.

No longer does the cost of printing information on paper force companies solely to seek mainstream audiences. And no longer do workers need to be tied to a central geographic location if they are equipped with a computer, modem, and fax.

In the past 10 years, the number of new computerized databases has grown almost 25 percent a year. During that same time, the number of consumer magazines has almost doubled, and thousands of small publishing companies have sprung up all over the country.

The public relations industry has also taken hold. Although public relations budgets suffer in poor economic times, the need for professional public relations services to polish images has been recognized by most institutions and is expected only to grow.

There has also been an increase in demand for people with skills to perform computer-aided research—librarians, researchers and information managers. Some newspapers are becoming information brokers on the side, selling their news articles to electronic databases and providing research services for a fee.

Financial wire services, with an affluent target audience of investors, flourished in the early 1990's, while other news organizations withered from lost advertising revenue during the recession.

Job prospects diminished for journalism and mass communications majors in the early 1990's. In 1992, unemployment for them held steady at around 16 percent, nearly double what it had been in 1988. Salaries also remained virtually frozen, representing a significant decline in earning capability from 1986.

About 33,000 to 34,000 students graduated in 1992 with bachelor's degrees in journalism or mass communications. Of these, only about half immediately found work in a communications field.

For these journalism school graduates, prospects seem to be best in the traditional field of print journalism. Of the media professions, print journalism offers more opportunities mainly because there are more newspaper jobs. Every burg and hamlet has its own newspaper; few have their own radio or television station. Many radio and television jobs also have little to do with news.

Two salary surveys found that in 1992–1993 print journalists made more than those in radio and television on the average.

But only 8 percent of journalism school graduates found work in the newspaper industry in 1992, according to a survey by Professor Lee B. Becker of the School of Journalism at Ohio State University.

Job satisfaction also decreased among journalists. According to a 1992 survey done by the Center for Survey Research at Indiana University's Bloomington campus, only 27 percent of journalists polled said they were very satisfied with their jobs, compared to almost 50 percent 20 years ago. About 20 percent said they expected to leave the profession within five years.

Growth within the newspaper industry is expected to take place in smaller publications, from an increase in small-town and suburban daily and weekly newspapers. The number of big-city dailies is expected to remain static. Only 35 newspapers in the country have circulations that exceed 250,000, and competition for jobs on them is stiff.

Of 1,700 daily newspapers in the United States, fewer than 200 have circulations of more than 100,000. Out of 5,000 weeklies, only two exceed that number.

The industry lost 10 daily newspapers in 1993, 13 in 1992, 19 in 1991, 9 in 1990 and 25 in 1989. Some of these suspended publication; others converted to weeklies or merged with other papers.

Tough economic times in the early 1990s also hurt job prospects in magazines, with salaries down and increased job duties for some positions.

Explosive growth in special-interest magazines resulted in a doubling in the number of consumer magazine titles in the past 15 years. Changes in printing technology reduced the cost of producing new magazines and enabled specialized magazines with relatively small circulations to be viable.

During the early 1990's, many of the specialized magazines folded as advertising dried up. Mergers and acquisitions added to the uncertainty of the job market.

More magazines are also going on-line, becoming available to subscribers over computer terminals. How this will affect the overall magazine industry remains to be seen.

Graduates looking for jobs in television and radio in the early 1990's had a harder time than graduates looking in print, public relations, or advertising. In 1993, television and radio salaries made moderate gains over inflation, regaining some ground that had been lost during the previous five years. About 6 percent of 1992 journalism school graduates found work in broadcasting. Competition for television jobs is intense.

Growth in radio and television should come from new stations and the growth of cable television systems. When compared to newspaper and television salaries, radio salaries ran a distant third.

Showing the popularity of "spin doctoring," more journalism school students majored in public relations for the past seven years than in print journalism and editing.

But this does not mean job prospects are better in public relations. The top 10 public relations companies cut their payrolls by an average of 7.5 percent in 1993.

About 11 percent of the 1992 graduates found work in either public relations or advertising. Public relations provided the weakest match between major and job found, a survey showed.

But salaries for recent graduates in public relations were slightly higher than for those in other specialities. As a relatively young industry, it is expected to continue to grow as emphasis on communications and information continues.

In advertising, mergers during the 1970s and '80s consolidated advertising agencies and reduced job opportunities. Entry-level opportunities are expected to remain good, but salary growth slowed during the early 1990's and advancement became quite competitive.

In this climate, job-jumpers seemed to do the best. Those who changed jobs frequently got bigger raises than those who stayed put. For those with salaries over $25,000, salary reviews were frequently stretched out to 18-month or more intervals.

Mergers and acquisitions also consolidated the number of book publishers serving as major players in the industry. There are now about six large publishers owned by major corporations. These six companies account for 60 percent of the industry's adult book revenues.

The book industry is marked by low salaries, limited advancement, and a salary gap between men and women in the same job.

But while employees in publishing may express some dissatisfaction with salaries, job satisfaction in this industry is high, according to a 1994 salary survey by *Publishers Weekly*. As with magazines, the center of this industry is in New York City.

Desktop publishing opened up new opportunities for small publishers, who can now produce an attractive, well-made book for a few thousand dollars. There are more than 40,000 publishers turning out books in the United States. Many smaller publishers develop books for tightly focused markets, and they are not necessarily based in New York City. (For example, *The Hunt for Red October,* Tom Clancy's first novel, was published in hardcover by the Naval Institute Press, a small, specialized publisher.)

While the Becker survey showed that minority journalism graduates fared no worse than white graduates in the job market, they also fared no better.

Competition remains stiff in the more glamorous fields of author, playwright, and screenwriter. Advances were high in the early 1990's for celebrity books or books by well-known authors, but in most other cases publishers were generally playing it safe.

Opportunities continued to be good for freelancers, especially those who offer multiple services. Businesses hurt by the bad economy tried to keep their staffs lean by sending work to be done "out-of-house." Computer technology also helped make at-home businesses viable with fax machines and modems.

Professionals and technical workers represented 12 percent of the temporary work force in 1992 and were the fastest-growing segment within it. In the past, traditional jobs offered enough comforts that people were not willing to leave them. Today, benefits packages are less generous and long-term job security is not guaranteed in most places, making it easier for people to decide to leave.

Freelancers in writing and communications specialties still do not make tremendous amounts of money, with the median gross income reported by members of the Editorial Freelancers Association about $25,000. Almost half the members reported making more money in 1992 than 1991, however.

Freelance income and workloads are often irregular and the uncertainty of work and pay require good sales skills, perseverance, self-discipline, organization, and financial management. Freelancers also have to invest in office equipment and bear the cost of running an office. Most freelancers are versatile and don't bank on a single market or type of work, as market needs can shift and contacts can be lost. Several years of experience in staff positions can provide a good background for a freelance career.

More than 75 percent of the Editorial Freelancers Association members are women; more than half said they would not take a full-time permanent job if one were offered. More than half of the membership also said they were overloaded with work some months and too idle in others. One in five had an appropriate amount of work each month; one in ten was swamped every month; and almost one in six needed more work every month.

While salaries might not be high in most writing or communications jobs, they are above average. The smaller the company, the lower the pay scale. Some entry-level jobs can pay as little as $12,000 a year. The Becker study of journalism majors found a median starting salary in 1992 of $18,200, somewhat less than the wage earned by the average American. In 1993, the average American earned a median of $24,076 a year.

The 1993 median for public relations specialists was $31,876; for editors and reporters, $29,848; and for technical writers, $37,440.

Salaries for experienced communications professionals were generally in the high twenties to mid-thirties. Women continue to experience pay gaps in most fields, especially at the senior levels. Salaries are more equal in journalism, where women and men make roughly the same in entry-level jobs; after this a pay gap develops, but remains smaller than in other sectors.

Whether you find your destiny in a cramped, messy newspaper office in some far-flung city, the ivy-covered halls of a distinguished university, or the buttoned-down boardrooms of corporate America, chances are you will find yourself in the company of creative, interesting people who influence the way other people think and feel.

The persuasive art of advertising, the clearheaded presentation of news, the loathed and loved business of image creation, and the lovely cadence of a poem all rely on the skillful manipulation of words for success.

Whatever kind of writing you find yourself doing, you may enjoy using your own creative skills and imagination to produce a work that informs, sells, entertains, and perhaps even changes the world.

MEDIA

NEWSPAPERS AND
NEWS SERVICES

COPY AIDE

CAREER PROFILE

Duties: Assist reporters and editors in minor news-gathering and editing tasks

Alternate Title(s): Editorial Assistant; Newsroom Assistant; Copy Assistant; Intern

Salary Range: $8,000 to $25,000

Employment Prospects: Fair

Advancement Prospects: Good

Prerequisites:
   Education—Undergraduate degree in journalism, communications, English, or liberal arts

   Experience—None

   Special Skills—Organization; writing; dealing with public

CAREER LADDER

```
┌─────────────────────────────┐
│   Journalist; Copy Editor    │
└─────────────────────────────┘

┌─────────────────────────────┐
│         Copy Aide            │
└─────────────────────────────┘

┌─────────────────────────────┐
│          College             │
└─────────────────────────────┘
```

Position Description

Copy aides, the lowest rung on the newsroom ladder, are jacks-of-all-trades. Most of them are journalism or communications students who are working at newspapers while enrolled in college; a few are graduates who've been unable to find jobs as reporters.

At one time, it was customary for all reporters to start out as copy aides. The job consisted primarily of running copy from reporters to editors, doing errands, and disseminating materials throughout the newsroom.

Today, with most copy transmitted electronically, the job of the copy aide has changed. Copy aides monitor the wire machines of news services and see that the right editors get the appropriate stories (called "ripping the wire"), act as newsroom receptionists, and perform general news-related tasks. The job can provide excellent entry-level training. For example, a copy aide may help a reporter with research by going through clips in the news library, may make routine phone calls to police and weather sources, and may write up obituaries and other small news items. Copy aides may work under the supervision of journalists or editors.

Enterprising copy aides can turn their jobs into full-fledged internships, accompanying reporters on assignments and eventually writing their own stories. Copy aides can also learn the duties of the copy desk, doing minor editing and headline writing.

Salaries

On unionized papers, top minimums for copy aides range from $8,000 to about $25,000, with even higher top minimums at some Canadian papers. Most aides make toward the lower end of the scale, however.

Employment Prospects

College programs and internships can lead to part- and full-time jobs as copy aides, though it is possible to get hired without help from a school. Many larger papers hire copy aides for evening and weekend work, which fits in with student schedules.

Advancement Prospects

Experience as a copy aide, particularly if the job involves research, writing, or editing tasks, can count heavily towards promotion to journalist or copy editor.

Education

Many copy aides are undergraduates in schools of journalism, communications, or liberal arts. Journalism study or background is desirable.

Experience/Skills

No experience is required to be a copy aide.

Unions/Associations

College students may join the Society for Collegiate Journalists; Quill and Scroll Society; and the collegiate chapters of the Society of Professional Journalists, and Women In Communications, Inc.

REPORTER SPECIALIST

CAREER PROFILE

Duties: Gather and report information about a specific area of expertise or "beat"; keep abreast of new developments in that area in an effort to become the newspaper's expert on the subject

Alternate Title(s): Beat Reporter, Journalist

Salary Range: $10,000 to $60,000+

Employment Prospects: Good

Advancement Prospects: Fair

Prerequisites:

Education—Undergraduate degree in journalism, communications, English, or liberal arts; a graduate degree or some advanced courses in the area of specialization may also be required

Experience—Several years as a general assignment reporter for a daily paper, with work displaying some expertise in the chosen specialization

Special Skills—Ability to write longer, in-depth "enterprise" stories; good writing skills; aggressiveness; persistence; good interpersonal relations; good research habits; organizational ability; self-discipline

CAREER LADDER

```
┌─────────────────────────────────┐
│       Reporter Specialist       │
└─────────────────────────────────┘

┌─────────────────────────────────┐
│  General Assignment Reporter    │
└─────────────────────────────────┘

┌─────────────────────────────────┐
│      Copy Aide; College         │
└─────────────────────────────────┘
```

Position Description

Unlike a general assignment reporter, who covers a wide range of stories at the discretion of an editor, a specialist covers a single area of expertise. A specialist also tries to stay abreast of developments in his or her field by developing sources, reading trade magazines, and taking courses.

For some specialties, larger papers may require a graduate degree. A business reporter may be asked to get a master's of business administration, or an education reporter may need a master's in education.

Reporters also cover geographic beats from outlying bureaus, but these jobs are generally given to less experienced reporters and resemble general assignment positions, in that a wide range of topics can be included. Bureau reporters often generate their own story ideas or field assignments from an editor.

Traditional "beats" or areas of specialization include courts, city hall, education, and police. However, as newspapers seek ways to remain interesting and relevant to a younger market that, as studies show, relies more on TV news to keep informed, beats such as health, environmental issues, ethics, and the family have started to appear.

Some newspapers expanded beat coverage into such areas as transportation, shopping, pets, and hobbies. The Orange County (California) *Register* created a position for a shopping mall reporter. The *Star Tribune* of Minneapolis added an ethics beat to its coverage, and other newspapers now have reporters covering traffic issues. In addition, a broad beat such as business may be broken down into smaller categories, such as insurance, banking, biotechnology, manufacturing, computer companies, etc.

Some of these specialty positions, usually added at the expense of general assignment positions, may not have survived the cutbacks brought by the recession in the early 1990s. But others, such as business, the environment, health, and science, have become standard at larger newspapers.

Beat reporters need to manage the beat—become acquainted with important news sources, monitor events, cover meetings, and look for stories of interest to the public. The reporter must keep editors informed of his or her activities and upcoming stories.

Beats are also generally long-term assignments, so journalists can build sources and expertise. Beat reporters work against deadlines on breaking stories. The number of deadlines varies with the size of the newspaper and the number of editions being put out, with larger papers having five or six deadlines per day, and smaller newspapers one or two.

Beat reporters are generally required to write longer, in-depth articles that require more research and interviewing. Work schedules change according to the demands of the business, but beat reporters are more likely to have regular hours.

But when a beat really heats up, that reporter could find him or herself working around the clock, on weekends or traveling to keep up with unfolding news. In sports, reporters often travel with the local teams during the season, working weeks without any days off and making up the extra time in the off-season.

Beat reporters sometimes still need to fill some less popular shifts, such as nights or weekends, or fill in as general assignment reporters if the newspapers is short of staff.

Salaries

Because specialists generally have more experience and training, they usually make more than entry-level journalists. Pay still varies widely. Even the smallest papers employ sports reporters (often at the entry level) and possibly business reporters, and often have low pay scales.

The 1993 median salary for reporters and editors in all fields (radio and television included) was $32,000. Two salary surveys—one done by Women in Communication, Inc. (WICI) in 1992–1993 and the other done by the Radio-Television News Directors Association (RTNDA) in 1993—found that print journalists make more than those in radio and television on average.

The WICI survey found print journalists to make about $5,000 more than broadcast journalists. The RTNDA survey found that except for television news anchors in major markets, print reporters made more than television reporters in comparable jobs.

The average top minimum for reporters represented by the Newspaper Guild in 1993 was $36,856 (reached after four or five years' experience); the average starting minimum was $23,872. Starting minimum at *The New York Times* was $60,265; starting minimum at the Battle Creek, Mich., *Enquirer* was $9,568.

The median salary for reporters with more than five years experience in 1993 was about $36,000 at newspapers with 100,000 to 150,000 circulation. Of 1,700 daily newspapers in the country, about 200 had circulations exceeding 100,000.

Employment Prospects

Employment of reporters is expected to grow about as fast as average for all occupations; however, much of this growth will come at the bottom—from an increase in small town and suburban daily and weekly newspapers. Small newspapers typically offer low salaries.

Other job openings will come from journalists leaving the field. The number of big city dailies is expected to be static, and the competition for jobs on them keen. Only 35 newspapers in the United States have circulations exceeding 250,000.

The industry is recovering from the recession, but lost 10 dailies in 1993, 13 in 1992, 19 in 1991, 9 in 1990, and 25 in 1989. Some of these papers shut down, some merged with other papers, and some converted to weekly publication.

In addition, journalists seemed less satisfied with their jobs in the early 1990s. According to a survey done by the Center for Survey Research at Indiana University's Bloomington campus in 1992, although salaries in journalism had improved, job satisfaction had declined and there was little growth in the workplace.

Only 27 percent of journalists surveyed said they were very satisfied with their jobs, compared to almost 50 percent saying that 20 years ago. More than a fifth said they intended to leave journalism within five years.

Advancement Prospects

Advancement prospects are fair. Specialists have more chances to move to larger newspapers than general assignment reporters. In addition, they may have good shots at becoming section editors or columnists, depending on their area of expertise. Those who handle highly specialized scientific or technical subjects will be at an advantage in the job market.

Education

This job generally requires an undergraduate degree in journalism, communications, English or liberal arts at a minimum. Specialists also often hold advanced degrees in subjects related to their area of expertise. An education reporter may need a master's degree in education, for example.

Experience/Skills

Good basic reporting skills are essential. Beat reporters must have a keen curiosity and sharp observational skills. They should feel comfortable dealing with and interviewing persons in positions of authority. They should know how to research and organize information and be able to explain complicated topics in a simple way. Speed, clarity, and accuracy are essential.

In addition, most specialized positions require several years of general reporting experience and some additional training in the area of specialization.

Unions/Associations

The Newspaper Guild is the primary union for print journalists. Professional associations include the Society of Professional Journalists; Newspaper Association of America; American Society of Journalists and Authors, Inc.; Associated Business Writers of America, Inc.; Asian-American Journalists Association; Association of Earth Science Editors; Aviation/Space Writers' Association; Construction Writers Association; Council of Biology Editors; Investigative Reporters and Editors; National Association of Hispanic Journalists; Outdoor Writers Association of America; National Turf Writers Association; Religion Newswriters Association; Society of American Travel Writers; and many others.

GENERAL ASSIGNMENT REPORTER

CAREER PROFILE

Duties: Gather and report information for news and feature stories on a wide variety of topics

Alternate Title(s):   Bureau Reporter; Journalist

Salary Range: $10,000 to $60,000+

Employment Prospects: Good

Advancement Prospects: Good

Prerequisites:

    Education—Undergraduate degree in journalism, communications, English, or liberal arts

    Experience—Work on a college publication or internship for small daily or weekly newspapers; minimum one to two years of experience for large dailies

    Special Skills—Aggressiveness; persistence; good interpersonal relations; good research habits; organizational ability; self-discipline

CAREER LADDER

```
┌─────────────────────────────────┐
│   Assistant Editor; Section Editor; │
│        Reporter Specialist          │
└─────────────────────────────────┘

┌─────────────────────────────────┐
│   General Assignment Reporter       │
└─────────────────────────────────┘

┌─────────────────────────────────┐
│       Copy Aide; College            │
└─────────────────────────────────┘
```

Position Description

General assignment reporters go to work not knowing exactly what they will be doing that day. If they work in the main newsroom, they find out from an assignment editor.

If they work in an outlying bureau covering a geographic territory or another city, they field assignments from a bureau chief, generate their own story ideas after making the rounds of their sources, or develop some combination of the two.

General assignment reporters need to work fast, meet deadlines, and switch gears smoothly as they move from one assignment to the next. Assignments may vary from covering a fire to a governmental meeting to interviewing a visiting celebrity. General assignment reporters often report on topics last covered by someone else. They need to quickly find and read through other stories on the topic and to follow all major stories appearing in the newspaper, even on days they don't work, so they can fill in at a moment's notice. On smaller newspapers or in bureaus, general assignment reporters may also take their own photographs, give assignments to freelance reporters (called stringers), and edit the resulting stories—or file from the scene of a breaking story with a portable computer or by dictating over the phone.

Because a general assignment reporter's wide-ranging duties help build skills in many areas, many newspapers require inexperienced reporters to work as general assignment reporters before considering them for a specialty or beat position.

Even plans to work on a long-range project can be disrupted by breaking news, making it hard to plan ahead. Night and weekend shifts are common. Deadline frequency depends on how many editions the newspaper prints, with deadlines around the clock at some large newspapers and one or two times a day on smaller dailies.

Salaries

The 1993 median salary for reporters and editors was $32,000. The average top minimum for reporters represented by the Newspaper Guild in 1993 was $36,856, reached after about four or five years of experience; the average starting minimum was $23,872.

The Guild figures cover a range from a low of $9,568 as the starting minimum for the Battle Creek, Mich., *Enquirer* to $60,265 at *The New York Times*.

A survey by Women in Communications, Inc. also showed that for 1992–1993, print journalists made about $5,000 more than their counterparts in broadcasting.

Employment Prospects

Most of the growth in newspapers is expected to come from small local newspapers. The number of large daily newspapers is expected to remain static, and competition for jobs on them is keen. Of 1,700 daily newspapers in the United States, 200 have circulations exceeding 100,000 and 35 have circulations over 250,000.

Other job openings are expected to be created by journalists leaving the field.

Advancement Prospects

Advancement prospects are fair. Bureau reporters generally move into city room jobs, starting as general assignment reporters and working their way into more specialized reporting jobs or management. The first promotion into management is likely to be either section editor or assistant editor.

Education

Most newspapers require an undergraduate degree in journalism, communications, English, or liberal arts. A survey done by the Center for Survey Research at Indiana University's Bloomington campus showed that 82 percent of journalists had bachelor's degrees; of those, 61 percent did not major in journalism. Some employers believe a general, well-rounded education prepares journalists best for the wide variety of topics they need to cover; others prefer the practical instruction offered by programs at journalism school.

Experience/Skills

General assignment reporter is generally an entry-level position. However, with more journalists losing jobs during the recession, newspapers that once hired inexperienced reporters can now choose from a more experienced field. Collegiate writing experience or internships help distinguish newcomers from the pack.

Journalists in these jobs need to be versatile, good listeners, and attentive to detail. They should not be intimidated easily and must be willing to ask questions.

They must be able to perform research and explain complex topics in a clear, simple way. Speed, accuracy, and clarity in writing are of the utmost importance.

Unions/Associations

The Newspaper Guild is the primary union for print journalists. Professional associations include the Society of Professional Journalists, and the American Society of Journalists and Authors, Inc. In addition, there are a number of associations that represent reporters in a wide variety of specialties or reporters of different racial or ethnic backgrounds.

WIRE SERVICE REPORTER

CAREER PROFILE

Duties: Report events quickly under constant deadline pressure; write summaries of stories for news digests; edit stories from local newspapers and broadcast stations for wire release

Alternate Title(s): none

Salary Range: $25,000 to $50,000+

Employment Prospects: Good

Advancement Prospects: Fair

Prerequisites:

Education—Undergraduate degree in journalism, communications, English, or liberal arts

Experience—None for a temporary position; 18 months or more at a newspaper or other news organization for a permanent job with some wire services

Special Skills—Ability to work fast and accurately under great deadline pressure; aggressiveness; good news judgment

CAREER LADDER

```
┌─────────────────────────────────────┐
│   Assistant Editor; Assistant Bureau │
│   Chief; Foreign Correspondent       │
└─────────────────────────────────────┘

┌─────────────────────────────────────┐
│      Wire Service Reporter           │
└─────────────────────────────────────┘

┌─────────────────────────────────────┐
│   Temporary Reporter; Intern         │
└─────────────────────────────────────┘
```

Position Description

For years, the traditional wire service job involved working for one of several worldwide services that supplied general news to newspapers. Because most newspapers do not have overseas or national bureaus, they rely on wire services for international and national news.

Now, with the advent of on-line computer services, people interested in a specific topic can subscribe to news services or "real-time" databases devoted to that field. Some of these services also provide copy to newspapers; others are strictly for subscribers.

Wire services differ from newspapers in that they are not restricted by printing deadlines. By providing news without relying on paper, stories can be continuously updated 24 hours a day.

At a general news wire service, reporters cover a wider scope of news than at most newspapers. When an event breaks, wire service reporters battle to be first to phone in a headline. Sometimes this means actually racing to a phone; other times, the reporters may carry cellular phones or portable computers to do the job. Then they race to provide a story. The pressure to be first is intense and constant. For specialized business wires providing information to investors on Wall Street, for example, a delay in getting the news out can mean a lost opportunity for financial gain for their subscribers.

Wire services maintain bureaus throughout the world. For general news wire services, such as the Associated Press, bureau reporters may be expected to generate routine copy, arrests, weather reports, commodity market prices, and the like, in addition to major news. Hours can be erratic, with night and weekend hours common.

Wire service reporters must be able to work both in the field, reporting stories, and at a desk, editing copy submitted by other reporters and member newspapers and broadcast stations.

Wire service reporters face great pressure, but they also can have the satisfaction of seeing their work reach a worldwide audience. The trade-off is that they may not get the time to write in-depth pieces or features.

Salaries

Salaries at wire services on the whole are higher than those at newspapers, according to a study done by the Center for Survey Research at Indiana University's Bloomington Campus in 1992. Salaries vary with the size of the organization and the experience of the journalist, with high salaries for high profile, knowledgeable stars.

Salaries may also depend on the city in which a reporter works. According to the Newspaper Guild, unionized wire reporter salaries range from a top minimum of $33,211 at United Press International to a top minimum of $51,549 at Reuters News Service.

Employment Prospects

Established wires maintain hundreds of bureaus around the world. In addition, new wires specializing in business and other topics have emerged, creating jobs. These jobs may be somewhat harder to obtain now than five years ago; some wires that maintained in-house training programs have abandoned them because the pool of experienced applicants is now so large.

A new wire reporter can expect to work on the desk, taking dictation from reporters in the field, editing stories submitted by member newspapers or broadcast stations, and performing clerical tasks.

Advancement Prospects

Experience on a wire service was once regarded as excellent training for those aspiring to work on larger dailies. In addition, reporters can move within a wire service to become news editors, bureau chiefs, assistant bureau chiefs, or work in foreign bureaus, capital bureaus, or the national capital.

Education

Wire service reporters are generally required to have a bachelor's degree in journalism or liberal arts. In addition, some services require applicants to take a vocabulary and news writing test.

Experience/Skills

Wire service reporters must be able to work under extreme deadline pressure. They must be both accurate and fast. Often, a wire service reporter must know what news has already been reported so he or she can make a split-second decision about an event's news value.

Wire service reporters may also be called upon to compose stories in their heads from notes, which they then dictate to an editor over the phone. They must be tenacious, aggressive, level-headed, and have good news judgment.

Wire services frequently require a minimum of 18 months full-time news experience on a daily newspaper or broadcast station. Those with less experience may qualify for temporary openings, which sometimes lead to full-time employment.

Proficiency in a foreign language can help if your goal is to work in a bureau overseas.

Unions/Associations

Employees at United Press International, Associated Press, and Reuters are represented by the Newspaper Guild. Other professional associations include the Society of Professional Journalists, Investigative Reporters and Editors, Women In Communications, Inc., National Association of Black Journalists, National Press Club, and the Information Industry Association.

FINANCIAL WIRE REPORTER

Duties: Follow the performance of companies and report changes that might affect the economy or the stock market; report economic developments and economic indicators; provide other financial information of interest to the wire service's customers

Alternate Title(s):   Real-time Financial Database Reporter

Salary Range: $20,000 to $65,000+

Employment Prospects: Fair

Advancement Prospects: Fair

Prerequisites:

  Education—Undergraduate degree in journalism, liberal arts, or communications; courses in business, economics, or computers helpful.

  Experience—None for entry-level positions. Otherwise, experience at a newspaper, wire service, or trade publication as a journalist or at a company working in public relations is needed.

  Special Skills—Must be able to work fast and accurately under deadlines; aggressive; able to explain complicated information simply and clearly without distorting its meaning.

```
┌─────────────────────────────────┐
│   Newspaper Magazine Business   │
│             Reporter            │
└─────────────────────────────────┘

┌─────────────────────────────────┐
│      Financial Wire Reporter    │
└─────────────────────────────────┘

┌─────────────────────────────────┐
│       Entry-Level Position      │
└─────────────────────────────────┘
```

Position Description

Financial wire reporters exist in the growing overlap between traditional news organizations and the specialized world of computerized information.

Some business wire reporters file reports intended for use by mainstream newspapers, which take them off the wire and print them. Others send their information directly to subscribers electronically, so the words never see print. This information helps money managers decide what investments to make, and when.

Because of this highly specialized audience, the pressure on financial wire reporters can be even more acute than it is for general wire reporters. Investors on Wall Street need information as soon as it becomes available. Any delay can mean a lost opportunity for them, and it could cost the wire service subscribers.

Any information that might affect the stock of a company must be put out immediately, even if only in the briefest headline form. Details follow as soon as possible as reporters race to be first with the news.

Financial wire reporters often work regular hours because so much of what they do is tied to the stock market. However, when a particular business or specialty topic becomes hot, a reporter can expect to put in the hours necessary to see that the news gets covered.

Many financial wires also offer general news, so reporters may have to work weekends writing news summaries or be on call during off hours in case of breaking events.

Each reporter may cover a different industry, tracking changes within that industry, following changes in stock prices and trying to find out why a change in stock price happened.

Salaries

Salaries for financial wire reporters are in line with salaries for general wire reporters, ranging from the low 20s for inexperienced reporters to the mid-30s and higher for those with more experience.

Employment Prospects

While other news organizations suffered cutbacks during the early 90s, financial wire services and other business databases blossomed. There are several services now competing for the same clients, and conventional wires have also added business reporting resources to stay in the game. Because the target market is specific and affluent, financial wires have a ready-made audience and money to sustain growth.

Opportunities in this field are better than in general news, which has experienced cutbacks. Some insiders believe that electronic information services targeting a select audience may be the future of reporting.

Advancement Prospects

At newer companies, advancement can be more rapid because growth is continually opening up new opportunities. Some financial wires maintain bureaus in major cities around the world, with large bureaus in New York and Tokyo to cover the stock markets there. Experience at such an organization may also lead to jobs at business magazines or other business or trade publications.

Education

As with most jobs in journalism, business reporters should have undergraduate degrees in journalism, communications, or liberal arts. Courses or degrees in business, computers, or economics are also desirable.

Experience/Skills

Some companies expect reporters to already possess a good understanding of the world's financial markets; others prefer to hire promising young writers and train them about the business world in-house. Previous experience as a business reporter elsewhere, or a background in business combined with good writing skills are good qualifications for this work. Proficiency in a foreign language can help land a job in a bureau overseas.

Unions/Associations

The Newspaper Guild represents employees of some companies with financial wire services. The Information Industry Association is the main trade association for businesses of this type.

COPY EDITOR

Duties: Edit reporters' copy for clarity, conciseness, organization, and grammar; write headlines and photo cutlines; lay out pages

Alternate Title(s): Copy Reader

Salary Range: $15,000 to $60,000+

Employment Prospects: Good

Advancement Prospects: Poor

Prerequisites:

Education—Undergraduate degree in journalism, communications, liberal arts, or English

Experience—Often an entry-level position; experience desirable for large papers

Special Skills—Grammatical knowledge; speed; ability to spot weaknesses in articles; creativity

```
┌─────────────────────────────────┐
│       Copy Chief; Editor        │
└─────────────────────────────────┘

┌─────────────────────────────────┐
│          Copy Editor            │
└─────────────────────────────────┘

┌─────────────────────────────────┐
│  Journalist; Copy Aide; College │
└─────────────────────────────────┘
```

Position Description

Copy editors are often the unsung heroes of the newspaper. The reporters may get the bylines, but the quality of their stories often depends on the copy editor.

The copy editor is often the last person to handle a reporter's story before it is typeset, after it has been read and edited by a news editor. For all but the smallest papers, there are usually several copy editors on duty who sit in a cluster or horseshoe near the news editor and copy chief.

Copy editors check the stories for spelling, punctuation, correct newspaper style, and other points of grammar. They may question reporters about vague sentences or inconsistencies. While substantial editing is the province of the news editors, copy editors can revise stories. Often the news editor is under too much pressure at deadline to spend a lot of time meticulously editing each story; consequently the task falls to the copy editor. Copy editors also write headlines and photo cutlines for the stories they handle, and they may do page layouts as well.

The work is fast-paced at deadline, and copy editors have to make quick and correct news judgment decisions. During slow times, enterprising copy editors research and write news or feature stories for the paper. In addition, copy editors may monitor wire service terminals.

Copy editors report to the copy chief, who works in coordination with the news editor in charge. Sometimes the copy chief is also the wire editor or page-makeup editor.

Salaries

Most copy editors make more than reporters; sometimes just a few dollars a week more, sometimes more significant amounts. On some newspapers, the starting pay is the same, but copy editors, who are in greater demand, move up the salary scale more quickly.

A novice copy editor on a small newspaper made a median of $20,000 in 1993. On newspapers of 20,000 to 30,000 circulation, less experienced copy editors made a median of $22,000, while those with more than five years' experience made $26,000. On newspapers of circulations from 100,000 to 150,000, the less experienced editors made $27,000, while the more experienced made $36,000.

At the largest newspapers, those with circulations over 500,000, the least experienced editors made a median of $41,000, and the more experienced a median of $52,000.

Employment Prospects

The overall journalism market is very competitive, but sometimes it's easier to get a job as a copy editor than as a journalist. In fact, many reporters take copy-editing jobs in order to get on a desired newspaper, then work their way into reporting by writing stories during slow periods or on their own time. Some papers require every journalist to spend a probationary period on the copy desk before he or she can join the reporting staff.

Advancement Prospects

Advancement for copy editors depends largely on individual career goals. Some copy editors enjoy working only with copy and have little interest in news reporting, while others aspire to move into reporter positions. Typical advanced copy editing positions are copy chief and wire editor. Copy editors with news reporting experience may be promoted to assistant news editor or assistant city editor, jobs which require supervising reporters and making decisions about news coverage. Most top level managerial jobs in the newsroom, such as executive editor or editor in chief, require news reporting experience.

Because good copy editors can be hard to come by, it may be easier to move into a copy editing position than to seek a reporting job. However, if your ultimate goal is to become a reporter, it may also be harder to make the switch to reporting later on unless you are willing to go to a smaller newspaper or move out of the main newsroom into a news bureau.

Education

An undergraduate degree in journalism or mass communications is preferred. A degree in English may be especially valuable to a copy editor. Liberal arts degrees also are acceptable.

Experience/Skills

Copy editing is often an entry-level job, although some large newspapers require experience. The copy editor must be skilled in grammar and be able to edit quickly and under pressure. Knowledge of type point sizes and column pica widths is needed for writing headlines and cutlines. The copy editor also should be creative in writing crisp headlines that influence people to read the stories. Most editing is done on a display terminal, requiring computer literacy.

Unions/Associations

The Newspaper Guild, affiliated with the AFL-CIO, represents copy editors on many newspapers. Related professional associations include Women In Communications, Inc., Society of Professional Journalists, and National Association of Black Journalists.

ASSISTANT EDITOR

CAREER PROFILE

Duties: Assist news or department editor in news gathering and editing operations; assign stories to reporters

Alternate Title(s):   Deputy Editor; Assistant City Editor; Assistant Metropolitan Editor

Salary Range: $20,000 to $56,000+

Employment Prospects: Fair

Advancement Prospects: Fair

Prerequisites:
　　Education—Undergraduate degree in journalism, communications, English, or liberal arts

　　Experience—Background as a journalist essential

　　Special Skills—Editing; directing and motivating others; news judgment

CAREER LADDER

```
┌─────────────────────────────────┐
│   News Editor; City Editor; Section │
│              Editor              │
└─────────────────────────────────┘

┌─────────────────────────────────┐
│         Assistant Editor         │
└─────────────────────────────────┘

┌─────────────────────────────────┐
│            Journalist            │
└─────────────────────────────────┘
```

Position Description

Most assistant editors serve on the general-news desk, while a smaller number serve section editors. Assistant editors are the front-line editors for nearly all copy, and they relieve editors of much work, giving the editors time for administrative and policy-making duties.

Assistant editors control the flow of copy through the editing process. They screen stories and do the preliminary editing. They have authority to ask reporters for changes and to decide on the importance of a story, determining its position in the newspaper. Decisions or editing that involves sensitive stories may be referred to the news editor or editor in charge.

Once assistant editors finish editing stories, they pass them along to the copy desk for additional editing and headline writing. They inform the makeup or layout editor of the positions the stories are to occupy on various pages and their approximate lengths.

Assistant editors help execute editorial decisions, field questions from reporters, and assign coverage of breaking stories. Some assistant news editors split their time between being journalists and working on the desk. The position is often a tryout to test a promising reporter's news judgment, editing, and management abilities.

Assistant editors may be assigned to work any shift, depending on the needs of the paper. In addition, assistant editors may write news stories and write headlines and cutlines.

Salaries

A salary survey by Women in Communications, Inc. placed assistant editors into the same median salary range as reporters—about $25,000 to $30,000. This job is not generally found at the smallest papers.

At newspapers from 20,000 to 30,000 circulation, the median for this job was $30,000 in 1993, according to a survey by the American Society of Newspaper Editors. The median pay went to $40,000 at papers from 100,000 to 150,000, and to $56,000 at newspapers with circulations over 500,000.

Employment Prospects

The assistant editor position is usually a training post, with candidates chosen from the reporting staff. Small papers offer the most and best opportunities for beginning assistant editors.

Advancement Prospects

The assistant editor's job is on track to middle and upper editorial management positions. Movement to another paper as assistant editor is unlikely; however, an assistant editor on a large paper may qualify for a news editor's post on a smaller paper.

Education

Most assistant editors have undergraduate degrees in journalism, communications, English, or liberal arts.

Experience/Skills

On small papers, a journalist with one or two years' experience may be promoted to assistant editor. On larger papers, four to six years' reporting experience is necessary.

Assistant editors should have good editing skills and news judgment. They should be able to meet deadlines and be well organized, in order to avoid copy bottlenecks at the last minute. They should be able to direct and motivate others.

Unions/Associations

Major professional associations include the Society of Professional Journalists; American Society of Newspaper Editors; Women In Communications, Inc.; National Association of Black Journalists; International Society of Weekly Newspaper Editors; Investigative Reporters and Editors; National Federation of Press Women; and National Association of Media Women.

NEWS EDITOR

CAREER PROFILE

Duties: Manage a news-gathering staff; determine the direction and content of the newspaper; make policy decisions

Alternate Title(s):   City Editor; Metropolitan Editor; Executive Editor

Salary Range: $20,000 to $83,000+

Employment Prospects: Fair

Advancement Prospects: Fair

Prerequisites:

   Education—Undergraduate degree in journalism, communications, or liberal arts

   Experience—Background in reporting and copy editing essential

   Special Skills—Ability to direct and motivate others; news judgment; editing

CAREER LADDER

```
┌─────────────────────────────────┐
│    Assistant Managing Editor;    │
│  Managing Editor; Executive Editor │
└─────────────────────────────────┘

┌─────────────────────────────────┐
│           News Editor            │
└─────────────────────────────────┘

┌─────────────────────────────────┐
│  Assistant Editor; Section Editor │
└─────────────────────────────────┘
```

Position Description

The quality of a newspaper often falls squarely on the shoulders of the news editor, who is in charge of the day-to-day operations of a newsroom. News editors must stay abreast of all major breaking and developing news stories, decide how the paper will cover them and play them on the page, and determine who will write the stories. They keep track of reporters' activities and make split-second decisions on how to handle breaking news.

News editors make story assignments and determine which reporters will handle what beats. In addition to editing copy, they monitor the progress of stories and the flow of copy through the editing process. They meet with high-level editors to determine the content and direction of the paper and discuss problems.

News editors are also administrators. They make up work schedules for reporters and assistants, arbitrate problems, write reports to upper management, and have a voice in the promotion, hiring, and firing of subordinates. They need to be informed on all labor laws pertaining to their employees. And, most important, they must be able to work within a budget.

Finally, news editors are community liaisons. Often they are called upon to speak for or represent the paper at civic functions and in the classroom.

On a small newspaper, the news editor may be in charge of the entire newsroom operation and have no assistant editors. On larger papers, news-editor positions are broken down into geographic areas, and each editor has one or more assistants.

The job is demanding, because a typical day can encompass a wide range of news and administrative tasks. News editors work regular business hours, but days run longer if a major story breaks. The counterpart of the news editor for the nighttime shift is the night editor, who oversees the operation of a daily paper after the news editor goes home.

Salaries

In 1993, the median salary for news editors at newspapers with circulations from 5,000 to 10,000 was $23,000, according to a salary survey done by the

American Society of Newspaper Editors. At newspapers with circulations from 20,000 to 30,000, the median was $33,000.

At those with circulations from 100,000 to 150,000, the median salary rose to $51,000; and at the largest newspapers, those over 500,000 in circulation, the median was $83,000.

Employment Prospects

Skilled news editors are always in demand on papers of all sizes, though opportunities are best with small dailies and weeklies. The pool of competitors is much smaller than for journalists, but opportunities may be greatly restricted by the size of the publication and relocation requirements.

Advancement Prospects

News editors are in an excellent position for advancement into upper management.

Education

Most news editors have undergraduate degrees in journalism, communications, English, or liberal arts. Advanced degrees are not necessary but can be helpful.

News editors should have additional training in management techniques.

Experience/Skills

On a very small paper, two or three years' experience as a journalist, section editor, or assistant editor can qualify someone for news editor. Five to ten years or more are required on larger papers. News editors should be adept at editing, rewriting, and making quick decisions, and they should be smooth in handling personnel matters. They must be detail-oriented and well organized in order to handle administrative tasks. Experience and ease in public speaking helps if the job involves community liaison work.

Unions/Associations

Major professional associations include the Society of Professional Journalists; American Society of Newspaper Editors; Investigative Reporters and Editors; Women In Communications, Inc.; National Association of Black Journalists; International Society of Weekly Newspaper Editors; National Federation of Press Women; and National Association of Media Women.

SECTION EDITOR

CAREER PROFILE

Duties: Supervise content and layout of special-interest section or page

Alternate Title(s): Business Editor; Life-Style Editor; Sunday Magazine Editor; Sports Editor; etc.

Salary Range: $17,000 to $80,000+

Employment Prospects: Fair

Advancement Prospects: Poor

Prerequisites:
  Education—Undergraduate degree in journalism, communications, English, or liberal arts; advanced degree desirable for specialized fields

  Experience—Background as journalist, copy editor, or assistant editor

  Special Skills—Staff supervision ability; news judgment; editing; graphics

CAREER LADDER

```
┌─────────────────────────────────┐
│  News Editor; Assistant Managing │
│             Editor               │
└─────────────────────────────────┘

┌─────────────────────────────────┐
│          Section Editor          │
└─────────────────────────────────┘

┌─────────────────────────────────┐
│  Journalist; Assistant Editor;   │
│            Copy Editor           │
└─────────────────────────────────┘
```

Position Description

Section editors are responsible for specialized sections or pages of a newspaper, such as business, life-style, arts and entertainment, real estate, suburban news, or Sunday magazine. They are responsible for determining content, assigning reporters and photographers to stories, monitoring deadlines, editing copy, and executing or overseeing page graphics. Most are expected to write for their pages as well.

Section editors may work under the direction of the news editor in charge, who may be called the city editor, metropolitan editor, or executive editor. Some section editors may be independent and work with other editors on a coordinating or advisory basis.

The job of section editor calls for a good sense of organization as well as the ability to manage others. The editor must monitor other sources of news, such as wire stories and magazines, for story ideas; work on both short-term and long-term stories; and coordinate the work of others.

On a typical day, a section editor may meet with other editors, review wire copy to determine which stories will be used in the section or page, assign stories, edit copy, and select photos and other artwork to illustrate the text. Many section editors do their own page layouts, while others work with the newspaper's art and photo departments. An editor of a daily page, such as business, must have good news judgment and be able to react to breaking news quickly.

The job can be especially rewarding, not only for the decision-making freedom that goes with it, but also for the leeway one has to put a personal "stamp" on part of a newspaper. Section editors tend to work regular business hours and usually are not subject to shift changes or weekend or night work.

Salaries

A survey done by Women in Communications, Inc. in 1992–1993 found that section editors fell into a median salary range of $30,000 to $35,000.

A 1993 survey done by the American Society of Newspaper Editors gave varying median base pays for section editors, depending upon the section of the newspaper they edited. On newspapers with circulations from 5,000 to 10,000, a lifestyle editor could expect a median base pay of about $17,500. A sports editor might make around $19,200; editorial page editors, $21,850; most papers of this size did not submit figures for business editors or Sunday editors.

At newspapers with circulations from 20,000 to 30,000, lifestyle editors made a median of $28,200; business editors, $27,600; sports editors, $31,400; editorial page editors, $37,800, Sunday editors, $30,700. At newspapers with circulations from 100,000 to 150,000, lifestyle editors made a median of $48,900; sports editors, $48,900; business editors, $47,300; editorial page editors, $58,500; Sunday editors, $49,100.

At the largest newspapers, those with circulations over 500,000, lifestyle editors made a median base pay of $76,200; sports editors, $88,000; business editors, $85,000; editorial page editors, $118,000; and Sunday editors, $78,500.

Employment Prospects

Most section editors are promoted from within. Some newspapers, however, conduct national searches for talent. Journalists and editors with advanced degrees or specialized education in certain fields, such as law, business, or science, have a hiring advantage. Jobs are highly competitive.

Advancement Prospects

Section editors are in excellent positions to be promoted to higher level jobs, but competition is keen.

Education

Section editors should have undergraduate degrees in journalism, communications, English, or liberal arts.

Experience/Skills

Background experience required depends on the size of the newspaper. A journalist with only one or two years of experience may become a section editor on a small paper, while larger papers require four or more years of experience. Many section editors have served time as copy editors or assistant news editors.

Section editors should be thoroughly knowledgeable about their subject areas and the audience they serve. They should be good writers and editors, and be able to lay out pages.

Unions/Associations

Major professional associations include the Society of Professional Journalists; Women In Communications, Inc.; National Association of Black Journalists; International Society of Weekly Newspaper Editors; National Association of Media Women; and National Federation of Press Women.

EDITORIAL WRITER

CAREER PROFILE

Duties: Research and write editorials on issues; screen columns, letters to the editor, and other editorial articles; help decide newspaper's position

Alternate Title(s):   Editorial Page Editor

Salary Range: $20,000 to $60,000+

Employment Prospects: Fair

Advancement Prospects: Fair

Prerequisites:
   Education—Undergraduate degree in journalism, communications, or liberal arts; advanced degree helpful

   Experience—Background as journalist and editor

   Special Skills—Logic; persuasiveness; excellent, clear writing; thoroughness; objectivity

CAREER LADDER

```
┌─────────────────────────────────────┐
│                                     │
│   Senior Editor; Managing Editor    │
│                                     │
└─────────────────────────────────────┘

┌─────────────────────────────────────┐
│                                     │
│         Editorial Writer            │
│                                     │
└─────────────────────────────────────┘

┌─────────────────────────────────────┐
│                                     │
│     News Editor; Section Editor;    │
│            Journalist               │
│                                     │
└─────────────────────────────────────┘
```

Position Description

Editorial writers work away from the daily hubbub of the newsroom; they are concerned with the issues generated by events rather than the news of the events. They are responsible for the contents of the editorial page and the page opposite, called the "op ed" page. The editorial page is a sensitive area because it represents the quality and character of the newspaper.

Editorial writers comprise an editorial board, which also includes members of senior management and the publisher. A small newspaper may have only one or two editorial writers to share all the duties, while a larger paper may allow particular editorial writers to focus on special areas of expertise. On a large paper, junior editorial writers may do research for senior members of the board.

Editorial writers examine issues that arise, research them, and decide on a position. Some editorials must be timely, reacting to the latest news. Others, on topics of current interest but not related to breaking news, may be researched and written more slowly. Editorial writers do research the same way as journalists do, by calling sources and consulting library clips and other published sources. They may ask a journalist for additional information.

In examining an issue, editorial writers must be thorough, objective, and accurate. In order to be fully informed of local, national, and international news, most editorial writers do extensive reading of other news and commentary publications. All sides of an issue must be carefully weighed in order to arrive at a position.

In addition, editorial writers screen letters and columns for publication on the editorial pages. The "letters to the editor" column is an important public forum. Columns may be written by the newspaper's own news staff or by syndicated writers.

Salaries

Smaller newspapers may only have an editorial page editor to write editorials, or the news editor may write them.

According to a 1993 salary survey by the American Society of Newspaper Editors, the median salary for an editorial page editor at newspapers of circulations from

5,000 to 10,000 was $22,000. There was not enough information to give a median for editorial writers at newspapers of this size.

At newspapers with circulations from 20,000 to 30,000, editorial writers made a median of $31,200. At newspapers with circulations from 100,000 to 150,000, the median for editorial writers was $43,200. At the largest newspapers—those with circulations over 500,000—editorial writers made a median of $62,000. Salaries for editorial page editors, who oversee the composition of the editorial page, can go up to a median of $118,000 on the largest newspapers.

Employment Prospects

Several years of seasoning are required to qualify for editorial writer. Candidates have to have demonstrated their reporting and analytical abilities as journalists first; editorial ability as newsroom editor is sometimes necessary as well.

Advancement Prospects

Fair opportunities exist to rise within the editorial board structure. Most senior managers, however, are selected from editors who run the daily operations of the newsroom. Many editorial writers, however, have no wish to leave the editorial department.

Education

Editorial writers should have at least undergraduate degrees in journalism, communications, English, or liberal arts. Degrees in business, economics, law, or other graduate degrees are likely to help career advancement because of the specialized nature of many editorial-writing positions.

Experience/Skills

Editorial writers have had at least several years' seasoning as journalists and, most likely, as newsroom editors as well. They have demonstrated their ability to write balanced, clear news analyses and accurate news stories. They have good news judgment, are objective, and are good editors. They do thorough research and stay abreast of public opinion through extensive reading.

Unions/Associations

Associations include the National Conference of Editorial Writers; American Association of Newspaper Editors; Society of Professional Journalists; Women in Communications, Inc.; National Association of Black Journalists; International Society of Weekly Newspaper Editors; National Federation of Press Women; and National Association of Media Women.

NEWS LIBRARIAN

CAREER PROFILE

Duties: Acquire, catalog, and maintain collections of information for use by journalists; perform research, including computer searches, for journalists under tight deadline pressure

Alternate Title(s):   News Information Resource Manager; News Library Director; Newspaper Library Manager

Salary Range: $12,000 to $68,000

Employment Prospects: Fair to good

Advancement Prospects: Fair to good

Prerequisites:

  Education—Graduate degree in library science for top jobs on larger papers; undergraduate degree needed for assistants

  Experience—Newspaper experience helpful, may be required if applicant has no library science degree or library experience; computer experience, especially familiarity with computer database searches, also a plus

  Special Skills—Research skills; good organizational skills; knowledge of newsroom operations; good oral and written communication skills; ability to work with journalists under deadline pressure

CAREER LADDER

```
┌─────────────────────────────────┐
│                                 │
│      News Library Director      │
│                                 │
└─────────────────────────────────┘

┌─────────────────────────────────┐
│                                 │
│         News Librarian          │
│                                 │
└─────────────────────────────────┘

┌─────────────────────────────────┐
│                                 │
│    Library Clerk; Researcher    │
│                                 │
└─────────────────────────────────┘
```

Position Description

Once a job filled by journalists near retirement (hence the traditional name for the library, the morgue) or newsroom managers in need of something to manage, the news librarian job earned new respect in the 1970s with the advent of on-line computer databases.

Where librarians once simply handed folders of clippings to reporters, news librarians now perform sophisticated computer searches under deadline pressure.

In addition, librarians at some papers, as the resident experts in computer technology, help put electronic versions of newspapers on-line. Some also act as the newsroom systems editors, choosing computer systems for use by reporters and editors.

Newsroom librarians, in their capacity as researchers, can even serve on Pulitzer Prize–winning investigative teams. In one case, a team of news librarians used databases to help flesh out coverage of a school bus accident that left 27 students dead. They compiled a list of all school bus accidents in the state, compared them to school bus accidents nationwide, and collected information about drunken driving laws, school bus design, and bus evacuation procedures.

News librarians can help with statistical analysis of election polls, or create a database to analyze the characteristics of a jury pool.

Marketing the information stored in newspaper libraries to the public provides a new source of revenue for companies feeling the recessionary pinch. Several newspapers around the country, including *The St. Petersburg Times, The Fort Lauderdale Sun-Sentinel, The Sacramento Bee* and *The Miami Herald,* now offer research services directly to the public for a fee.

These operations charge either by the article or by the hour and generally require full-time positions separate from the librarians serving the newsroom.

Most major newspapers also market their stories through electronic databases available to subscribers or libraries. Newsroom librarians edit and prepare the data for public release.

Librarians code the contents of the paper for the electronic library each day. At larger papers, they also maintain archives of digital photographs within the computer system.

Newspapers with circulations of under 30,000 often do not hire librarians, instead relying on each reporter to keep his or her own files.

Salaries

Top minimums paid by newspapers represented by the Newspaper Guild in 1993 ranged from $67,946 for the chief librarian at the *New York Times* to $11,580 for a library clerk at the Terre Haute, Indiana, *Tribune-Star*.

Librarians at larger newspapers can expect to make more; non-union papers may pay less. The median salary for news librarians at newspapers of 30,000 circulation or less is around $20,000; at newspapers with circulations of 100,000 to 150,000, it's $36,000, and at newspapers larger than 500,000, the median is $56,000.

Job Prospects

Employment of librarians in general is expected to grow more slowly than for all occupations through the year 2005. However, many traditional librarians work for school, public, or university libraries, which face budgetary constraints.

Librarians in nontraditional settings can expect increased job opportunities, especially in information management. With newspapers beginning to provide a variety of electronic information services, librarians can expect increased responsibility and better job prospects.

Advancement Prospects

Good for those with the right combination of skills. Assistant librarians can also use their research skills to move into free-lance book research or other research jobs. More opportunities exist at larger newspapers.

Librarians may also take over systems editor positions, buying computer systems for the newsroom.

Education

Most journalism jobs require a bachelor's degree in journalism, communications, liberal arts, or English. A master's of library science (MLS) is required for library management jobs at larger papers. The M.L.S. includes advanced courses in cataloging, indexing, computer automation, abstracting, and library administration. Other recommended courses include those dealing with business management, computer use, statistics, and databases.

Many large newspapers now hire library professionals from outside their ranks for top jobs, but smaller papers still often move newsroom employees into the library to be trained "in house." Traditional library science programs generally don't offer courses in newspaper librarianship.

More specialized training can be obtained from the Special Libraries Association's News Division, which offers books, guides, newsletters, presentations, research, seminars, workshops, conferences, and consultation services.

Assistant librarian or clerk jobs are generally populated by those unable to find newsroom jobs or those who like to do research. No experience may be required for entry-level jobs. Experience in news is a plus. Those who hope to move up may want to get a MLS degree.

Experience/Skills

Knowledge of computer systems, an understanding of newsroom operations, the ability to find information fast and good organizational skills are all important. Previous news experience, preferably in newspapers but also in other media, can help.

Unions/Associations

The Special Libraries Association has a division for news libraries. News librarians are also represented by the Newspaper Guild at unionized newspapers. The American Library Association and the American Society for Information Science provide support to librarians.

COLUMNIST

CAREER PROFILE

Duties: Write daily or weekly columns

Alternate Title(s): None

Salary Range: $17,000 to $75,000+

Employment Prospects: Poor

Advancement Prospects: Poor

Prerequisites:

Education—Undergraduate degree in journalism, communications, English, or liberal arts; advanced degrees if specialized

Experience—Background as journalist

Special Skills—Good storytelling ability; creativity

CAREER LADDER

```
┌─────────────────────────────────┐
│  Assistant Editor; Section Editor │
└─────────────────────────────────┘

┌─────────────────────────────────┐
│            Columnist             │
└─────────────────────────────────┘

┌─────────────────────────────────┐
│    Journalist; Copy Editor       │
└─────────────────────────────────┘
```

Position Description

Columnists are regarded as having plum jobs on newspapers, but their job is harder than it appears. And, because they are showcased, they are also subject to more criticism.

Most columnists have human-interest, around-the-town or social-notes beats. Their columns may be collections of short, gossipy, or newsy items, or they may each consist of a single feature story built around an interesting person or someone's dilemma. Also common on most papers are political columnists who analyze or comment on the activities of politicians. A few columnists are nationally syndicated (see "Syndicated Columnist" in Section XIII).

Specialized columnists can write about any topic that catches the public's fancy—computers, pets, health, love and romance, plants, bridge, medicine—the list goes on and on.

Columns may be daily or weekly. Columnists are expected to generate their own material, which sometimes is not all that easy. The column goes to press regardless of material at hand.

Columnists usually operate autonomously and have a great deal of freedom. They become "personalities" and build up audiences, thus becoming promotional assets to their newspapers; consequently, some of them can negotiate higher pay than their fellow journalists. The position is usually an end goal rather than a stepping-stone to something else. Few columnists want to give up their domain and their audience for something else.

Not all columnists work at their columns fulltime. Many report for the general-news pages as well.

Columnists who become syndicated can earn a good deal of money. Art Buchwald, humorist, and Jack Anderson, investigative reporter, reportedly earn well over $200,000 a year from their columns.

Salaries

Not enough smaller newspapers hire full-time columnists for salary data to be available. At smaller newspapers, many reporters write columns in addition to their reporting duties in the hope that this experience and visibility may catapult them into full-time columnist positions later.

At newspapers with circulations from 20,000 to 30,000, columnists made a median base pay of $28,300 in 1993, according to a salary survey conducted by the American Society of Newspaper Editors. At newspapers with circulations of 100,000 to 150,000, columnists made a median of $43,400. And at the largest newspapers, those with circulations over 500,000, columnists made a median of $74,000.

A particularly prestigious or popular columnist may command an even higher salary at a large newspaper or in syndication.

Employment Prospects

Most newspapers do not hire journalists to be columnists unless they have established a track record and audience. The best bet is to use a journalist's position as the launching point to build a local readership for one's work.

Advancement Prospects

Few columnists aspire to managerial jobs; the column is the sought-after position. A popular column, however, can establish a writer as an authority in a certain area, and that can lead to syndication.

Education

Like their fellow journalists, most columnists have undergraduate degrees in journalism, communications, English, or liberal arts. A columnist writing about a specialized area, such as economics or medicine, should have the appropriate education and credentials.

Experience/Skills

Most columnists are experienced journalists; experience varies according to the market. Columnists must be creative. For human-interest subjects, they need to be good storytellers. Political columnists are expected to have good analytical skills. Since most columns are short, columnists must write concisely.

Unions/Associations

Many columnists are members of the Newspaper Guild union. Professional associations include the Society of Professional Journalists; Women In Communications, Inc.; National Association of Black Journalists; National Association of Media Women; National Federation of Press Women.

CRITIC

CAREER PROFILE

Duties: Review artistic performances, recordings, exhibits and books; write columns

Alternate Title(s):   Reviewer

Salary Range: $15,000 to $55,000+

Employment Prospects: Poor

Advancement Prospects: Poor

Prerequisites:

   Education—Undergraduate degree in journalism, communications, English, or liberal arts; specialization in a particular field

   Experience—Background as a journalist and expertise in the area reviewed

   Special Skills—Good writing ability; thorough knowledge of subject matter

CAREER LADDER

```
┌─────────────────────────────┐
│                             │
│      Section Editor         │
│                             │
└─────────────────────────────┘

┌─────────────────────────────┐
│                             │
│          Critic             │
│                             │
└─────────────────────────────┘

┌─────────────────────────────┐
│                             │
│   Journalist; Copy Editor   │
│                             │
└─────────────────────────────┘
```

Position Description

Critics can wield a great deal of influence with the public and can affect the success of artists, films, plays, books, and musical and/or dance productions. Bad reviews can keep an audience away and close a play or kill a film.

Critics, many of whom work evenings and weekends, review plays, films, concerts, operas, exhibits, dance productions, books, records, nightclub acts—anything connected with the arts and entertainment field—and write their opinions in columns. They may be highly specialized; for example, a music critic may not handle films or plays. Some small to medium-sized papers, however, have one or two persons who handle all reviewing.

Critics are expected to be knowledgeable about their subjects and keep abreast of trends and news. They interview performers and celebrities, and they do extensive reading, even studying in their respective areas. They must be objective and have good judgment. Like columnists, they develop audiences who trust their views.

Besides review columns, critics often write celebrity interviews, feature stories, and in-depth articles on trends or other aspects of the arts.

Salaries

Critics earn roughly the same as, or sometimes more than, their fellow experienced journalists—approximately $15,000 to $55,000 or more. High salaries depend heavily on experience, credentials, and the size of the newspaper.

Employment Prospects

Many critics start out as journalists and work their way into full-time critic posts by doing occasional reviews. A position as a staff writer or assistant editor for the life-style or arts-and-entertainment sections is an excellent place to start. Once a critic is established, it is possible to change employers, though the job market is very small.

Advancement Prospects

Like columnists, many critics don't wish to do any other kind of news work. The most likely advancement is to become editor of the arts-and-entertainment section or book-review section.

Education

Critics are expected to have a background in their area of expertise; this may involve specialized or advanced degrees. Basic education is an undergraduate degree in journalism, communications, liberal arts, or other areas pertaining to the arts.

Experience/Skills

Critics should be thoroughly familiar with their specialization in order to give fair and objective reviews. This requires extensive reading and often periodic study. They should be good interviewers and be able to write quickly on deadline.

Unions, Associations

Professional associations include the American Theater Critics Association; Dance Critics Association; Music Critics Association; National Book Critics Circle; Television Critics Association; Society of Professional Journalists; Women In Communications, Inc.; National Association of Black Journalists; National Federation of Press Women; and National Association of Media Women. The Newspaper Guild negotiates wages for many journalists, including critics.

MAGAZINES

EDITORIAL ASSISTANT

CAREER PROFILE

Duties: Clerical and receptionist duties; errands; minor editorial and production tasks; research

Alternate Title(s):   None

Salary Range: $13,000 to $15,000+

Employment Prospects: Fair

Advancement Prospects: Good

Prerequisites:

Education—Undergraduate degree in communications, journalism, English or liberal arts; courses in publishing

Experience—None, for many positions

Special Skills—Editing; proofreading; secretarial skills; writing

CAREER LADDER

```
┌─────────────────────────────────────┐
│   Associate Editor; Assistant Editor │
└─────────────────────────────────────┘

┌─────────────────────────────────────┐
│          Editorial Assistant         │
└─────────────────────────────────────┘

┌─────────────────────────────────────┐
│          College; Secretary          │
└─────────────────────────────────────┘
```

Position Description

Editorial assistant is the entry-level position on a magazine's editorial staff. The job is more secretarial than editorial, but beginners are given a chance to learn on the job and work their way into more responsible editorial positions.

Editorial assistants report to higher-level editors, including assistant and associate editors, senior editors, and editors. They do library research for superiors who are writing articles, and they check the accuracy of facts in articles written by outside authors. They are responsible for reviewing other magazines and newspapers and clipping articles of interest for editors. Such articles may generate story ideas or provide helpful information on stories in progress.

They also proofread galleys and write headlines, photo cutlines, and "deck" copy, which consists of several lines of large type excerpted from the article to break up the gray type on a page. Secretarial functions include opening and routing the mail, answering the telephone, running errands, filing, and typing letters.

As experience is gained, editorial assistants are given more editorial responsibilities, such as editing manuscripts and suggesting article ideas. They may also be given a chance to write short bylined articles or columns for the magazine or be responsible for collecting short items for news-roundup columns.

In addition, editorial assistants may:

- handle production details, including trafficking copy, galleys, and artwork;
- give a first reading to unsolicited manuscripts;
- work with freelancers involved in writing and production;
- screen job applications.

Salaries

Most editorial assistants earn between $13,000 and $15,000. Some top magazines pay as much as $21,000. Trade publications sometimes pay more than average for those who have specialized education or experience, such as technical or computer-science backgrounds.

Employment Prospects

Competition for magazine editorial jobs is keen, even at the entry level. Beginners who have taken skill-oriented journalism or publishing classes in high school and college—writing and editing—and have had school newspaper or intern experience have an advantage.

Advancement Prospects

Editorial assistants have a good chance of working their way up the editorial ladder, though competition remains stiff at all levels.

Education

An undergraduate degree in communications, journalism, English, or liberal arts is necessary. In some cases, a master's degree in communications or publishing may be advantageous. Technical and trade journals may require specialized education in such fields as engineering, computer programming, science, law, or economics.

Experience/Skills

Although no experience is required for many editorial-assistant jobs, the candidates with the best chances of employment are those who've taken writing/editing journalism and publishing courses in school, been actively involved in school publications, and have had internships or summer jobs in the field.

Editorial assistants should demonstrate both editing and writing ability, though they may not immediately write articles. Production knowledge also is useful.

Unions/Associations

The American Society of Magazine Editors; American Society of Journalists and Authors, Inc.; and Women In Communications, Inc. are among the major professional associations open to magazine editors. Some editors also join specialized authors' groups or trade and industry associations. Those who work for major news and feature magazines may belong to The Newspaper Guild.

RESEARCHER

CAREER PROFILE

Duties: Read all stories and mark facts to be verified; check with author and sources; keep records of any changes and apprise editor of changes.

Alternate Title(s): Fact Checker; Research Editor; Editorial Assistant

Salary Range: $12,000 to $30,000+

Employment Prospects: Poor

Advancement Prospects: Poor

Prerequisites:

Education—Undergraduate degree in journalism, communications, English, or liberal arts; advanced degrees or course work for technical/scientific/business publications

Experience—Entry-level researcher does not necessarily require any previous experience; background as journalist, writer, or editor helpful

Special Skills—Meticulous attention to detail; organization; telephone skills; editing; writing

CAREER LADDER

Associate Editor; Assistant Editor

Researcher

Editorial Assistant; College

Position Description

Researcher is often an entry-level position with a magazine, but one that is usually understood to lead to more editorial responsibility. Researchers must verify each piece of information in a reporter's story and make sure that all corrections are made. Both the reporter and the assistant editor should be informed of any changes the researcher makes.

Smaller publications usually do not hire researchers but depend on their own reporters to verify facts and information. At larger magazines, the researcher not only checks data but shepherds stories under his or her responsibility through the entire production process, making sure that everything remains correct at each step.

To groom them for reporting and other editorial positions, editors may assign small, bylined stories or column features to researchers. Write-ups of personnel changes or new-business columns may be the regular responsibility of a researcher. Researchers may also be responsible for proofreading galleys and writing headlines and captions.

In addition, researchers may:

- handle other production details;
- attend seminars, workshops, and trade shows to keep up with industry trends.

Salaries

In 1993, the Newspaper Guild top minimum for a researcher at *Newsweek* was $23,244, reachable after three years. The top minimum for a researcher at *Maclean's* was $30,798, also reachable after three years. However, most researchers make less, sometimes as little as $10,000, and are often not represented by a union.

Employment Prospects

Since researcher is an entry-level job, there is more turnover at such positions than at higher ones. People who have patience and are capable of meticulous attention to detail are not always easy to come by, yet a magazine's credibility depends on the accuracy of its stories. Beginners with journalism skills and great organizational ability have less trouble breaking into the editorial staff by acquiring such researcher positions. Not all magazines employ researchers.

Advancement Prospects

Most researchers have fairly excellent advancement prospects. Often a researcher is hired with the understanding that, if everything works out all right, promotion to assistant or associate editor is quite likely in about two years. On smaller publications, a researcher may move up even sooner. As with all editorial jobs, however, competition is stiff.

Education

An undergraduate degree in journalism, English, communications, or liberal arts is essential. Any secretarial training that gives the researcher organizational skills is also a boon. Advanced course work, sometimes even an advanced degree, is necessary for researcher jobs on specialized publications, such as those for law, medicine, or high technology.

Experience/Skills

While no formal experience in journalism is necessary, aspiring researchers who have taken writing and editing courses, have been involved in school publications, and who have had summer jobs or internships have a leg up on other applicants. Many editors think a good researcher should have a background in liberal arts and have a strong interest in reading in general. Attendance at summer seminars or workshops is also advantageous.

Researchers should demonstrate good organizational skills, plus editing and writing abilities. Knowledge of magazine production is very helpful.

Unions/Associations

Researchers are eligible to join the American Society of Magazine Editors, American Society of Journalists and Authors, Inc., and other writers' trade groups. All women journalists may join Women In Communications, Inc. The Newspaper Guild represents employees on some major news and feature magazines.

COPY EDITOR

CAREER PROFILE

Duties: Oversee all editorial copy for grammar and style; prepare copy for production; check facts

Alternate Title(s): Copy Chief; Assistant Managing Editor; Production Assistant; Proofreader

Salary Range: $15,000 to $45,000+

Employment Prospects: Fair

Advancement Prospects: Fair

Prerequisites:

Education—Undergraduate degree in English, communications, liberal arts, or journalism; advanced course work or knowledge of specialized fields necessary for certain technical publications

Experience—Not necessary for entry-level jobs; otherwise, work as editorial assistant or professor's assistant beneficial

Special Skills—Good command of English punctuation, grammar, and spelling; organizational skills; patience; attention to detail

CAREER LADDER

```
┌─────────────────────────────────────┐
│  Associate Editor; Assistant Editor; │
│        Reporter; Researcher          │
└─────────────────────────────────────┘

┌─────────────────────────────────────┐
│                                      │
│             Copy Editor              │
│                                      │
└─────────────────────────────────────┘

┌─────────────────────────────────────┐
│                                      │
│      Editorial Assistant; College    │
│                                      │
└─────────────────────────────────────┘
```

Position Description

The copy editor takes each article through the successive steps of accuracy and fit, readying it for typesetting and, finally, print. He or she checks each story for grammar and magazine style, and may be responsible for fact-checking as well. On smaller publications without separate researchers, the copy editor handles fact research, working directly with the writers and editors.

Copy editors must have a good working knowledge of magazine production. If a story is too long or too short, the copy editor is usually the person responsible for cutting or lengthening it. If the piece is too short, the copy editor will prefer to go back to the original writer, but he or she may have to act alone if pressured by production deadlines. Copy editors often write headlines, captions, and "decks" (the large quotes which highlight a page of copy). They check relentlessly for typographical errors, misspelled words, and incorrect usage in the original manuscript, and proofread galleys and final page proofs for errors that may have slipped by earlier or have been incorrectly set by the typesetter. Other production duties may include working with the layout or managing editor to decide article placement, determining use of photos and other artwork, and giving final approval of page layouts. In addition, copy editors may spend time with managing editors at typesetters' or printers' shops, and substitute for the managing editors when necessary.

Large publications usually employ several copy editors for individual sections, but one copy editor may serve for an entire small magazine. Copy editors are valued for their unruffled personalities and meticulous attention to the smallest details.

Salaries

Most small trade magazines start copy editors at about $15,000, while large consumer publications start copy editors at about $23,000. A typical proofreader for

Time, Inc. earned about $19,000 in 1993, but a good copy editor with experience can generally earn about $45,000.

Employment Prospects

Competition is stiff and is characterized by high turnover. Many copy editors work on a part-time basis for more than one publication, or work as freelancers (for freelance rates, see Section 8).

Advancement Prospects

Advancement potential for copy editors is fair. A beginning copy editor can move on to associate or assistant editor, perhaps eventually to senior editor. Knowledge of magazine production is always helpful at higher editorial positions, and the copy editor is in a perfect position to acquire such information.

Education

As with all magazine-writing jobs, an undergraduate degree in English, journalism, communications, or liberal arts is a must. After that, a copy editor would do well to brush up on grammar and writing skills through course work and/or seminars and internships. Advanced course work for specialized publications gives the copy editor familiarity with technical concepts and jargon connected to a particular field.

Experience/Skills

Although a background in writing or journalism is helpful, the copy editor's most important skill is a thorough command of English grammar, punctuation, and style. Copyediting work for any general-interest publication stands as a good recommendation for any other general-interest magazine. Secretarial skills acquired along the way, for organizational purposes, are also helpful.

Finally, a copy editor would do well to learn how to communicate easily and courteously with people, since some writers are not predisposed to hear about their sloppy grammar, incorrect information, and terrible spelling.

Unions/Associations

There are no unions for magazine editorial personnel. Professional organizations available include the American Society of Magazine Editors, as well as writers' trade groups.

ASSOCIATE EDITOR

CAREER PROFILE

Duties: Assign, read, and edit articles; write articles, columns, and copy; handle production

Alternate Title(s): Assistant Editor

Salary Range: $15,000 to $50,000+

Employment Prospects: Fair

Advancement Prospects: Fair

Prerequisites:

Education—Undergraduate degree in journalism, communications, or liberal arts; advanced or specialized degrees for technical, scientific, or business publications

Experience—None for entry level; otherwise, background as journalist, editorial assistant, or as associate editor on a smaller publication is needed

Special Skills—Editing; organization; production skill; graphics sense

CAREER LADDER

```
┌─────────────────────────────────┐
│     Editor; Senior Editor       │
└─────────────────────────────────┘

┌─────────────────────────────────┐
│        Associate Editor         │
└─────────────────────────────────┘

┌─────────────────────────────────┐
│ Editorial Assistant; Journalist;│
│        Writer; College          │
└─────────────────────────────────┘
```

Position Description

Associate editors have varying degrees of responsibility, depending on the size of the magazine. On a small trade magazine, for example, an associate editor can be second in command, reporting to an editor. On a larger publication, an associate editor may work under a senior editor and be assigned to a particular department.

Associate editors screen the unsolicited manuscripts that are initially screened and routed to them by editorial assistants; in some cases, they may do all the screening themselves. They assign articles to freelance writers, edit manuscripts, plus write headlines, cutlines, and other copy as needed. They are responsible for assigning photographic coverage or art illustrations to accompany articles. They either direct editorial assistants in research and fact-checking or are responsible for those duties themselves.

Associate editors participate in regular editorial meetings at which ideas are suggested and content for future issues planned. They may be assigned responsibility to generate articles on certain topics, which they in turn assign to writers.

In addition, associate editors may:

- handle production tasks, such as proofreading galleys;
- represent the magazine at professional functions;
- attend workshops, seminars, and trade conventions to stay abreast of industry trends and techniques.

Salaries

The Newspaper Guild, which negotiates the salaries for unionized magazines, reported that the top minimum for an associate editor at *Scholastic* magazine in 1993 was about $32,500. At the *Nation,* the top minimum for this job was $31,300 after six years. Associate editors generally earn less than this, somewhere between $15,000 and $20,000.

Employment Prospects

The best job opportunities are on small and special-interest magazines, though job security is low. Many trade publications do not require experience or education in the industry they serve; background information is learned on the job.

Advancement Prospects

Work as an associate editor provides the necessary skill and background for higher editorial positions. There is a great deal of movement from one publication to another, especially in cities such as New York, which have a high concentration of publications. It is also possible to move into book-publishing editorial jobs.

Education

Associate editors are expected to have undergraduate degrees in communications, journalism, or liberal arts. Courses in publishing and advanced degrees in communications provide one with a competitive edge. Degrees in specialized fields are required by many technical, law, economics, scientific, and medical publications.

Experience/Skills

Prior experience as an editorial assistant, writer, or journalist is necessary for most associate-editor posi-

tions, though some jobs are at entry level. Also, work as an associate editor on a small magazine may be necessary to advance to associate editor on a large magazine.

Associate editors should be organized and deadline conscious. They should write and edit well, and understand the production process. They must be able to manage and direct others.

Unions/Associations

The Newspaper Guild represents employees of some major news and feature magazines, but by and large magazine editors are non-union. The principal professional association is the American Society of Magazine Editors. Many editors join trade associations and are auxiliary members of writers' groups. Women In Communications, Inc. is open to women in all media.

SENIOR EDITOR

CAREER PROFILE

Duties: Supervise major editorial department; manage lower-level editors, freelancers, and/or photographers; write some articles and columns

Alternate Title(s):   Executive Editor; Associate Editor

Salary Range: $22,000 to $115,000

Employment Prospects: Fair

Advancement Prospects: Poor

Prerequisites:

 Education—Undergraduate degree in journalism, English, communications, or liberal arts; advanced degree in journalism or specialized degrees for technical, scientific, or business publications

 Experience—Background as journalist, writer, or editor essential; academic career sometimes beneficial

 Special Skills—Editing; organization; managerial skills; knowledge of a particular field or specialty; production and graphics knowledge

CAREER LADDER

```
┌─────────────────────────────────┐
│   Editor; Executive Editor      │
└─────────────────────────────────┘

┌─────────────────────────────────┐
│        Senior Editor            │
└─────────────────────────────────┘

┌─────────────────────────────────┐
│       Associate Editor          │
└─────────────────────────────────┘
```

Position Description

Senior editors may have almost as much responsibility for a magazine's content as the editor. On small trade magazines, senior editors usually write the longest, most comprehensive articles as well as news. They offer story ideas and may even pass these ideas on to other writers. On larger publications, especially consumer magazines, senior editors manage a single major editorial department. In fact, the senior editor's title may reflect his or her area of responsibility, such as sports editor or fashion editor.

Although associate editors under the senior editor's supervision may handle all of the day-to-day tasks—reading unsolicited manuscripts, working with freelancers—the senior editor has ultimate responsibility for this work. Senior editors may deal directly with freelancers and occasionally assign photographs and illustrations for particular stories. If there are any changes in an assigned article's composition, or if the writer is having problems, the senior editor should—and must—know about them.

Senior editors participate regularly in editorial meetings, keeping the editor informed of the department's progress and suggesting story ideas. On a large publication, the senior editor may have the freedom to assign stories or columns without first getting the editor's approval. Such assignments may be the senior editor's ideas, but it is usually the associate editor's responsibility to write the stories or hire freelancers for the task.

Particularly on smaller magazines, the senior editor also writes. He or she may have a regular column or may produce articles or features as assigned. Senior editors for larger magazines rarely write; their supervisory and editorial duties take up a great deal of time.

In addition, senior editors may:

- handle production tasks, such as editing manuscripts and proofreading galleys;
- attend workshops, seminars, and trade shows to keep abreast of trends in the industry;
- represent the magazine at professional meetings and functions;

- handle day-to-day dealings with the printer.

Salaries

Senior editors earned a median of $40,000 in 1992. They also reported expecting an average salary for 1993 of around $43,500, a 5.9 percent increase, faring better than many magazine employees, according to a salary survey by *Folio* magazine.

However, although *Folio*'s survey found about the same number of women as men in editorial jobs, women made lower salaries even when they had comparable experience. Female senior editors with four to 10 years of experience made a median of $37,554, while male senior editors made $41,552.

Employment Prospects

The best job opportunities for senior editors are on small and special-interest publications, especially trade magazines. Such publications have smaller staffs and often need people who are experienced writers and editors. Background information may be learned on the job, but familiarity with a given industry is preferable.

Advancement Prospects

Opportunity to move up the ladder to executive editor and/or editor depends on the publication. Although senior editors at smaller magazines have more visibility and perhaps perform more duties—both writing and editing—advancement may be stymied if the longtime editor has no plans to step down. At a larger magazine, senior editors have more chance to change departments (often with more responsibility) or to be promoted to executive editor. This is because editors at large publications tend to move more frequently to other magazines or even decide to start their own publications.

Education

Senior editors should have degrees in journalism or English; communications or other liberal-arts fields are also acceptable. An advanced degree can give the senior editor an edge. For specialized fields, such as law, economics, medicine, science, or technology, course work or degrees in that specialty are essential.

Experience/Skills

Prior experience as a journalist or lower level editor is often required to become senior editor. Academic experience as a professor or researcher is often acceptable as one's only qualification for becoming a senior editor in a specialized field, such as medicine or science—particularly if he or she will be writing a regular column.

Since so much of the senior editor's duties are supervisory, he or she must be well organized and able to manage people well. Senior editors have to have excellent editing skills and should write well also.

Unions/Associations

The American Society of Magazine Editors is the principal professional organization for editors. Writers and editors also often join writers' groups, such as the American Society of Journalists and Authors, Inc. All women writers and editors are eligible to join Women In Communications, Inc. Editors of large news and feature magazines may belong to The Newspaper Guild.

EDITOR

Duties: Supervise magazine preparation; manage staff; rewrite and edit

Alternate Title(s): Editor-in-Chief; Editorial Director

Salary Range: $22,000 to $136,000

Employment Prospects: Poor

Advancement Prospects: Poor

Prerequisites:

Education—Undergraduate degree in communications, journalism, or liberal arts; specialized degrees for scientific and technical publications

Experience—Background as editor and journalist or writer essential

Special Skills—Grammar and editing knowledge; self-motivation; intellectual curiosity; administrative ability

```
┌─────────────────────────────┐
│                             │
│         Publisher           │
│                             │
└─────────────────────────────┘

┌─────────────────────────────┐
│                             │
│          Editor             │
│                             │
└─────────────────────────────┘

┌─────────────────────────────┐
│                             │
│ Senior Editor; Associate    │
│ Editor; Assistant Editor    │
│                             │
└─────────────────────────────┘
```

Position Description

The editor has complete responsibility for the editorial content and production of a magazine. He or she reports to the publisher; in some cases, the editor may be the publisher as well.

Responsibilities depend on the size of publication. On a small magazine, the editor may perform many of the day-to-day editing and production tasks. On a larger publication, those tasks are all delegated, and the editor concentrates on broad administrative duties. Some editors may be in charge of groups of publications under a common ownership.

The typical magazine editor divides working time between editorial, production, and administrative duties. Editorial duties include planning future issues, making assignments to the staff and freelance writers, editing and rewriting manuscripts, and assigning photo coverage. Editors supervise the activities of subordinate editors, as well as monitor work-in-progress against deadlines. They have ultimate approval of all articles and copy.

Production duties include working with a layout editor to decide placement of articles, use of photos, and other artwork, plus final approval of page layouts. On small publications, the editor may have sole responsibility for production; this may entail proofreading galleys and spending time at the typesetter's shop.

Administrative duties include hiring and firing staff members, planning and managing budgets, negotiating freelance contracts, writing reports, answering letters from readers, and other managerial tasks.

In addition, editors may:

- attend trade conventions;
- participate in promotional and publicity activities for the publication;
- write signed or bylined columns or editorials.

Salaries

Editors reported an average salary of $46,893 in 1993, down 6 percent from the previous year, as magazines continued to be hurt by tough economic times, according to a salary survey by *Folio* magazine. Those who worked on consumer magazines were hurt most, with salaries falling nearly 24 percent from 1992. Business magazines, on the other hand, saw their editors receive a 17 percent salary increase to an average of $50,613.

Editors responsible for one magazine also earned more than those responsible for more than one. Editors working for magazines with circulations of more than 100,000 earned average salaries of more than $50,000; those in the 50,000 to 99,000 circulation range made about $48,000 on average; and those on magazines with circulations under 49,999 made about $40,000 on average.

Women editors also made lower salaries than men, even when they had the same amount of experience. Male editors with 4 to 10 years of experience made a median of $41,137, while female editors with the same amount of experience made a median of $37,409. The gap widened to a $9,000 difference between the sexes when both had 11 to 20 years of experience, with men making a median of $56,399 and women making a median of $47,472, according to the *Folio* survey.

Employment Prospects

The market is competitive and characterized by high turnover. The best opportunities will be in business and trade publications, especially those serving growth industries such as executive management, computers, and health. The consumer field is unstable.

Advancement Prospects

Editor is the top position of many magazines, directly under the publisher (who almost always comes from the advertising and marketing side of the business). Since editor usually is the top position, advancement can only be made by moving on to bigger, more prestigious publications. Such advancement opportunities can be slow in coming—turnover is less frequent at higher editorial positions.

Education

As with many writing and editing jobs, there is little agreement as to the preferred major. Many editors have undergraduate degrees in communications or journalism, while others have degrees in liberal arts, history, philosophy, or the social sciences. Some editing jobs require business, economics, science, or engineering degrees.

Experience/Skills

The amount of experience required to be editor depends on the publication. Three to five years may be necessary for some jobs; ten years or more for others. Experience can include work as a journalist, assistant news editor, copy editor, or section editor; work in book publishing as a junior editor or editor; or work on a magazine staff in lower editorial positions.

Editors should have good judgment about what to publish and what to reject; they should have tact and the ability to direct and motivate staff members and freelance writers. They should be creative, highly self-motivated, and have a strong sense of curiosity. They should be able to meet deadlines and manage budgets. Production knowledge is also important.

Unions/Associations

Major professional associations include the American Society of Journalists and Authors, Inc.; American Society of Magazine Editors; and Women In Communications, Inc. Other writer associations as well as trade and industry groups are open to magazine editors. The Newspaper Guild represents some employees on major news and feature magazines.

EXECUTIVE EDITOR

CAREER PROFILE

Duties: Supervise magazine preparation; manage staff; assign stories; rewrite and edit

Alternate Title(s): Editor; Senior Editor; Managing Editor

Salary range: $22,000 to $55,000

Employment Prospects: Fair

Advancement Prospects: Fair

Prerequisites:

Education—Undergraduate degree in journalism, English, communications, or other liberal arts; advanced or specialized degrees for scientific, technical, or specialty publications

Experience—Several years' background as journalist, writer, or editor is essential

Special Skills—Knowledge of editing and grammar; good organization; knowledge of a particular field or specialty; ability to manage and direct people

CAREER LADDER

```
┌─────────────────────────────────┐
│            Editor               │
└─────────────────────────────────┘

┌─────────────────────────────────┐
│        Executive Editor         │
└─────────────────────────────────┘

┌─────────────────────────────────┐
│  Senior Editor; Associate Editor; │
│        Assistant Editor         │
└─────────────────────────────────┘
```

Position Description

The executive editor is a title more closely associated with larger publications, since smaller magazines allocate the executive editor's duties to senior editors and the top editor. The executive editor may have total responsibility for a particular magazine, reporting to the editor-in-chief in charge of a magazine group under common ownership. The structure of magazine staffs varies greatly from one publication to another.

Like senior editors, executive editors supervise lower-level editors and may take responsibility for freelancers, photographers, and illustrators. Executive editors assign stories, monitor the department or entire magazine's work, and have ultimate responsibility for final editing. They may also write features or articles, but usually they confine their responsibilies to editing. They are responsible for meeting deadlines.

Usually second-in-command to the editor, executive editors delegate authority and story assignments often without prior approval. Should the editor be out of town or ill, the executive editor takes over complete control of the magazine.

In addition, the executive editor may:

- represent the magazine at professional meetings or functions;
- attend workshops, annual meetings, seminars, and trade shows to stay abreast of industry trends;
- work with the editor on budget and give approval for editorial expenses;
- handle production skills, such as page-checking and proofreading.

Salaries

Median salaries are in the mid-thirties. Executive editors at large publications earn $55,000 to $100,000 or more. About 20 to 25 percent of executive editors receive bonus incentive compensation.

Employment Prospects

The best opportunities for an executive editor are with large publications, since smaller magazines often have no executive editorial position. Competition is strong, however. It is less likely that an executive editor will be hired from outside than promoted from within the organization.

Advancement Prospects

Since the executive editor is directly under the editor or editor-in-chief, advancement prospects are less promising than for senior editor. If the editor has been with a publication for many years and has no intention of leaving, an executive editor may have to move to another publication to advance to the editor's slot. Editors do move though, often to start their own magazines.

Education

Any executive editor worth his salt will have an undergraduate degree in journalism, English, communications, or liberal arts. Most have probably acquired advanced degrees in journalism or technical fields along the way as well or, at least, have taken advanced course work. Specialized publications, such as those for medicine, science, law, or high technology require advanced education.

Experience/Skills

Prior experience as a senior editor or editor of a smaller publication is usually necessary for most executive-editor positions. Work as a professor or academic researcher may be sufficient for certain spots, especially if there is more writing and less editing involved. In these cases, the executive editor's title reflects background and expertise more than editing and managerial functions.

Good writing and editing skills, as well as the ability to manage people effectively, are vital to an executive editor. Depending upon the executive editor's level of responsibility, he or she must also deal with the publisher, the advertising department, and the readers.

Unions/Associations

Executive editors, like their counterparts, may belong to the American Society of Magazine Editors or writers' trade organizations.

NEWS LIBRARIAN

CAREER PROFILE

Duties: Organize a library containing books, clippings, and databases to support research of magazine articles; assist writers and researchers; share information with other libraries

Alternate Titles(s): Information Manager; Library Director; Director of Information Services; Information Specialist, Supervisor of Information Services

Salary Range: $18,000 to $60,000+

Employment Prospects: Fair

Advancement Prospects: Poor

Prerequisites:

Education—For higher-level jobs, a master's degree in library science; a second advanced degree in another field is also helpful, such as a degree in English or political science

Experience—A part-time or summer job in a newsmagazine library or other library, or familiarity with computer databases and database research

Special Skills—Ability to work with journalists on deadline; good organizational skills; good research skills

CAREER LADDER

```
┌─────────────────────────────┐
│   News Library Director     │
└─────────────────────────────┘

┌─────────────────────────────┐
│      News Librarian         │
└─────────────────────────────┘

┌─────────────────────────────┐
│  Library Clerk; Researcher  │
└─────────────────────────────┘
```

Position Description

The most extensive libraries maintained by magazines can be found at news magazines, where a given week's editorial content can be extremely diverse. Although automation through computers has eliminated some library jobs, the use of computer databases and information networks with other librarians has made computer skills increasingly important. In fact, the field is evolving from traditional librarianship into information management.

Within a news magazine library, staffers are divided into different areas of expertise, where they field requests for information from the magazine's researchers and writers. Writers for overseas editions of the magazine may deal with a librarian assigned to that edition.

Lower-level jobs, such as filer, may be part-time or summer jobs with no experience needed. Higher-level jobs, however, invariably require library training, unlike the old days of the "morgue," when library staffers were generally magazine staffers who were near retirement, with no special training.

Librarians oversee collections of print material, still very important since most pre-1975 material is not available in computer databases. They are also responsible for collections of pictures and photographs. Librarians also may field requests from the public for specific stories that appeared in the magazine, finding the edition they appeared in and mailing them out.

Because news is continuously evolving, research often has to be done on a moment's notice to meet deadlines.

Salaries

A filer at one of the major news magazines may start at $18,000. A clerk may start at slightly more, around $20,000. Librarians start around $23,000, and senior librarians at $26,300.

Unionized librarians, represented by the Newspaper Guild, have their raises negotiated, usually about $15 or more per week per year.

Employment Prospects

While the use of computer technology may have initially reduced the number of library staffers needed at news magazine libraries, as magazines go on-line and the use of computer-aided research increases, there may be more call for people skilled at finding information fast.

Employment in special libraries, such as news magazine libraries, in-house private libraries for businesses or law libraries, is expected to be more promising than employment in traditional public libraries.

Advancement Prospects

Staffers may have to wait a long time to advance. At some news magazines, employees stay within the library for 10 years or more. However, many of these employees began as filers or summer interns and rose within the library as they obtained more training. Many hold dual degrees—one in library science, one in an area of expertise.

Library employees can also move on to become researchers or writers, or go on to work in other "specialty" libraries, such as an in-house library at a business or a law firm.

Education

To rise within a news magazine library, a master's of library science is essential. A second degree in a specialty area, such as political science, is also very helpful. Computer research experience is also increasingly important.

Experience/Skills

Library jobs require specific combinations of skills. Librarians need to know the news magazine business and what journalists require to satisfy their deadlines. They also must be versed in the techniques of research and library management. Many news librarians also are experts in a specific field. They must be well-organized, respond well to pressure, and have good communications skills.

Unions/Associations

The Special Libraries Association has a division for news libraries. News librarians are also represented by the Newspaper Guild at unionized magazines. Other organizations include the American Library Association and the American Society for Information Science.

TELEVISION

DESK ASSISTANT

CAREER PROFILE

Duties: Provide clerical and general assistance to television newsroom personnel

Alternate Title(s):   News Desk Assistant

Salary Range: $10,000 to $15,000

Employment Prospects: Fair

Advancement Prospects: Good

Prerequisites:

Education—High school diploma; some college preferred

Experience—None necessary, but news-related work is helpful

Special Skills—Clerical skills; writing ability; organization skills

CAREER LADDER

News Writer; Reporter; Production Assistant

Desk Assistant

High School; College

Position Description

Persons who are interested in careers in television news often begin as desk assistants, general apprentices who perform routine office and clerical tasks while learning the trade.

Generally this job is found only at medium and large stations and networks, where staffs are large enough to need desk assistants. Desk assistants may work part- or full-time, any hours of the day or night, any days of the week.

Duties include fielding telephone calls, distributing messages and mail, running errands, typing letters, reports, and scripts, and filing them. Desk assistants may be responsible for maintaining office supplies and seeing that equipment such as typewriters and copiers are serviced and repaired.

Duties relating directly to news operations include monitoring and ripping the copy from wire service printer terminals, and disseminating it among reporters and editors, as well as filling requests for information and tapes from the library or videotape storage room. Tapes must be logged in and out. Desk assistants may also handle the sending and receiving of tapes to and from sister stations and affiliates; they themselves may be required to act as couriers.

Desk or production assistants help with script preparation. "Breaking script," as it is called, is done for every news broadcast; this includes typing, updating, and delivering scripts to all appropriate persons. It's not unusual for multiple updates to be done for each broadcast, especially when major stories happen.

In addition, desk assistants may:

- do research work for reporters, such as collecting background information and updating facts, sports scores, and weather reports;
- learn production work by assisting in the control room;
- learn reporting by accompanying reporters on assignments.

Salaries

Entry-level jobs in television pay low salaries. Most desk assistants earn between $10,000 and $15,000, even at large stations and networks. Earnings over $15,000 are rare. Desk assistants are paid either a weekly rate or, if part-time, an hourly rate.

Employment Prospects

Most desk-assistant jobs are concentrated in medium to large market cities, including network headquarters and bureaus. Cable is opening more opportunities for desk assistants. Finding a job may be difficult and time-consuming, but once in the field, prospects are good for advancement because of high turnover.

Advancement Prospects

The desk assistant is in an excellent position for internal promotion to production, newswriting, or reporting work. The successful candidate for advancement must demonstrate a knowledge of broadcasting operations, good writing and speaking skills, and good news judgment. He or she should be highly motivated, seeking assignments beyond the normal range of the desk assistant's duties.

Education

A college degree is not necessary for desk-assistant jobs, but it is preferred for higher positions. Some desk assistants work part-time while they attend college. Studies should include communications, liberal arts, history, social sciences, and courses in broadcasting.

Experience/Skills

Any kind of experience in a news-related job is helpful, such as working on a community newspaper, or school publication, radio, or TV station. Clerical and office skills are paramount for desk assistants, who must type and file reports, correspondence, and scripts. Good organization also is important; desk assistants may have to quickly locate or handle information for someone under deadline pressure. Those who aspire to newswriting or reporting jobs should have good journalistic research and writing skills, as well as strong self-motivation.

Unions/Associations

At many major stations and the networks, desk assistants belong to such unions as the National Association of Broadcast Employees and Technicians, American Federation of Television and Radio Artists, or Writers Guild of America.

RESEARCHER

CAREER PROFILE

Duties: Assist television staff with background research for news and other programs

Alternate Title(s): None

Salary Range: $14,300 to $35,000

Employment Prospects: Fair

Advancement Prospects: Good

Prerequisites:

Education—Undergraduate degree in communications or liberal arts

Experience—Any background in the media helpful

Special Skills—Accuracy; good organizational skills; attention to details; good writing ability; curiousity

CAREER LADDER

```
┌─────────────────────────────────┐
│ Reporter; News Writer; Associate │
│            Producer              │
└─────────────────────────────────┘

┌─────────────────────────────────┐
│            Researcher            │
└─────────────────────────────────┘

┌─────────────────────────────────┐
│ College; Desk Assistant; Production │
│            Assistant             │
└─────────────────────────────────┘
```

Position Description

Most researchers employed at television stations work in the news department. The job is an entry-level position, though there may be levels of junior and senior researchers at large stations and networks.

Researchers assist reporters, news writers, and news directors or editors with gathering background information for stories. A half-hour broadcast can contain anywhere from 14 to 30 stories, and a single researcher may be assigned to work on several stories for each broadcast.

They do most of their work by telephone, pre-interviewing sources to find the best ones for the reporter to then interview on tape. They also interview sources in order to gather and check information pertaining to stories, then write summary reports of their findings for reporters or news writers to use. The job is often demanding and pressured, and researchers must be able to absorb a wide range of information quickly, sorting out the most important material.

Researchers also generate ideas for stories. They maintain contact with news sources, and they scan magazines and newspapers. They may be assigned a geographic area of responsibility or to certain topics, such as education, business, or government.

Researchers help reporters assemble audio and visual materials for stories, searching library files or contacting other stations to acquire film or videotape footage.

In addition, researchers may:

- do follow-up work on stories to check for new developments;
- work on other programs or documentaries;
- work in the marketing department, tracking ratings.

Salaries

Researchers are likely to be paid on a weekly or hourly rate, with extra compensation for overtime. Some may work only part-time. Junior researchers earn roughly $14,300 to $16,000 a year, while senior researchers with more than three years of experience can earn up to $35,000, including overtime. The best-paying jobs are at large stations and the networks.

Employment Prospects

Researcher usually is considered an entry-level position in the news department, though large stations and networks may require some experience. Part-time openings, if offered, should be seriously considered; they may lead to full-time work.

Advancement Prospects

It may be difficult to find a job as a researcher but, once established, advancement opportunities are good. Researchers have several avenues open to them: reporting the news; writing scripts for the news; or assisting in the production of news and other programs.

Education

Undergraduate degrees in communications, history, social sciences, or liberal arts are preferred for jobs in the news media. Also acceptable are degrees in political science or business. Courses in broadcasting are helpful.

Experience/Skills

Any experience in the news media is helpful for competing for researcher positions, including school or community publications. Researchers may have previously worked as desk or production assistants, reporters, or news writers for newspapers or radio stations.

Researchers should be adept at quickly gathering information. They should be well organized, detail-oriented, and comfortable with interviewing over the phone. They should be able to handle pressure well, and provide clearly written reports and summaries of their findings. News judgment also is important.

Unions/Associations

Researchers may belong to such unions as the American Federation of Television and Radio Artists, Writers Guild of America, or National Association of Broadcast Employees and Technicians. Some researchers may join professional associations as well, such as the National Academy of Television Arts and Sciences or the Academy of Television Arts and Sciences.

REPORTER

Duties: Prepare news and feature stories; report on air

Alternate Title(s): Newscaster; Correspondent

Salary Range: Under $15,300 to $69,500+

Employment Prospects: Fair to good

Advancement Prospects: Poor to fair

Prerequisites:

Education—Undergraduate degree in communications, liberal arts, history, social sciences, or political science

Experience—Work as news writer or researcher helpful

Special Skills—Good reporting, writing, and speaking ability; self-motivation; astute news judgment

```
┌──────────────────────────────────┐
│    Anchorperson; Assistant News  │
│             Director             │
└──────────────────────────────────┘

┌──────────────────────────────────┐
│             Reporter             │
└──────────────────────────────────┘

┌──────────────────────────────────┐
│  News Writer; Researcher; Assistant; │
│             College              │
└──────────────────────────────────┘
```

Position Description

The prime responsibility of a television reporter is to gather news and prepare stories for broadcast. The work involves interviewing sources, researching facts, directing a film crew, writing a script, delivering news on the air, and working with film editors.

Time pressures are enormous. Not only do reporters work against the clock for scheduled news programs—they are limited severely in the amount of time they have to present a news story. A major story typically runs about two minutes; many stories run 90 seconds or less. Reporters must strive to summarize highlights, give important information, and make the story visually interesting as well.

Reporters are assigned stories and estimated time allotments by an assignment editor or news director. Editors often rely on a reporter's news judgment to determine the slant and length of a story. Some reporters, especially those at large stations, may specialize in certain areas, such as business or politics, and have more control over the stories they generate.

Gathering information involves interviewing people by phone and in person. Some stations employ researchers and assistants to do background legwork and

news writers to write scripts. Otherwise, reporters do those tasks themselves.

Reporters then go on location with a camera crew and direct the shooting. Their on-air report may include portions of a taped interview, a voice-over of the visuals, and a stand-up summary. Live reports have gained increasing popularity as new technology has made smaller, more portable cameras available.

Stories can run the gamut from city council meetings to major disasters. They can be features or investigative pieces. Some reporters occasionally prepare special series.

Salaries

The early 1990s saw salaries at typical television and radio stations stagnating or losing ground. Graduates of journalism schools seeking jobs in television or radio in those years also had a harder time finding jobs than graduates looking in print, public relations or advertising.

In 1993, television and radio salaries made moderate gains over inflation, with the most impressive increases in the smallest television markets, where pay had been declining for the previous five years.

The median pay for television reporters in 1993 was $21,440. However, market size has a great deal of influence over television salaries. Commercial stations also pay more than public broadcasting.

The typical reporter in the largest markets made a median of $51,250 in 1993. In the smallest markets, the median was $15,230. Salaries are expected to continue to grow modestly.

The best salaries are offered in the east, and the lowest in the midwest and south.

Salaries in television news in every market are lower than their counterparts in print, with only television anchors in major markets doing better than comparable print journalists, according to the Radio-Television News Directors Association. This is partly because competition for advertising revenues is greater when three or more television stations exist in the same area, where most daily newspapers enjoy a monopoly.

Growth in the profession should be provided by new radio and television stations and the growth of cable television systems. Most openings for announcers will come from announcers leaving the field or the labor force.

Reporter jobs will be hard to come by, as the field attracts more job seekers than there are jobs. Those who specialize in such areas as business, consumer, and health news may have an advantage in the job market.

Advancement Prospects

Reporters generally begin at a station in a small community and then try to move to a job in a large city. Many reporters also aspire to anchor positions, jobs with semi-celebrity status, high salaries, and glamour. Prospects for obtaining these jobs are poor, with intense competition for limited openings.

Off-camera jobs that might interest ambitious reporters include assistant news director or news director.

Education

Formal training in this field, an undergraduate degree in communications or liberal arts, is almost always required, but taped auditions also weigh heavily. Specialized degrees in business, health or law may be advantageous. Communications courses should include study in broadcasting.

High school or college courses in English, public speaking, drama, foreign languages, and electronics may also prove valuable.

Experience/Skills

At very small stations and cable operations, it may be possible to get a reporting job right out of college. At such small stations, a reporter may be required to shoot his or her own film, edit it, and deliver it on air.

However, most reporters have had some kind of experience before they go on the air. Good entry-level jobs include production assistant, researcher, production secretary, or newswriter. Some newspaper reporters are also able to switch to television.

Experience on college publications or radio and television stations is also an asset. A reporter should have a pleasant and well-controlled voice, good timing, good pronunciation, use correct English, and appear neat and well-groomed. Knowledge of a wide variety of subjects also helps, as reporters are often required to ad-lib on the air.

Television reporters also need the same skills as all journalists—accuracy, astute news judgment, ability to work under pressure, and strong self-motivation.

Unions/Associations

The Writers Guild of America, National Association of Broadcast Employees and Technicians, and American Federation of Television and Radio Artists are major unions representing many TV reporters. Small stations may not be unionized. Professional associations include Radio-Television News Directors Association; International Radio and Television Society; Radio and Television Correspondents Association (for Congressional reporters); National Academy of Television Arts and Sciences; Women in Communications, Inc.; Academy of Television Arts and Sciences; and Society of Professional Journalists, Sigma Delta Chi.

ANCHOR

CAREER PROFILE

Duties: Host news or other shows; read the news or other copy on air; interview guests; may also go on location for coverage of major events

Alternate Title(s): Anchorperson

Salary Range: Under $21,300 to $400,000+

Employment Prospects: Poor

Advancement Prospects: Poor

Prerequisites:

Education—Undergraduate degree in communications or political science with emphasis on liberal arts; graduate degree may be preferred

Experience—Many years as reporter, correspondent, or other television positions

Special Skills/Attributes—Pleasing appearance on camera; good voice; competitiveness; ability to work under pressure; ability to be spontaneous

CAREER LADDER

```
┌─────────────────────────────┐
│     Major Market Anchor      │
└─────────────────────────────┘

┌─────────────────────────────┐
│           Anchor             │
└─────────────────────────────┘

┌─────────────────────────────┐
│    Reporter, Correspondent   │
└─────────────────────────────┘
```

Position Description

The anchor job is the brass ring sought by many who start careers in television reporting. Competition for these coveted jobs is fierce. Anchors earn their jobs by putting in years of hard work as reporters or correspondents, and by becoming well-versed in politics and other issues of great public concern.

The anchor serves as host to a news or entertainment show and reads the news, introduces the stories, and interviews the guests who appear on the show. Essentially, the entire show revolves around the anchor or anchors. These individuals become public personalities and celebrities.

In small markets, anchors do their own research, writing and work with production on editing videotape for broadcast. In larger markets, these functions are performed by supporting staff, and the anchor's primary job is to read the copy and perhaps interview guests. Prior to broadcast time, all anchors review the contents of the broadcast with staff. The anchor has a say in determining the content and in giving time priority to various stories. Increasingly, news and entertainment shows provide time for anchors to question reporters and exchange conversation and banter. Some of this is orchestrated and some is spontaneous.

In addition to the regular show, anchors may go on location for major events, such as conferences and conventions, and may work on documentaries or specials to be broadcast at different times.

Salaries

As with other television news jobs, salaries of anchors largely depend on the size of the market in which they work. In 1993, anchors earned a median of $36,750; high or star anchors, who have demonstrated ratings pull, $55,250.

However, these salaries ranged from a median of $227,500 for an anchor in the top markets and $101,770 for rank-and-file anchors in those markets, down to $21,345 for a typical anchor in the smallest markets and $25,185 for the station's highest paid anchor in the smallest markets.

A small number of star personalities earn $400,000 and up. But star anchors saw their 1993 salaries drop to an average of $250,000, a 5 percent setback.

Anchors in major markets have the only jobs in television news that pay better than comparable print positions, according to the Radio-Television News Directors Association.

Employment Prospects

Only a small percentage of television reporters ever become anchors. The typical station hires two or more anchors, while major stations and networks have numerous anchors. The constant emphasis on ratings creates high turnover as anchors don't make the grade or are picked off by competing stations or higher-paying stations in larger markets. The expansion of cable television news programs is likely to increase employment opportunities in the future. Job openings are somewhat better for women and minorities, as stations seek to provide a balance in highly visible positions.

Advancement Prospects

The anchor job is the highest position for a reporter or correspondent, and the only advancement then can be achieved by moving up to larger markets or the networks.

Education

Virtually all jobs in television news require an undergraduate degree in communications or one of the liberal arts; some posts may require a graduate degree. Other fields of study can include political science.

Experience/Skills

Reporters typically spend many years in the field before becoming eligible for promotion to anchor. Grooming is of paramount importance. Anchors must have a pleasing on-camera appearance and personality and a good, clear voice. They must convey authority to the viewer. They also must be able to ad-lib and think on their feet in the event something unexpected happens live on the air. When major stories break, they must be able to react quickly. Because competition for these jobs is keen, anchors must be tough and stay on their toes.

Unions/Associations

Anchors may belong to the Writers Guild of America, the American Federation of Television and Radio Artists, the RTNDA, and the Society of Professional Journalists.

NEWS WRITER

CAREER PROFILE

Duties: Write scripts for news programs

Alternate Title(s): Senior Editor

Salary Range: $20,000 to $50,000+

Employment Prospects: Fair to good

Advancement Prospects: Fair to good

Prerequisites:

Education—Undergraduate degree in liberal arts, history, social sciences, or communications

Experience—None to several years in similar or related position

Special Skills—Good news judgment; script-writing ability; speed

CAREER LADDER

```
┌─────────────────────────────────────┐
│                                     │
│   News Editor; Reporter; Producer   │
│                                     │
└─────────────────────────────────────┘

┌─────────────────────────────────────┐
│                                     │
│            News Writer              │
│                                     │
└─────────────────────────────────────┘

┌─────────────────────────────────────┐
│                                     │
│  College; Desk Assistant; Researcher │
│                                     │
└─────────────────────────────────────┘
```

Position Description

News writer is a fast-pace, high-pressure job in television news departments. It requires quick, sound news judgment, good reportorial skills, and the ability to write for the ear rather than the eye.

News writers may be assigned any shift around the clock, any day of the week, depending on the station's needs. They usually begin their work day by reviewing wire copy, newspapers, and stories aired on previous newscasts. They attend one or more editorial meetings each day; decisions at these meetings are made on what stories to cover and who will be responsible for tracking and updating breaking stories.

A single news writer may be responsible for writing copy for a major newscast and one or more regularly scheduled news breaks or digests (which typically include about 30 seconds of news). News writers often do their own research, corroborating other news sources and checking out conflicting reports, such as differences in the number of fatalities in a disaster or accident. They interview sources by phone and research information in the station's library. Often they are aided by researchers and desk assistants. They also coordinate graphics and tapes to be used during newscasts, working with artists, producers, and representatives of other television stations.

News writers must be able to write tight scripts that are easy to read and easy for listeners to understand— and also fit a teleprompter screen. They are restricted by time—news stories seldom run over 90 seconds and may be as short as 10 seconds for news breaks—and their scripts must match what viewers see on their sets. News writers either preview tapes or receive "shot sheets" that describe visuals and time lengths. Scripts are written down to the second, a skill that can only be developed over time, with experience.

The daily workload for news writers often varies. Reporters write their own scripts, and anchors often write scripts for the lead stories. The workload also depends on the day's news—a news writer may work on a few big stories or on many small ones.

News writers work under the supervision of an editor, assistant news director, or news director. Overtime is often required, and shifts of 10 to 11 hours are not uncommon.

In addition, news writers may:

- produce news digests, documentaries, or other programs;
- supervise tape editing for news reports;
- write promotional scripts to publicize upcoming broadcasts.

Salaries

The average starting pay for a news writer was $24,759 in 1992; the average pay, $31,326; and the average top pay, $42,236.

Employment Prospects

Job prospects for news writers are fair to good, though beginners usually will have to go to small stations. Networks and large stations hire only seasoned news writers who have worked their way up the markets. Cable and independent stations may offer the best prospects for beginners.

Advancement Prospects

News writers have fair to good chances for advancement, either as news editors, news directors, or as producers. Some experienced news writers take on production assignments as part of their development.

Education

News writers must be able to handle wide ranges of topics and need some historical perspective of news events. A broad education in liberal arts, social sciences, history, or political science can be better preparation than a degree in communications or broadcasting. Broadcasting courses are helpful for learning the technical end of the business.

Experience/Skills

At small stations, news writer is often an entry-level position. Large stations and networks require experience and proven skills. Candidates typically work as desk assistants or researchers before becoming news writers.

News writers must be able to condense important information into scripts written for the ear. They seldom have time to revise. They must be good, accurate, detail-oriented researchers. News writers also must be adaptable and versatile, able to understand many different topics and issues.

Unions/Associations

News writers in large markets usually are members of a union, such as Writers Guild of America, National Association of Broadcast Employees and Technicians, or American Federation of Television and Radio Artists. Major professional associations are the National Academy of Television Arts and Sciences; Academy of Television Arts and Sciences; Radio-Television News Directors Association; and Society of Professional Journalists, Sigma Delta Chi.

ASSISTANT NEWS DIRECTOR

CAREER PROFILE

Duties: Assign news coverage; manage news operations

Alternate Title(s): Assistant News Editor; Assignment Editor; Managing Editor; City Editor

Salary Range: $19,925 to $77,000+

Employment Prospects: Poor

Advancement Prospects: Good

Prerequisites:
Education—Undergraduate degree in communications, liberal arts, history, social sciences, or political science

Experience—Several years' experience as reporter

Special Skills—Good news judgment; managerial ability; organizational skills

CAREER LADDER

```
┌─────────────────────────────┐
│        News Director        │
└─────────────────────────────┘

┌─────────────────────────────┐
│   Assistant News Director   │
└─────────────────────────────┘

┌─────────────────────────────┐
│          Reporter           │
└─────────────────────────────┘
```

Position Description

Assistant news directors are middle managers responsible for the day-to-day supervision of television station newsrooms. They work under the supervision of a news director, executing the director's decisions. Depending on the size of staff, they have a certain amount of their own decision-making authority for assigning reporters and crews to stories. They evaluate suggestions for stories and monitor the reports made by reporters.

Assistant news directors are responsible for many of the nuts and bolts of daily operations. They may make up work schedules so that the newsroom has adequate personnel at all times and complies with any union regulations concerning varying shifts in a given period of time. They also monitor assignments and work-in-progress. They may assume complete responsibility for fast-breaking stories.

Managerial responsibilities include coordinating the work of various departments, solving problems, and handling complaints. Assistant news directors are in complete charge of the newsroom in the absence of the news directors.

At some small stations, assistant news directors may do some of the writing, editing, and reporting for newscasts.

Salaries

The 1993 median salary for assistant news director was $44,500. This range extended from $19,925 for an assistant news director in the smallest markets with a full-time staff of less than 10 to $77,000 in the largest markets with a staff of more than 50.

Employment Prospects

Job turnover is high, but candidates for assistant news director have poor employment prospects due to keen competition. Small stations may not have this middle-management position, but large stations or networks may have several. Assistant news directors usually are promoted from within, from the ranks of reporters. More opportunities are becoming available in the rapidly growing cable industry.

Advancement Prospects

Assistant news directors are directly in line for news-director positions, which undergo high turnover. The best opportunities are in commercial and cable television; public television staffs are shrinking due to cutbacks in federal support. Assistant news directors may also advance their careers by switching to a related field, such as newspapers, wire services, or government.

Education

An undergraduate degree in communications, English, liberal arts, history, or social sciences is considered the minimum educational requirement. Other degrees include political science, economics, or business.

Experience/Skills

Assistant news directors typically have worked for several years as reporters, researchers, or news desk assistants. They may also have had experience in radio or print journalism. They should be familiar with video and studio operations.

Sound news judgment and leadership qualities are important for this job. Decisions must be made quickly and often under pressure. Assistant news directors need to be able to edit, write, and even report, as needed. They should have managerial and leadership qualities. In addition, they should understand Federal Communications Commission regulations governing fairness and equal-use time, as well as laws concerning copyright and libel.

Unions/Associations

The major professional associations are the Radio-Television News Directors Association, National Academy of Television Arts and Sciences and Academy of Television Arts and Sciences. Women may join Women in Communications, Inc. Assistant news directors who write or report on air may belong to such unions as the American Federation of Television and Radio Artists; Writers Guild of America; or National Association of Broadcast Employees and Technicians. In addition, some assistant news directors may belong to the Society of Professional Journalists, Sigma Delta Chi.

NEWS DIRECTOR

CAREER PROFILE

Duties: Assign news coverage; manage entire news operations of a TV station; determine policy

Alternate Title(s):   News Editor

Salary Range: Under $28,895 to $97,625+

Employment Prospects: Poor

Advancement Prospects: Poor

Prerequisites:

Education—Undergraduate or graduate degree in communications, liberal arts, history, social sciences, or political science

Experience—Several years in TV or radio news work

Special Skills—Good news judgment; managerial and administrative ability

CAREER LADDER

```
┌─────────────────────────────────┐
│   General Manager; News Vice    │
│           President             │
└─────────────────────────────────┘

┌─────────────────────────────────┐
│         News Director           │
└─────────────────────────────────┘

┌─────────────────────────────────┐
│ Assistant News Director; Reporter│
└─────────────────────────────────┘
```

Position Description

Television news directors have overall responsibility for stations' news operations. They decide and coordinate the content of news programs, including what will be covered, how the stories will be presented, and which reporters will be assigned to them. They edit and review scripts and file reports. Ultimate responsibility for and authority over what appears on the air is theirs.

An average station has a news staff of about 10; larger stations typically have 40 or more. In addition, news directors coordinate the technical operations of news production. This involves assigning camera crews to stories and camera operators to work in the studio.

News directors report to station general managers or, in the case of large stations, to vice president of news. They often work long hours under great pressure, and their jobs are heavily dependent on ratings. In breaking major stories, they must make quick decisions.

News directors hire and promote news staffs. They are involved in determining budgets, and they handle many administrative responsibilities. At small stations, news directors may also take part in news gathering and reporting, or they may act as talk show hosts.

In addition, news directors may supervise public-affairs programs; they may also coordinate news activities with programming and other departments.

Salaries

The median 1993 salary for news director was $48,655. In the largest markets, the median was $97,625; in the smallest, with a staff of under 10, the median was $28,895.

In addition, 1993 saw the pay gap between male and female news directors decrease. The median for female news directors was $40,500, 19 percent less than for male directors. In 1992, women in the job made 31 percent less than men. According to the Radio-Television News Directors Association, such gaps tend to close as women catch up in experience.

Employment Prospects

Though the federal government projects moderate overall growth in TV jobs during the next decade, competition will remain strong for news-director positions, particularly in major cities. Turnover is high, especially at large stations where news directors seldom stay more than two to three years. Aggressive job candidates, however, are many. More opportunities are available in the rapidly growing cable industry.

Advancement Prospects

News directors face limited opportunities for advancement; at many stations their job is the highest on the news side. Some may be promoted to general managers, though sales managers are the most likely candidates for that position. Large stations and networks offer vice president and assistant vice president positions in news.

Education

An undergraduate degree in communications, liberal arts, history, English, or social sciences is considered the minimum educational requirement. Many news directors have degrees in political science. A master's degree may be helpful for employment and advancement.

Experience/Skills

Television news directors generally have had at least several years' seasoning as reporters or assistant news directors in TV or radio. Large stations require more experience than small stations. News directors need sound news judgment and the ability to make quick decisions. They should understand Federal Communications Commission regulations governing fairness and equal-use time, as well as laws concerning copyright and libel.

Unions/Associations

The major professional associations are the Radio-Television News Directors Association, National Academy of Television Arts and Sciences, and Academy of Television Arts and Sciences. Women may join Women In Communications, Inc. Since news directors are managers, they generally do not belong to unions.

NEWS LIBRARIAN

CAREER PROFILE

Duties: Catalog and maintain a library of reference materials and an archive of videotape; provide background information and previously shot videotape for news segments; license archival material for sale to viewers who request a taped copy of a story or to production companies who need footage for films, documentaries, or other media productions

Alternate title(s):   News Information Resource Manager; News Library Director; Information Manager

Salary Range: $24,000 to $60,000

Employment Prospects: Poor

Advancement Prospects: Fair

Prerequisites:
  Education—A master's degree in library science is necessary for top positions

  Experience—Familiarity with television and video helpful; computer-aided research experience another plus

  Special Skills—Ability to work quickly on deadline; good organizational skills; knowledge of television news production needs and news journalism; good oral and written communication skills

CAREER LADDER

```
┌─────────────────────────────────┐
│     News Library Manager        │
└─────────────────────────────────┘

┌─────────────────────────────────┐
│         News Librarian          │
└─────────────────────────────────┘

┌─────────────────────────────────┐
│   Library Clerk; Researcher     │
└─────────────────────────────────┘
```

Position Description

A good library with professionally cataloged videotape is a vital component of larger television news operations. Although some television libraries rely on staffers with backgrounds in video, larger libraries now hire professional librarians with degrees in library science, and train them in television.

Television news librarians function as broadcast journalists, part of a production team that includes writers, editors, technicians, producers, graphic artists, and reporters.

They must ensure that every news video cataloged includes the necessary journalistic elements of who, what, where, and when. Much of the video included in the library contains "raw" or unedited footage, which is more valuable than polished, edited footage for future production and historical purposes.

News librarians also provide background information for news segments, researching the lives of key figures in a news event and happenings leading up to the story. Often the reference librarians have two hours or more to answer questions, but sometimes they are left with just a minute or two.

Computer databases, such as DIALOG and NEXIS, are used for research, as are books, newspapers, magazines, and clipping files.

The library also coordinates sales of videotape, a money-maker for news organizations. The tapes are sought by people who want copies of a specific news segment and those seeking tape of a historic nature for documentaries, films, and other media productions.

The library staff must decide which tape to save and document and which to discard. Videotape not properly documented can be history lost.

Salaries

Salaries can range from $24,000 to $60,000. Pay at network news stations can be higher.

Job Prospects

Job prospects can be good for those with the right combination of education and skills. News librarians need both a knowledge of library management techniques and a good understanding of television journalism. Libraries provide a range of job opportunities, starting with tape sales and library assistant jobs that may not require much training or experience, to reference librarian jobs and, at the top, the library manager and director positions. Smaller television stations may not hire any professional library staff.

Employment prospects for news librarians are better in newspapers than in television.

While news libraries employ relatively small numbers of people, the need for information and the importance of good library systems to news organizations is likely to grow. Because libraries can also sell videotape at a profit, staff will be needed to provide this service as well.

Advancement Prospects

Advancement can be slow as those in the limited number of high-level jobs hang on to them for some time. With the proper education, employees who start in entry-level jobs can hope to advance, move to other types of television jobs, or move to other types of special libraries.

Education

A master's degree in library science is increasingly required for higher-level library jobs. In the past, experience with video might have been good enough. Smaller stations also might not require professional library training.

Experience/Skills

Computer research skills, good organizational skills, and knowledge of the basics of journalism are needed for this position in addition to training in basic information storage and retrieval.

Unions/Associations

The Special Libraries Association has a division for news libraries. News librarians may also belong to the National Academy of Television Arts and Sciences.

COMMUNITY AFFAIRS DIRECTOR

CAREER PROFILE

Duties: Write and produce public-service announcements and programs; meet with community groups

Alternate Title(s): Community-Relations Director; Public-Service Director

Salary Range: $15,000 to $30,000+

Employment Prospects: Poor

Advancement Prospects: Fair

Prerequisites:

 Education—Undergraduate degree in social sciences, liberal arts, or communications

 Experience—Background in nonprofit or service organizations

 Special Skills—Good writing ability; interpersonal skills

CAREER LADDER

```
┌─────────────────────────────────────┐
│                                      │
│      Program Director; Producer      │
│                                      │
└─────────────────────────────────────┘

┌─────────────────────────────────────┐
│                                      │
│      Community-Affairs Director      │
│                                      │
└─────────────────────────────────────┘

┌─────────────────────────────────────┐
│                                      │
│    Nonprofit-Organization Director   │
│                                      │
└─────────────────────────────────────┘
```

Position Description

The Federal Communications Commission (FCC) requires all licensed commercial and public television stations to devote a certain amount of air time to community affairs and public-service announcements (PSAs). At many stations, the responsibility for managing and coordinating these operations is given to community-affairs directors.

Community-affairs directors plan—and in many cases write and produce—public-affairs programs on local news and issues. These may include talk and panel shows or documentaries. Sometimes the community-affairs directors work on-air as hosts, moderators, or narrators of programs. In addition, they develop, prepare, and supervise the production of public-service announcements—short spots that feature upcoming community events or highlight the services of particular groups. The station's public-service activities and feedback from the community are documented for the FCC.

Community-affairs directors spend much of their time meeting with local nonprofit and service groups to discuss proposals and concerns, which they then evaluate for air time. They also represent the station at group meetings, sometimes as featured speakers. They may also plan special public-service events sponsored by their stations.

Community-affairs directors generally work regular business hours, though evening and weekend work is often required for organization meetings. They report either to program directors or general managers.

In addition, community affairs directors may:

- perform publicity and promotion duties;
- conduct station tours for the public;
- coordinate speaking engagements for other station personnel.

Salaries

Community-affairs directors earn moderate salaries, averaging about $20,000 to $25,000. Small stations pay considerably less, as low as $15,000, while large stations pay up to $30,000 or more.

Employment Prospects

Job opportunities are poor, due to limited job openings in commercial television and budget cutbacks in public television. Opportunities may be further limited by locale. Stations frequently select candidates who already are familiar with local community groups and concerns. Many small stations do not have designated positions for community affairs.

Advancement Prospects

Prospects are fair for advancement into programming or producing; these jobs, however, require additional skills. Community-affairs directors may also advance by moving to positions in other fields, such as nonprofit organizations or the federal government.

Education

A broad education in liberal arts or social sciences is ideal for service work. The minimum requirement is an undergraduate degree. Other areas of emphasis include urban affairs, government, public relations, and communications.

Experience/Skills

Most community-affairs directors enter television with at least two years of experience in a nonprofit organization, as director or as manager of public information. They are familiar with local businesses and government units. They understand local social issues and concerns.

Community-affairs directors are personable and sensitive in their relationships with the community. They also must be good writers and speakers, and understand television production.

Unions/Associations

Community-affairs directors may belong to a variety of associations, depending on their communities and major interests. They may also belong to the Public Relations Society of America, Inc.; Women In Communications, Inc.; National Academy of Television Arts and Sciences; or Academy of Television Arts and Sciences.

RADIO

REPORTER

CAREER PROFILE

Duties: News gathering, rewriting, and editing; announcing

Alternate Title(s):   Newscaster

Salary Range: Under $14,280 to $50,000+

Employment Prospects: Good

Advancement Prospects: Good

Prerequisites:

Education—High school diploma sufficient for some entry-level jobs; undergraduate degree in communications, broadcasting, or liberal arts necessary for most positions

Experience—None to one or more years

Special Skills—Sound news judgment; concise writing; good speaking ability; tape editing skills

CAREER LADDER

```
┌──────────────────────────────────┐
│                                  │
│   News Director; Air Personality; │
│            Announcer             │
│                                  │
└──────────────────────────────────┘

┌──────────────────────────────────┐
│                                  │
│            Newscaster            │
│                                  │
└──────────────────────────────────┘

┌──────────────────────────────────┐
│                                  │
│    Continuity Writer; College;    │
│           High School            │
│                                  │
└──────────────────────────────────┘
```

Position Description

Radio reporters generally have two primary responsibilities: to collect and prepare news stories for broadcast, and to read their copy on the air. At large stations, these responsibilities may be divided into two jobs held by different persons—one who collects, writes, and edits; and one who announces.

Reporters do most of their work in the studio, where they monitor incoming wire-service copy and other news sources. They select stories for the newscasts, and they rewrite and edit the copy to fit time limitations and the interests of their audiences. Some reporters may do their own news gathering, by taping interviews over the phone or in person. Some may actually be sent out of the studio to cover disasters or major news events. The tapes, called "actualities," are edited for quotes to be aired. It's not uncommon to have to rewrite copy just before airtime.

Most radio stations air news breaks on the hour, giving shorter, periodic updates as well, especially for major, breaking stories. Many AM radio stations are all news/talk, a format that has gained considerable popularity in recent years. The news/talk format allows longer and more in-depth stories, providing more opportunities for feature stories and personality interviews as well.

Reporters work under the direction of a news director who assigns coverage and responsibilities. Working hours can range anywhere around the clock, seven days a week; most beginners usually draw evening, night, and weekend shifts. Overtime is often required.

Most radio stations have small facilities and staffs. At smaller stations, reporters are more likely to either work part-time or share other duties, such as ad copywriting or programming.

In addition, reporters may prepare and read news analyses or editorials, and research stories for major air personalities.

Salaries

The median annual salary for radio reporters in 1993 was $14,930. Stations in the smallest markets with one-person staffs paid a median of $14,280; major market stations paid a median of $22,900. A radio anchor in a major market could expect a median salary of $30,025.

Salaries were best in the East and worst in the South. Radio salaries also ran a distant third when compared to television and newspaper salaries.

Employment Prospects

Most of the nation's 4,500 AM radio stations and 4,000 FM stations have at least one full-time newsperson. Most have more than one, and medium to large stations have news staffs of 10 to 40 persons or more. Other broadcast news jobs are available at the major networks and news wire services. Beginners will find their best opportunities at small stations. Competition is keen.

Advancement Prospects

Turnover in radio jobs in general is high. In addition, according to industry sources, openings occur more frequently in news and clerical positions than in such other areas as programming and ad copywriting. A reporter can advance to news director, or build an audience to become an air personality or announcer.

Education

A high school diploma is the minimum requirement for many entry-level jobs. A college degree in broadcasting or mass communications is strongly recom-mended to be competitive for more prestigious, higher paying positions.

Experience/Skills

Beginners who have had experience at school newspapers or radio or TV stations have significant advantages for acquiring reporter jobs. Most large radio stations, however, hire experienced newscasters from smaller stations rather than novices fresh from college. Continuity writing, which is writing advertising copy for broadcast, is excellent experience.

Reporters should have good news judgment and be able to work quickly under deadline pressure. They should be able to write "for the ear" and know how to handle studio taping and broadcasting equipment. Good speaking ability is essential—with clear enunciation and using correct grammar.

Unions/Associations

Many broadcast professionals are represented by unions, such as the American Federation of Television and Radio Artists; National Association of Broadcast Employees and Technicians; or Writers Guild of America. Other major professional associations include American Women in Radio and Television, Inc.; Radio-Television News Directors Association; National Association of Educational Broadcasters; National Association of Broadcasters; and Women In Communications, Inc.

NEWS DIRECTOR

CAREER PROFILE

Duties: Supervise content of newscasts; report, write, edit, and deliver news as needed

Alternate Title(s): News Editor

Salary Range: $18,000 to $31,000+

Employment Prospects: Fair to good

Advancement Prospects: Fair

Prerequisites:

Education—Undergraduate degree in communications, English, history, or liberal arts

Experience—Several years in broadcast journalism

Special Skills—Decision-making; managerial ability; sound news judgment

CAREER LADDER

```
┌─────────────────────────────────────┐
│                                     │
│   Program Director; General Manager │
│                                     │
└─────────────────────────────────────┘

┌─────────────────────────────────────┐
│                                     │
│            News Director            │
│                                     │
└─────────────────────────────────────┘

┌─────────────────────────────────────┐
│                                     │
│          Reporter; College          │
│                                     │
└─────────────────────────────────────┘
```

Position Description

Radio news directors are in charge of their station's news operation. They supervise other newscasters or news writers, assign coverage of stories, and make decisions concerning the content of news broadcasts. They set news-gathering and writing policies. They are often called upon to make quick decisions on breaking news stories. Many news directors have production responsibilities as well, which include tape editing and overall supervision of a program.

At large stations, radio news directors may be in charge of staffs of 30 to 40 persons. Most stations have much smaller staffs; at some stations, the news director is the entire staff—reporter, editor, director, and newscaster all rolled into one.

News directors have hiring and firing responsibility. They report to general managers or station managers. Their responsibilities also include administrative tasks, correspondence, reports, and paperwork.

In addition, radio news directors may also act as working reporters—gathering, editing, and rewriting news stories. Occasionally, they deliver the news on the air.

Salaries

The median annual salary for radio news directors in 1993 was $19,685. Those in the largest markets made a median of $31,250, while those in the smallest markets made a median of $15,450.

Salaries were highest in the East and lowest in the Midwest.

Male and female radio news directors were paid comparably on average in 1993, although male directors out-earned their women counterparts in major markets.

News directors at very small stations may be their own one-person staff, earning a 1993 average of $18,225 and doing all jobs from reporting to editing to delivering the news. Such jobs may require little or no experience.

Employment Prospects

Small and medium markets offer the best job prospects for persons seeking news-director positions. Turnover in radio is high, and news directors average one to two years in a particular job. Competition is tougher for jobs at stations and networks that have large news staffs.

Advancement Prospects

The increasing importance and profitability of news operations in recent years has greatly enhanced opportunities for advancement for radio news directors. Most general managers of stations typically have come from the sales and programming operations, but more and more are coming from the news department. Ambitious news directors should become familiar with all station operations, including sales, programming, engineering, and production.

Education

An undergraduate degree in communications, liberal arts, or other fields is preferred. Some broadcast journalists have graduate degrees in communications.

Experience/Skills

Most radio news directors have had several years' experience as radio newscasters or news writers; some start their careers as directors at very small stations that have one-person news operations. In addition to newswriting, some also have experience in production.

Skills for this job include the ability to supervise others, make decisions and assignments, and have good news judgment. News directors should be good writers and editors, with good speaking skills. A familiarity with other station operations is advantageous.

Unions/Associations

Many broadcast professionals are represented by such unions as the American Federation of Television and Radio Artists; National Association of Broadcast Employees and Technicians; or Writers Guild of America. Other major professional associations include American Women in Radio and Television, Inc.; Radio-Television News Directors Association; National Association of Educational Broadcasters; National Association of Broadcasters; and Women In Communications, Inc.

BOOK PUBLISHING

EDITORIAL ASSISTANT

CAREER PROFILE

Duties: Clerical, secretarial, and minor editorial tasks

Alternate Title(s): Editorial Secretary; Editorial Trainee

Salary Range: $15,000 to $24,000

Employment Prospects: Fair

Advancement Prospects: Good

Prerequisites:
 Education—Undergraduate degree in liberal arts, English, history, or communications

 Experience—Secretarial training helpful

 Special Skills—Organizational ability; office skills; knowledge of grammar

CAREER LADDER

```
┌─────────────────────────────┐
│      Assistant Editor        │
└─────────────────────────────┘

┌─────────────────────────────┐
│     Editorial Assistant      │
└─────────────────────────────┘

┌─────────────────────────────┐
│     College; Secretary       │
└─────────────────────────────┘
```

Position Description

Editorial assistant is the entry-level editorial job in a publishing house. It is largely a training position for more advanced editorial posts. Most of the duties revolve around office tasks, such as receptionist duties, filing, typing, and running errands. Editorial assistants usually work for one or more editors, such as an editorial director and assistant or associate editors, depending on the size of the publishing house.

Publishing houses receive thousands of manuscripts every year. Most are unsolicited and relegated to what is called the "slush pile." In some major publishing houses, the slush pile can fill an entire storage room. Editorial assistants usually are responsible for the initial handling of all incoming manuscripts, directing some to the appropriate editors and assigning the rest to the slush pile.

Reading the slush to search for publishable manuscripts is a job often shared by editorial assistants as well as lower-level editors. In some houses, editorial assistants may not be allowed to read the slush, while in others they may have the entire responsibility for it. First readings of most manuscripts are quick and partial, due to limited time. Rejected manuscripts are returned, usually with form letters. For manuscripts that look promising, editorial assistants write summary reports on the plots, including their opinions and recommendations. They then pass the manuscripts and reports to the appropriate higher editors for evaluation.

Editorial assistants also act as coordinators and liaisons for a variety of functions. For example, they work with copy editors and proofreaders, who may either be on staff or be hired freelancers. They monitor production schedules for editors—researching and relaying information on cost estimates for design work and typesetting, as well as giving the status of production work for various manuscripts. They may also act as liaisons with authors, handling phone calls and correspondence, and typing book contracts.

In addition, editorial assistants may have responsibility for copyright applications, and route requisitions for author advances, editorial expenses, freelancer invoices, and other bills.

Salaries

In 1994, the average salary for editorial assistants was $21,000. Those working for a company with revenues of less than $50 million averaged $15,000; those working for companies with revenues of more than $50 million averaged $24,000.

Employment Prospects

Publishing is a glamour industry and attracts many job applicants. Competition is fierce, however, because jobs are limited and the industry has suffered a downturn in recent years. Most jobs are in the New York City area, the center of publishing.

Advancement Prospects

Job turnover in publishing is high, especially at the lower editorial levels. Editorial assistants have good chances of moving up to assistant or associate editors.

Education

Persons interested in careers as book editors should have well-rounded undergraduate educations in liberal arts, English, history, or communications, including publishing courses. Some universities have specialized publishing curricula. A number of summer institutes offer intensive publishing programs. For work in educational publishing, a degree in education is desirable but not necessary.

Experience/Skills

Any kind of editing experience, such as working on school publications or taking summer jobs on local magazines or newspapers, is helpful. Working in a bookstore also provides excellent experience and understanding of the marketing end of pubishing, as well as a sense of what type of books sell well.

Editorial assistants should have good office skills, and be well organized, and be able to monitor many projects at once. They should possess a thorough understanding of grammar and use of the English language.

Unions/Associations

District 65 of the United Auto Workers represents editors of some large book publishers. Major professional associations include the Women's National Book Association, Inc.; P.E.N. American Center; Manhattan Publishing Group; and Women In Communications, Inc. Editors may also belong to a variety of authors' groups.

ADMINISTRATIVE ASSISTANT

CAREER PROFILE

Duties: Assist publicity, promotion, or advertising managers with routine tasks and minor writing activities

Alternate Title(s): Executive Assistant; Publicity Assistant; Promotion Assistant; Advertising Assistant; Marketing Assistant

Salary Range: $14,000 to $22,500

Employment Prospects: Fair

Advancement Prospects: Fair

Prerequisites:

Education—Undergraduate degree in communications, liberal arts, advertising, or marketing

Experience—Background in publishing, media, advertising, or public relations helpful

Special Skills—Writing; organization; clerical skills

CAREER LADDER

```
┌─────────────────────────────────────┐
│  Publicity Specialist; Promotion     │
│  Specialist; Advertising Specialist; │
│  Marketing Specialist                │
└─────────────────────────────────────┘

┌─────────────────────────────────────┐
│  Administrative Assistant            │
└─────────────────────────────────────┘

┌─────────────────────────────────────┐
│  College                             │
└─────────────────────────────────────┘
```

Position Description

Administrative assistant is an entry-level position found in almost all publishing departments. Many of the duties usually are low-level, routine clerical and secretarial tasks, although they can involve higher responsibilities. The job does provide one with an excellent background and training in how books are publicized, advertised, and marketed. With experience, one's responsibilities increase; this can lead to more interesting work and, in some cases, direct contact with prominent authors.

Administrative assistants may be assigned to one department and limited to tasks in a particular function, such as publicity, advertising, or promotion. Some assistants work in the sales and marketing department. Other assistants may be shared by several departments and have broader, more versatile responsibilities.

Routine tasks common to all departments include typing, filing, answering the telephone, placing calls, running errands, and performing general office duties.

Administrative assistants also maintain mailing lists, updating them as necessary; handle correspondence, including routing letters and writing letters for their supervisors to sign; stuff envelopes, press and sales kits; and prepare materials for meetings and conferences.

They also maintain records, such as sales figures, price changes, as well as ad and publicity campaign results. They distribute review copies and press releases.

Writing duties may include departmental reports; material for press kits; promotional or advertising copy; and copy for sales catalogs, which describes books, gives the track records and expertise of authors, and the commitment the publisher expects to make for advertising, publicity, and promotion.

In many cases, administrative assistants act as liaisons between departments, helping coordinate various activities that support the marketing of books. Administrative assistants often work long hours and have many deadline pressures. They must be flexible and able to accommodate last-minute changes. Travel is seldom required.

In addition, administrative assistants may:

- help organize sales conferences, publicity, and promotional events;
- work with film and television contacts concerning movie and TV tie-ins;
- assist in the booking of author tours and speaking engagements.

Salaries

Administrative assistant salaries vary from department to department, and also depend on the size of the publishing house and the geographic location. Average salaries are in the $17,000 to $18,000 range in the editorial and art departments, while advertising and publicity departments pay an average of about $20,000. Salaries can start as low as $14,000, even in advertising/publicity.

Employment Prospects

Job candidates have a fair chance of finding entry-level assistant positions. In some publishing houses, the job may be limited to publicity functions, while in others it may cover other departments as well, such as advertising and promotion.

Advancement Prospects

Administrative assistants have few opportunities to advance in publicity, due to the limited number of managerial positions in the industry. Some may find more opportunities in the sales promotion and advertising departments in publishing. Advancement may also be achieved with lateral moves to other fields, such as magazines, news media, or corporations.

Education

An undergraduate degree in communications, especially journalism, or liberal arts provides a good background for publicity work. Publishing courses are not as helpful as media courses. Familiarity with advertising and public relations is advantageous.

Experience/Skills

Most administrative-assistant jobs are entry-level positions and require no experience. Candidates who've had college internships, summer jobs, or experience on school publications have significant competitive advantages. Some assistant jobs—particularly at major publishers—are more advanced, carrying greater responsibilities. One or two years' experience at another publisher is often required for such positions.

Publicity assistants should be able to juggle many projects at the same time, paying close attention to detail and follow-through. They should have good written and oral communications skills, and be self-motivated and disciplined.

Unions/Associations

Among major professional organizations are the Publishers' Ad Club; Public Relations Society of America, Inc.; Publishers' Publicity Association, Inc.; American Publicists Guild; and Women In Communications, Inc. District 65 of the United Auto Workers represents some employees at major publishers.

COPY EDITOR

CAREER PROFILE

Duties: Edit manuscripts for grammar, style, and consistency; proofread

Alternate Title(s): None

Salary Range: $20,000 to $46,000+

Employment Prospects: Fair

Advancement Prospects: Fair

Prerequisites:
  Education—Undergraduate degree in liberal arts or communications preferred

  Experience—Background as editorial or production assistant preferred

  Special Skills—Thorough knowledge of grammar and style; attention to detail; production knowledge

CAREER LADDER

```
+-----------------------------------+
| Production Editor; Managing Editor |
+-----------------------------------+

+-----------------------------------+
|           Copy Editor             |
+-----------------------------------+

+-----------------------------------+
| Editorial Assistant; Production   |
| Assistant; College                |
+-----------------------------------+
```

Position Description

Once book manuscripts have been accepted, edited, and revised to the satisfaction of authors and editors, they are turned over to copy editors for final editing and checking. This vital part of the editing process protects both authors and publishers by ensuring the accuracy and quality of the final end product.

Much of the copy editors' work is meticulous and detail-oriented. They carefully go over each manuscript (including indexes, glossaries, and bibliographies), correcting spelling, punctuation, and other points of grammatical style. Each publishing house has its own internal style for such things as abbreviations, titles, capitalizations, use of italics, etc., and copy editors must make certain all manuscripts conform to that style.

Copy editors may also check for inconsistencies in fact and logic, a time-consuming process that is not always possible at many publishing houses. Copy editors consult reference sources and may even contact authors to verify information in question. They may also consult with other editors over questions about the manuscript.

Copy editors do not change the substance of a manuscript or alter an author's style or "voice." Revisions or rewrites are the prerogative of the authors and their "line" editors—assistant, associate, or senior editors.

While copy editors must be thorough in their editing, they also must adhere to production schedules, delivering manuscripts on time for typesetting. In other stages of production, copy editors usually proofread galleys for typographical errors and check to see that typesetting instructions have been followed. They also proofread mechanicals and check any layouts, such as artwork and captions.

Copy editors work under the direction of a production editor or managing editor, and may themselves supervise production assistants and freelance copy editors and proofreaders. They are a liaison between editorial and production functions. Their work can be tedious, requiring patience and great attention to detail. Errors should be caught early in the production process to avoid delays and costly corrections.

Publishers have begun to experiment with editing manuscripts on computer terminals. In the future, manuscripts are likely to be transmitted electronically from one department to another, and perhaps outside—to author and typesetter—as well. Ambitious copy editors would be wise to learn how to use computer technology.

Salaries

The average salary for copy editors in 1994 was $37,250, with those working at smaller publishers making more and men making considerably more than women. (In many smaller publishing houses, higher-level employees are also taking on copyediting duties.)

Men made an average of $46,000, while women in comparable jobs made $34,330; those working for companies with revenues of less than $50 million made an average of $46,000 while those working for companies with revenues of more than $50 million made $34,500.

Employment Prospects

Most publishers employ copy editors. Many copy editors start as production assistants. The greatest job opportunities are in New York City, the center of the publishing industry, although the rise of small and moderate-sized publishers throughout the country offers prospects elsewhere, albeit usually at lower pay.

Advancement Prospects

The most likely advancement opportunities for copy editors are on the production side of publishing—to production or managing editors. Computer technology is creating new growth in production-oriented jobs, and copy editors who have experience in using computer systems will have an advantage for advancement. It is possible, but difficult, to switch to the editorial side and become an assistant editor.

Education

Copy editors should have a minimum of three years of college, though preference is given to those who have earned undergraduate degrees. Areas of study include liberal arts, communications, and publishing. Additional training in editing and production is valuable.

Experience/Skills

A production background is preferred for copyediting positions. Work as a production assistant, or any editing and production work done in college, is helpful for getting a job.

Copy editors must be familiar with production stages and with typesetting symbols and terminology. They should be excellent spellers and know rules of grammar and style. Also, they should have a high tolerance for detail work. Copy editors who can work with computer systems will be more in demand as publishers increasingly computerize their operations.

Unions/Associations

Industry associations include the Manhattan Publishing Group; Women's National Book Association; and Women In Communications, Inc. Copy editors who freelance on the side may belong to the Editorial Freelancers Association. Some at large publishing houses may be represented by a union, District 65 of the United Auto Workers.

ASSISTANT EDITOR

CAREER PROFILE

Duties: Screen, edit, and occasionally acquire manuscripts; monitor production

Alternate Title(s): Editorial Assistant

Salary Range: $16,000 to $20,000

Employment Prospects: Fair

Advancement Prospects: Fair

Prerequisites:

   Education—Undergraduate degree in liberal arts, English, history, or communications; publishing courses

   Experience—Work as editorial assistant or trainee

   Special Skills—Editing; organization

CAREER LADDER

```
┌─────────────────────────────┐
│                             │
│      Associate Editor       │
│                             │
└─────────────────────────────┘

┌─────────────────────────────┐
│                             │
│      Assistant Editor       │
│                             │
└─────────────────────────────┘

┌─────────────────────────────┐
│  Editorial Assistant; Editorial  │
│       Trainee; College      │
└─────────────────────────────┘
```

Position Description

The assistant editor position usually is one step above editorial assistant, who is essentially a clerk and secretary. In large publishing houses with big and highly structured staffs, assistant editor may be the equivalent of editorial assistant.

Most assistant editors have learned the editorial process, know how to screen manuscripts, and can edit them according to the in-house style of the publisher. They assume more responsibilities than editorial assistants.

Typical duties include reading queries and proposals submitted by authors through agents, and screening unsolicited manuscripts for publishable material. Assistant editors are responsible for helping publish a specified number of books a month or year; this means shepherding the product from manuscript to finished book. The work involves editing and coordinating proofreading and production. Much of the work is routine. Editing is done under the supervision of a higher-level editor. Assistant editors may or may not have direct contact with authors concerning revisions and rewrites. If a staff is small, job duties may be broad enough to include writing jacket copy, as well as proposing publicity and promotion ideas.

Assistant editors report to associate editors, senior editors, managing editors, or editorial directors, depending on the size of the house. They help plan deadlines and production schedules, and they may delegate work to editorial assistants.

In many cases, assistant editors recommend manuscripts for acquisition, and they may even make the initial offer to the author. Actual contract negotiation usually is done by more experienced editors. Assistant editors generally do not work on the most important books.

In addition, assistant editors may write reports and make presentations to recommend manuscripts for purchase, and attend trade and professional meetings.

Salaries

Salaries for assistant editors range from $16,000 to $20,000, depending on their experience, responsibilities, and employer.

Employment Prospects

Job applicants have a fair chance of getting low-level editing jobs. The best opportunities are at small publishing houses. Employment agencies which specialize in publishing can be helpful in a job search. Employment prospects in educational publishing are decreasing due to school budget cutbacks.

Advancement Prospects

Assistant editors have a good chance of being promoted in-house, due to the high turnover typical of the publishing industry.

Education

An undergraduate degree in liberal arts, history, English, or communications is preferred, though virtually any degree is acceptable. Job candidates benefit from courses in book publishing.

Experience/Skills

Prior experience as an editorial assistant, trainee, editor, or writer in another field is necessary for many assistant-editor jobs. Some positions, however, are entry-level for persons right out of college.

Assistant editors should have good editorial and grammatical skills, and understand the entire editorial process. They should have a good sense of the book marketplace and know what has sales potential. Oral presentation skills are advantageous for editorial and sales meetings.

Unions/Associations

Major professional associations include the Women's National Book Association, Inc.; Women In Communications, Inc.; Manhattan Publishing Group; and various authors' organizations. Editorial employees at some large publishers are members of District 65 of the United Auto Workers.

ASSOCIATE EDITOR

CAREER PROFILE

Duties: Screen, edit, and rewrite manuscripts; manage projects; recommend acquisitions

Alternate Title(s): Editor; Project Editor

Salary Range: $18,000 to $55,000+

Employment Prospects: Fair

Advancement Prospects: Poor

Prerequisites:

Education—Undergraduate degree in communications, liberal arts, English, or history

Experience—One to two years in editorial work

Special Skills—Good editing and organization; supervisory ability; business knowledge; presentation skills

CAREER LADDER

```
┌─────────────────────────────────────┐
│              Editor                  │
└─────────────────────────────────────┘

┌─────────────────────────────────────┐
│          Associate Editor            │
└─────────────────────────────────────┘

┌─────────────────────────────────────┐
│  Assistant Editor; Editorial Assistant │
└─────────────────────────────────────┘
```

Position Description

Associate editors may delegate much of the routine work in a publishing house to subordinates, concentrating more on the screening, acquisition, and editing of manuscripts. Their responsibilities are likely to include screening the slush pile of unsolicited manuscripts and evaluating manuscripts that have passed a first screening by a lower level editor or assistant. Associate editors are not likely to do the actual acquiring and contract negotiating, but they do make acquisition recommendations to the editorial board. They must have a clear sense of the needs of the publisher as well as the conditions in the book marketplace. If a publisher is seeking an author to write a book, they may recommend or search for candidates.

Associate editors usually work under the direction of senior editors or editorial directors. They may help plan long-range projects for series of books; this involves scheduling deadlines for acquisitions, editing, production, and promotion, and working within a budget.

They also edit manuscripts and work directly with authors concerning revisions and rewrites (subject to the approval of a superior editor). They may oversee the work done by copy editors.

Associate editors attend regular in-house editorial meetings, during which potential books are discussed and decisions made. They may be asked to make informal or formal presentations explaining why particular manuscripts should be purchased. They make periodical progress reports.

On large staffs, associate editors are likely to have one or more subordinates who help with routine work and correspondence.

In addition, associate editors may maintain contact with literary agents, supervise special editorial projects, write jacket copy, and help plan publicity and promotion.

Salaries

Salaries for associate editors are traditionally modest, generally ranging from $18,000 to $30,000 for jobs that often involve long hours.

Employment Prospects

Turnover is high in publishing. Most low and middle positions, including associate editor, are filled from within. Though much smaller publishing "centers" exist in the areas around Chicago, Boston, San Francisco, Los Angeles, the Pacific Northwest, and Florida, most publishers are located in the New York City area.

Advancement Prospects

Competition is very keen for editorial positions above associate editor. At higher levels, many jobs are filled by outside candidates rather than those promoted within.

Education

Most associate editors have undergraduate degrees in communications, liberal arts, English, or history. Additional courses in publishing are desirable.

Experience/Skills

Most associate editors have had at least one or two years of experience in lower editorial positions; some have worked as editors of magazines and newspapers. Associate editors should have strong editing skills and a good business sense of a book's potential commercial appeal. They should be able to work within budgets and supervise others. Oral presentation skills and the ability to be persuasive are invaluable.

Unions/Associations

Major professional associations include Women In Communications, Inc.; Manhattan Publishing Group; Women's National Book Association, Inc.; and authors' groups. District 65 of the United Auto Workers represents employees of some large publishers.

EDITOR

CAREER PROFILE

Duties: Develop ideas for books, recommend books for acquisition, negotiate deals, work with authors, supervise staff

Alternate Title(s): Developmental Editor

Salary Range: $25,000 to $70,000+

Employment Prospects: Poor to Fair

Advancement Prospects: Poor to Fair

Prerequisites:

Education—Undergraduate degree in communications, publishing English, liberal arts, humanities; special publishing courses advantageous

Experience—Work as editorial assistant, assistant editor or associate editor

Special Skills—Creativity; organization; knowledge of all phases of publishing process; ability to work well with others and to work under pressure

CAREER LADDER

```
┌─────────────────────────┐
│                         │
│      Senior Editor      │
│                         │
└─────────────────────────┘

┌─────────────────────────┐
│                         │
│         Editor          │
│                         │
└─────────────────────────┘

┌─────────────────────────┐
│                         │
│     Associate Editor    │
│                         │
└─────────────────────────┘
```

Position Description

Editors perform may of the same duties as associate editors, but have more responsibility and work on more important books. Editors read manuscripts and proposals submitted by authors and agents, and make presentations to the editorial board to recommend acquisitions. When they receive the green light to proceed, editors negotiate the terms. Editors also generate book ideas, and then work with agents and authors to develop them into acceptable proposals.

Once a proposal or manuscript is acquired, editors shepherd it through the editing and production process. Editing responsibilities vary considerably according to publishing house. At a large house, an editor does a general edit and asks for revisions if they are necessary. Once the manuscript is acceptable, it is turned over to line and copy editors who read for consistency, grammar, and style. At a small house, the editor may do all of those functions.

The editor coordinates with art, production, marketing, and publicity departments to help meet their needs and deadlines, and contributes information and ideas that will help the success of the book.

Editors talk and meet with agents frequently to discuss ideas and potential book projects. They work closely with authors. They supervise other editors and delegate tasks, and report to a senior editor, editorial director, or executive editor. They attend staff meetings, and spend a certain amount of time reading the "slush," or unsolicited manuscripts and proposals. At a large house, an editor may be responsible for dozens of books a year, requiring constant juggling and attention to detail. Publishing is fraught with delays—especially from authors—and editors must work under pressure.

Salaries

The average salary for an editor was $57,180 in 1994. The average for men was $61,330; the average for women was $52,200. Those working for companies with revenues under $50 million averaged $50,500; those working for companies with revenues above $50 million was $92,500.

Employment Prospects

Major publishing houses, most of which are concentrated in Middle Atlantic and Northeastern United

States, are expected to remain under financial pressure throughout the 1990s, thus limiting job opportunities. Many jobs have been lost due to mergers, acquisitions and consolidations, and also to ill-conceived spending that has left some houses with piles of debt. The best opportunities may be in the lower end of the market, the small presses and moderately sized independent presses. Although the pay is lower, the opportunities may be greater.

Advancement Prospects

Promotion opportunities are limited for the same reasons.

Education

Most editors have an undergraduate degree in communications, publishing, liberal arts, English, or humanities. Many have taken additional courses in publishing and marketing.

Experience/Skills

The editor's job requires prior experience as an editorial assistant, assistant editor, or associate editor—or two of those positions, depending on the house and the nature of the editor's job.

Editors must be able to work well with a wide variety of people and temperaments. They must be able to supervise, delegate, and work under pressure. They are creative and intuitive when it comes to anticipating trends and interests in the marketplace. They are well organized and able to work with budgets and deadlines.

Unions/Associations

Editors may belong to the Women's National Book Association, the Manhattan Publishing Group, Women In Communications, Inc., or other groups related to publishing. Some may belong to a labor union.

SENIOR EDITOR

CAREER PROFILE

Duties: Acquire and develop major books and authors; supervise other editors; plan and execute editorial policies

Alternate Title(s): Acquisitions Editor; Project Editor

Salary Range: $30,000 to $73,000+

Employment Prospects: Poor

Advancement Prospects: Poor

Prerequisites:

Education—Undergraduate degree in liberal arts, communications, English, or history

Experience—Three to five years or more in editing

Special Skills—Negotiation and supervisory ability; business and decision-making skills

CAREER LADDER

```
┌─────────────────────────────────────┐
│                                     │
│  Editorial Director; Executive Editor │
│                                     │
└─────────────────────────────────────┘

┌─────────────────────────────────────┐
│                                     │
│            Senior Editor            │
│                                     │
└─────────────────────────────────────┘

┌─────────────────────────────────────┐
│                                     │
│           Associate Editor          │
│                                     │
└─────────────────────────────────────┘
```

Position Description

Senior editors play influential roles in the editorial policies, directions, and products of publishing houses. They are heavily involved in the marketing and business aspects of publishing, and they usually handle the most prestigious books.

Senior editors work under the direction of editorial directors or publishers. They help develop comprehensive, long-range publishing plans, which include acquisition and publishing schedules, budgetary analyses, and sales projections. They have overall responsibility for the completion of book projects, including supervision of editing done by other editors, production work, adherence to schedules and deadlines, and use of frelance and consultant help.

Most senior editors are also responsible for acquisitions, though some large houses may delegate this task to specialized acquisitions editors. Acquisition involves deciding which manuscripts should be purchased, then negotiating the contracts with authors and agents. Each publisher has a standard contract, and senior editors must know the limits of negotiable points. Senior editors often work closely with in-house legal staff and subsidiary-rights editors in contract negotiations. The actual sale of a book's subsidiary rights to foreign publishers, magazines, or paperback publishers may be handled by a senior editor.

Senior editors also work with marketing and publicity/promotion staff to persuade them which titles deserve the most sales, advertising, and publicity support. They make many presentations, some informal at weekly editorial and sales meetings, and others formal, at major sales conferences.

In addition, senior editors may accompany sales representatives on sales calls, and represent their publisher at major industry conventions.

Salaries

The average salary for senior editors was $64,430 in 1994. Men in this position averaged $72,990, while women made an average of $59,650. Those working for companies with revenues less than $50 million made an average of $54,110, while those working for companies with revenues of more than $50 million made an average of $62,000.

Employment Prospects

Senior-editor positions are highly competitive and require years of experience in the publishing industry. It is often necessary to change employers in order to get a job at this level.

Advancement Prospects

A tight job market in publishing makes advancement to editorial director or executive editor very difficult. There is much less turnover at this level than at lower editorial levels. Advancement usually is made by changing employers.

Education

Senior editors are expected to have undergraduate degrees, most preferably in liberal arts, English, history, or communications. Education ideally should include publishing courses. Additional study at a publishing summer institute is advantageous.

Experience/Skills

Three to five years' experience in editing is required for most senior-editor posts; large publishers may require more experience. A background at one or more publishers is advantageous. Most publishers do not fill senior editor positions from within but instead hire from the outside.

Senior editors should understand publishing contracts and be able to negotiate them. They should have a good grasp of the business and financial side of publishing, be able to develop budget plans, and know how to supervise other employees.

Unions/Associations

Women In Communications, Inc. and Women's National Book Association are among the principal professional groups for book editors. In addition, senior editors may belong to authors' organizations, or, at some major publishers, to District 65 of the United Auto Workers.

COPYWRITER

CAREER PROFILE

Duties: Write copy for advertising, promotion, and directmail campaigns; create flap copy and press releases

Alternate Title(s): None

Salary Range: $16,000 to $35,000

Employment Prospects: Fair

Advancement Prospects: Fair

Prerequisites:

Education—Undergraduate degree in communications, advertising, or liberal arts

Experience—Background in advertising or marketing

Special Skills—Sales orientation; graphic-arts knowledge

CAREER LADDER

```
┌─────────────────────────────────┐
│  Promotion Manager; Advertising  │
│    Manager; Sales Manager        │
└─────────────────────────────────┘

┌─────────────────────────────────┐
│          Copywriter             │
└─────────────────────────────────┘

┌─────────────────────────────────┐
│     Administrative Assistant     │
└─────────────────────────────────┘
```

Position Description

Copywriters create many of the materials that help sell books, not only to the public but to book sellers, wholesalers, and the media as well. They usually work under the direction of managers of advertising, sales, or promotion. They write copy for print ads and book catalogs, and scripts for radio commercials. Television ads are uncommon for books but may be required for special, major campaigns or for lines of books. Some romance publishers, for example, advertise their lines in TV commercials. Other sales-oriented material includes literature for the sales force (such as information on discounts to booksellers, sales records of authors' previous books, special displays available, and advertising and publicity plans) plus posters, flyers, and displays for use in bookstores.

In some highly structured publishing houses, copywriters also handle certain editorial copy tasks that might otherwise be done by junior editors. These include creating press releases for the media and book reviewers, material for press kits, and jacket copy. Jacket copy consists of a synopsis of a book's plot, and it is intended to entice customers into a purchase. Some-

times information on the author and his or her previous books is included as well.

Copywriters coordinate their work with others, such as advertising and promotion representatives as well as editors. They may do their own research for projects or may delegate the work to assistants. They often work with graphic artists in designing and laying out ads, brochures, and catalogs. They must be able to work with space limitations. For example, jacket copy for paperback books must fit the space allowed by the illustration, type, and universal price code. Some copywriters may specialize in certain areas, such as direct mail.

Salaries

Most copywriters earn in the low to mid-twenties, though salaries can range from $16,000 to $35,000, depending on experience, responsibilities, and employer. On the average, copywriting jobs at publishing houses do not pay as well as those at ad agencies or businesses.

Employment Prospects

Copywriting jobs aren't as glamorous as editorial jobs in publishing. However, they may be easier to get, due to the increasing importance of effective book marketing.

Advancement Prospects

Skilled copywriters can advance to managerial positions in sales, advertising, or promotion. Some publishers have direct-mail specialists as well. These business-oriented jobs also lead to higher executive positions overall in publishing houses.

Education

An undergraduate degree in communications or advertising is preferred for copywriting jobs. A degree in liberal arts also is acceptable.

Experience/Skills

A background in advertising or sales-promotion work is usually required for this type of job. Some copywriters come from jobs in advertising agencies, while others start as entry-level assistants.

Copywriters should be able to write crisp, persuasive sales copy. They should also have some knowledge of graphic arts—layout and production.

Unions/Associations

Major professional organizations include the American Advertising Federation; Publishers' Ad Club; the Direct Mail/Marketing Association, Inc.; Copywriters Council of America; and Women In Communications, Inc. Employees of some major publishers belong to District 65 of the United Auto Workers.

PUBLICITY MANAGER

Duties: Generate publicity for books and authors; arrange for book reviews and author tours

Alternate Title(s): Publicist

Salary Range: $20,000 to $88,000

Employment Prospects: Fair

Advancement Prospects: Poor

Prerequisites:
  Education—Undergraduate degree in communications, English, or liberal arts

  Experience—Background as publicity assistant or journalist essential

  Special Skills—Good writing and organizational skills; salesmanship

```
┌─────────────────────────────┐
│                             │
│    Director of Publicity    │
│                             │
└─────────────────────────────┘

┌─────────────────────────────┐
│                             │
│     Publicity Manager       │
│                             │
└─────────────────────────────┘

┌─────────────────────────────┐
│                             │
│     Publicity Assistant     │
│                             │
└─────────────────────────────┘
```

Position Description

Publicity managers have highly visible jobs in publishing houses. They represent their publishing houses to the media, and they are responsible for generating favorable press coverage of books and authors.

Most books receive minimal publicity support, but a certain few are identified for receiving special effort. The amount of publicity can vary from a mailing of review copies with press releases to a full-blown campaign that includes an author tour, as well as advertising and sales promotion.

Planning for publicity begins long before a book is finished and ready to be delivered to the stores. Publicity managers coordinate their plans with editorial, advertising, sales, and promotion staffs. Budgets and deadlines are set for materials, mailings, travel, and other expenses.

For a major campaign, the publicity manager works with the author to develop press-kit material, such as author's biography and photograph, questions for interviewers to ask, press releases, and clips of early reviews or other notable news coverage an author may have received previously.

Review copies and press releases are mailed to book reviewers in advance of publication. Publicity managers are responsible for maintaining up-to-date lists and for seeing that books are sent to appropriate reviewers. A technical book, for example, would require a different mailing list than a novel.

In addition to reviews, publicity managers try to generate news or feature stories in the media. They send press releases and follow up with phone calls to arrange interviews for the authors. They also book speaking engagements and autograph signings at bookstores, libraries, and other places.

For author tours, publicity managers may do the bookings themselves or may hire freelance publicists to make all arrangements. Tasks include deciding tour cities; contacting the media for interviews; setting up schedules; arranging for transportation, accommodations, and travel advances for authors' out-of-pocket expenses. Tours are complicated, time-consuming, and involve a great many last-minute changes.

Publicity managers may be in charge of their publishers' entire publicity operation, or they may report to directors of publicity. They are likely to supervise assistants who handle much of the routine writing, stuffing, and mailing jobs.

In addition, publicity managers may:

- be responsible for maintaining clipping files on all authors and books;
- maintain good relations with the media through regular contact;
- plan and direct company publicity functions, such as dinner and cocktail parties.

Salaries

Salaries for publicity managers averaged $49,540 in 1994. Men averaged $87,500, while women averaged $42,640. Those working for companies with revenues under $50 million averaged $43,000, while those working for larger companies averaged $85,500.

Employment Prospects

The job market in this field is very tight, due to the competitive nature of such desirable jobs and the fact that publicity is one of the first areas to be cut back in bad economic times. Many openings at this level are not openly advertised. The best bet is to start as a publicity assistant and make industry contacts.

Advancement Prospects

Opportunities for promotion are limited in this field. At some publishing houses, publicity manager is the top position, supervised by a director or vice president of sales and/or advertising. In others, the next highest position is director of publicity. Advancement is usually achieved by changing employers rather than being promoted from within. Competition is strong.

Education

An undergraduate degree in communications or journalism is preferred for publicity jobs in publishing. Also acceptable are degrees in liberal arts and social science.

Experience/Skills

Three to five years of experience usually is required for publicity-manager positions, either as a publicity assistant or journalist for a newspaper or magazine. Publicity managers should understand the needs of the media and know what constitutes good publicity material. They should have good newswriting skills, and be outgoing and personable in their relations with the media. Publicity managers also should be persuasive, as they must "sell" their ideas to the press.

Unions/Associations

Major professional organizations include the American Publicists Guild; Publishers' Ad Club; Public Relations Society of America, Inc.; Publishers' Publicity Association, Inc.; and Women In Communications, Inc. District 65 of the United Auto Workers represents some employees of large publishing houses.

PROMOTION MANAGER

Duties: Supervise promotional projects to help book sales

Alternate Title(s):   Sales Promotion Manager

Salary Range: $25,000 to $65,000

Employment Prospects: Poor

Advancement Prospects: Poor

Prerequisites:

Education—Undergraduate degree in advertising or marketing preferred

Experience—Two to five years in copywriting, promotion, or marketing

Special Skills—Sales orientation; copywriting ability; marketing knowledge; supervisory skills

```
┌─────────────────────────────────────┐
│                                     │
│    Director of Marketing or Sales   │
│                                     │
└─────────────────────────────────────┘

┌─────────────────────────────────────┐
│                                     │
│          Promotion Manager          │
│                                     │
└─────────────────────────────────────┘

┌─────────────────────────────────────┐
│                                     │
│   Copywriter; Researcher; Publicity │
│              Assistant              │
│                                     │
└─────────────────────────────────────┘
```

Position Description

Promotion is an important part of the overall marketing support given books once they are published. Other elements of support include media advertising, publicity, and direct-sales efforts. The most visible work of the promotion department can be seen in bookstores, where certain titles are out in special floor displays or emphasized by shelf tags, wall posters, buttons, and bookmarks at the cash register.

Other promotion products include direct-mail brochures and order blanks, sales literature, exhibits at industry conventions, and tie-ins such as T-shirts, tote bags, caps, key rings, and other items that are given away to the public.

Promotion managers work with editorial, advertising, and sales staffs to identify the books that will be supported. They develop and coordinate promotion plans, including scheduling, deadlines, and budgets. They then delegate work to copywriters, researchers, and assistants, and approve the final products. If specialty items such as T-shirts and note pads are to be used, they supervise their purchase and distribution.

Promotion managers often play an instrumental role in determining whether certain manuscripts are purchased by publishers. If a book is not promotable, in terms of getting attention and attracting a big enough audience, it may be rejected. Promotion managers sometimes sit in on editorial meetings at which buying decisions are made.

Promotion managers usually report to directors or vice presidents of marketing or sales. They may work with outside advertising agencies, if their publishers use such agencies, in the development of copy and materials. They may also supervise freelance copywriters in addition to their own staff.

In addition, promotion managers may supervise publicity efforts, supervise jacket copywriting, and assist in the preparation of sales catalogs.

Salaries

The average salary for a promotion manager in 1994 was $48,330. Those at smaller companies averaged $38,750; those at larger ones averaged $61,250.

Employment Prospects

Not all publishing houses have separate job positions for promotional work. Duties may be folded into another job, such as advertising manager.

Advancement Prospects

Promotion managers face stiff competition from their peers in sales and advertising for promotion to director or vice president of sales/marketing. Sales experience is an asset for advancement.

Education

An education in marketing or advertising is preferred for sales-promotion work. Also acceptable are undergraduate degrees in communications, liberal arts, or social sciences.

Experience/Skills

Two years of experience in copywriting, market research, publicity, or sales is considered the minimum for sales-promotion manager; ideally, job candidates should have at least five years of experience.

Sales-promotion managers should be knowledgeable in advertising and marketing techniques, and should be skilled copywriters themselves. Managerial skills include preparing budgets and long-range plans, and hiring, training, and supervising staff.

Unions/Associations

Major organizations include the Publishers' Ad Club; Publishers' Publicity Association, Inc.; American Publicists Guild; American Advertising Federation; and Women In Communications, Inc.

PROMOTIONAL ASSISTANT— ELECTRONIC PUBLISHING

CAREER PROFILE

Duties: Write promotional copy about electronic publishing products such as on-line databases, data collections, and telephone information services

Alternate Title(s): Publicity Assistant

Salary Range: $15,000 to $30,000

Employment Prospects: Good

Advancement Prospects: Good

Prerequisites:

    Education—Undergraduate degree in liberal arts, communications, English, or history

    Experience—Familiarity with computer databases as a user of on-line services; any background in book promotion or publishing a plus

    Special Skills—Ability to communicate technical information clearly and precisely; familiarity with products; computer literacy; ability to adjust to change

CAREER LADDER

```
┌─────────────────────────────────┐
│   Assistant Product Manager;     │
│       Promotion Manager          │
└─────────────────────────────────┘

┌─────────────────────────────────┐
│       Promotion Assistant        │
└─────────────────────────────────┘

┌─────────────────────────────────┐
│ College; Researcher; Library Clerk │
└─────────────────────────────────┘
```

Position Description

Because electronic publishing is a relatively new field, most jobs related to it still do not have well-defined descriptions.

Electronic publishing involves producing on-line versions of reference books, magazines, and other works traditionally found in print. There are several reasons to convert books into electronic products. Some books have been turned into electronic databases to overcome the limitations of print. Electronic versions of books can be continuously updated up until "loaded" onto a computer. Information in traditional books is generally at least one year old by the time it hits print.

Also, online information is not restricted to a specific number of pages. If a computer user wants to use information from a book in his or her computer, it does not have to be retyped into the machine.

Information can also be put into the format a customer needs, merged with information from other sources, or combined with a software product that allows a customer to rearrange it to suit him- or herself.

Other books naturally lend themselves to a computerized form because of their content. If a book is invariably used in conjunction with a computer program, it works best if published in a form that can integrate with the program.

Other electronic publishing products include full-text databases of magazines, journals, or books, complete with reference citations that can be used to produce the whole text of the article that was referenced; company databases, with information about companies and their business activities; financial wire services, with stock quotes and other financial information; fax and telephone information services; and others.

Most jobs in electronic publishing resemble traditional publishing jobs, but require a good knowledge of the target customer for online services and a familiarity with databases. As a result, it can be hard to find people with the right combination of skills to write promotional material about electronic products.

Promotional assistants in this field would work with the product manager to define who the target audience of the product might be, what features of the product might appeal to these customers, and how to present the product to them.

They might also become involved with using market research to develop project design, learning what customers want and adapting books to meet those needs.

Salaries

Pay varies according to the size of the publisher, the size of the electronic publishing operation within the company, and the actual job duties. Such a job would probably pay somewhere within the $20,000 to $25,000 range.

Advancement Prospects

The next step up for someone in this job might be to assistant product manager, project coordinator, or to another promotional job within the publishing house.

Education

A communications or liberal arts degree would be preferred. Formal education with computers is not necessary, but could be a plus.

Experience/Skills

While this may be an entry-level job, familiarity with computer databases is a must. This can be self-taught. Librarians or other researchers would have the type of familiarity with computer-aided research necessary. Experience in book promotion would also be a plus.

An ability to communicate clearly and translate technical information in everyday language is also necessary.

Unions/Associations

The Information Industry Association is the main trade association for electronic publishing. The Association of American Publishers also has an electronic publishing division.

ELECTRONIC PUBLISHING PRODUCT MANAGER

CAREER PROFILE

Duties: See the idea for an electronic version of a book through to a completed product; decide how best to market and promote the product

Alternate Title(s): Varied

Salary Range: $30,000 to $40,000

Employment Prospects: Fair

Advancement Prospects: Fair

Prerequisites:

Education—Undergraduate degree in communications, liberal arts, history, or English; a master's degree in library science, with training in computer-aided research, would be a plus

Experience—Several years' experience as a promotional assistant, project coordinator, or assistant product manager within electronic publishing; experience working in a library or using computer databases in a corporation is also helpful

Special Skills—Familiarity with users of computer databases; an ability to see what books might lend themselves to electronic form; knowledge of what information users of computer databases might need and how that information should be packaged

CAREER LADDER

```
┌─────────────────────────────────────┐
│   Director of Marketing or Sales     │
└─────────────────────────────────────┘

┌─────────────────────────────────────┐
│          Product Manager             │
└─────────────────────────────────────┘

┌─────────────────────────────────────┐
│    Assistant Product Manager;        │
│       Promotion Assistant            │
└─────────────────────────────────────┘
```

Position Description

Because electronic publishing is still emerging, job descriptions within it are far less static than those in traditional publishing, and a lot of a product manager's job within electronic publishing is experimental.

This position could be described as a cross between promotional manager and editor. The product manager is responsible for cradling an electronic product along from the original idea for the product to promoting and marketing it.

The product manager also must ensure that the final product properly integrates writing with pictures and sound, so that the completed product looks finished. He or she must obtain the necessary permissions to use video clips or other features added to the book.

Many electronic products are online versions of books that benefit from continuous updating, or contain too much information for a traditional book format. Many reference works, such as encyclopedias and directories, lend themselves to database form and can be periodically updated with new CD-ROM disks (which subscribers can obtain by turning in their old disks).

Others are computerized versions of books designed to be used with computer programs, or computerized products designed to be used with books. Electronic publishers also produce audio versions of books.

The product manager needs to be familiar with who might use the company's products and what they need the product to do. Because libraries and major corporations are the largest customers for these products, a background in using databases or computer systems in one of these settings can be helpful.

The product manager also has to be familiar with market research or speak to users of computer databases directly to define who they are and what they need.

He or she must then determine what marketing approach would work best. Unlike traditional publishing, where there are several defined ways to promote a book, this area can be more experimental in electronic publishing. Familiarity with traditional book promotion is important, however.

Many electronic products can be cross-promoted with books. Others can be more difficult to promote because they require the use of computer bulletin boards and other outlets not traditionally used by publishers. Because advertising is discouraged on some computer services, the problem of reaching the customers for a product can be more complicated.

Salaries

Salaries vary according to the size of the publisher and the electronic publishing division. Typically, they fall in the $30,000 to $40,000 range.

Employment Prospects

With the right background, landing this type of job might be easier than getting a similar job in traditional publishing. Many people now employed in non-technical electronic publishing jobs come from publishing backgrounds.

Advancement Prospects

Someone in this job might advance through the publishing company's traditional marketing department into a more conventional marketing job. The product manager might also advance within the electronic publishing unit to become the unit manager.

Education

A bachelor's degree in communications, English, journalism, marketing, advertising, or liberal arts is generally required. Formal knowledge of computer systems and computer-aided research is also advantageous.

Experience/Skills

Several years' experience as an assistant product manager or another job within the electronic publishing unit is required for most product manager jobs. Experience in marketing, copywriting, market research, publicity, or sales may also be required.

Unions/Associations

Product managers may belong to the same associations that promotion managers do. In addition, the trade association for electronic publishing is the Information Industry Association. The Association of American Publishers also has a division for electronic publishing.

ARTS AND ENTERTAINMENT

AUTHOR

CAREER PROFILE

Duties: Research and write nonfiction or fiction books and articles

Alternate Title(s): Writer; Novelist

Income Potential: $0 to no limit

Work Prospects: Fair

Prerequisites:

Education—None required; undergraduate or advanced degrees in specialized fields desirable for nonfiction credentials

Experience—Background as a journalist or professional writer helpful

Special Skills—Creativity; self-motivation; persistence; good writing ability

Position Description

Authors enjoy an envied, glamorous image. Many people think writers don't really "work" for a living, merely spending a few hours a day at their typewriters composing whatever strikes their fancy.

In truth, most authors work hard, spending long hours researching, writing, editing, and rewriting. A good portion of their work is done on speculation—that is, they don't get paid unless their finished work is accepted—and rejections are far more common than acceptances.

Most professional authors work on nonfiction books and articles, which in general earn more money than fiction. Nonfiction includes textbooks, encyclopedias, and academic works as well as topical books. Some authors also write novels, and a very few write nothing but novels.

The author's work is a solitary pursuit requiring strong self-discipline and motivation. Authors treat their writing like any other job—it must be done daily, and deadlines must be met. Authors do have an advantage in being able to choose their working hours. Some authors gauge their work by hours per day, while others measure it by numbers of pages or words written. They spend a great deal of time searching for ideas by reading periodicals and books, as well as by being naturally curious and observant.

Established authors seldom complete manuscripts before trying to sell them. They make a sale based on a proposal, which consists of an introductory pitch, an outline and sometimes a sample chapter; or a partial, which is generally three or more chapters, a synopsis and an outline. Beginners may be asked by publishers to complete their manuscripts before they are purchased, especially in fiction.

Most authors prefer to have agents handle their material. The agent sends manuscripts or proposals, called properties, to publishers. Agents also negotiate contracts, collect payments on behalf of the author, and often mediate in any problems that arise. Agents also find work for their clients by being aware of editors' interests.

The author's work is not done once a book is written and sold. Revisions must be completed and galleys proofread. Authors often spend their own time and money in helping publishers promote and advertise their books.

Authors may work on more than one project at a time, including developing ideas for sale while working on books under contract. Authors essentially run a small business, and must keep track of tax deductible expenses.

In addition, authors may supplement book income with freelance writing or part- or full-time jobs, and speak or teach at writers' conferences, colleges, and universities.

Income Potential

Authors earn anywhere from $3,000 a year to $100,000 or more. The average author in the early 1990s earned about $6,000 annually.

Because most authors write part-time, statistics on their earnings are hard to come by. Only the best-sellers garner the big money, however. Beginning novelists can earn advances of $500 to $10,000 or more, but most novels never earn royalties (a percentage of the retail price) beyond the advance.

Genre novels such as mysteries, science fiction, romances, and westerns fare the best. Authors of these types of novels can earn up to $50,000 a year or more.

Nonfiction books, especially if they are on "hot" topics, can bring high advances and earn royalties over a long period of time. Most books, however, are out of print within a year of publication. Scientific and technical authors are able to earn more money than many other nonfiction authors.

Work Prospects

More than 40,000 books are published every year in the U.S., but that number represents only a fraction of the total number of manuscripts, proposals, and queries submitted by authors. Most ideas are rejected. Authors can wait months, even years, to sell their books. It's not uncommon to collect dozens of rejections before making a sale, even with the help of an agent.

Education

For nonfiction, an undergraduate degree of any kind is helpful. If the author is writing as an expert in a specialized field, an advanced degree is helpful. Fiction depends more on creativity and imagination than education.

Experience/Skills

Any kind of writing experience, such as school newspaper, a creative-writing class, or a media job, is good training. Professional writing experience as a news journalist or magazine staff writer is an asset for nonfiction credentials.

Authors must be imaginative, very self-disciplined, and able to spend long periods of time alone. They must possess a high degree of perseverance, both in perfection of craft and against the odds of rejection. They cannot afford to be easily discouraged.

Knowledge of publicity and promotion is helpful in aiding publishers in selling published books.

Unions/Associations

Major national authors' associations include the Authors Guild; P.E.N. American Center; American Society of Journalists and Authors, Inc.; National Writers Union; Authors League of America, Inc.; and National Writers Club, Inc. Other organizations serve a wide range of specialized interests. Major women's groups include the International Women's Writing Guild and National League of American Pen Women. The Writers Guild of America is a union representing radio, TV, and film scriptwriters.

GHOSTWRITER/COLLABORATOR

Duties: Work with others to write, rewrite, and edit books and articles

Alternate Title(s): None

Income Potential: $400 to $4,000 for trade articles; $100 per page or full advance and half of author's royalties for a book; $25 to $100 per hour; or $200 per day plus expenses

Work Prospects: Fair

Prerequisites:

Education—High school diploma or undergraduate degree in communications, journalism, English, or liberal arts

Experience—Background as an author, journalist, or novelist helpful

Special Skills—Good organization and research; editing skill; ability to imitate another's style or "voice"

Position Description

Ghostwriting carries little glamour but can be very lucrative. Many books and articles that appear under celebrities' or experts' names are in fact written, rewritten, or edited by professional writers who receive little or no credit for their role. The celebrity or expert provides the raw material; the writer molds it into a salable work.

The amount of work performed by ghostwriters varies. They may do all the researching, interviewing, writing, and editing, or they may write only a first draft. Some ghostwriters are hired to fix manuscripts by rewriting and editing.

The job of the ghostwriter is to become the voice of the subject. Thorough research is required in order to become familiar with the subject's manner of expression.

Most ghostwriting is nonfiction, such as articles or papers written for business officials, politicians, professionals, or scientific and academic leaders who wish to gain prestige through authorship. Many celebrities hire ghostwriters to write their first-person autobiographies. The ghostwriter may also write a textbook and nonfiction book for publication under an expert's name.

Some ghostwriters write novels for well-known authors. This is much more difficult than nonfiction.

Ghostwriters may be acknowledged in the introduction for "help in preparing the manuscript," or receive credit on the cover and title page under the guise of "with" or "as told to." Many ghostwriters prefer to remain invisible or are required to do so by their contracts. While they receive scant public recognition for their work, they can build reputations within publishing circles.

Collaboration is a more visible form of ghostwriting, often involving working in a partnership with another writer or celebrity. Collaborators usually share the research, writing, and revising.

Ghostwriting or collaboration can be an excellent way for writers to break into publishing and earn book credentials. Some ghostwriters build big reputations and do no other kind of writing.

In addition, ghostwriters and collaborators may:

- write their their own books and novels;
- write magazine articles, short stories, scripts, screenplays, or other freelance material;
- work as freelance editors.

Income Potential

Income varies according to the project, the celebrity or expert involved, and the experience of the ghostwriter. If a book is being ghostwritten but published under a celebrity's name, it generally earns more. Business articles for trade journals can earn from $400 to $4,000 if published under someone else's byline.

In general, fees for ghostwriting business articles are $25 to $100 per article or $200 a day plus expenses. Ghostwriting an article for a physician can bring in $2,500 to $3,000; ghostwriting a corporate book over the course of six months generally garners a fee of $20,000 to $40,000.

For books, fees vary according to whether the author is self-publishing or has a publisher lined up, and whether the ghostwriter receives an "as told to" line or not. For a book with "as told to" credit, the fee includes a portion of the advance and up to 50 percent of the royalties. If the subject is self-publishing, the fee is $25 to $50 per hour.

If the subject is either self-publishing or does not have a publisher lined up, a ghostwriter who is not getting "as told to" credit would charge a flat fee of $5,000 to $35,000, with payment at regular intervals throughout the project.

Work Prospects

The ongoing popularity of celebrity books, plus the increasing number of specialized and trade publications that require expertise, provide a fair number of opportunities for ghostwriters and collaborators. Most of these writers tend to live in major cities near publishing and entertainment centers.

Education

There are no minimum education requirements unless a writer is working in business, professional, or technical fields.

Experience/Skills

Most ghostwriters and collaborators are experienced journalists, freelance business and magazine article writers, or novelists. Even with a writing background, it can be difficult to get one's own book published. Many writers break into publishing by ghosting or collaborating, and then use the credentials to help sell their own books.

Good interviewing, researching, writing, and editing skills are necessary. Above all, collaborators and ghostwriters are able to mimic others writing styles.

Unions/Associations

Major national authors' associations include the Authors Guild; American Society of Journalists and Authors, Inc.; National Writers Union; Authors League of America, Inc.; and National Writers Club, Inc. Other organizations serve a wide range of specialized interests. Major women's groups include the International Women's Writing Guild and National League of American Pen Women.

SCRIPTWRITER/SCREENWRITER

CAREER PROFILE

Duties: Write scripts and screenplays for film, television, and radio

Alternate Title(s): None

Income Potential: $9,000 to $100,000+ a year

Work Prospects: Poor

Prerequisites:

    Education—Undergraduate degree in fine arts, English, or communications

    Experience—Writing for any medium helpful

    Special Skills—Creativity; writing talent; production knowledge

Position Description

Writing scripts and screenplays for the entertainment industries, particularly for film and television, is prestigious and glamorous—and can be quite lucrative. The business also is extremely unpredictable, high-pressure, and intensely competitive. Many scripts and screen plays that are commissioned are killed before production, which means lower fees for writers, if any at all. And many scripts that are produced undergo so many changes by so many writers that the original writer may not be credited with the final product. (Some even request no credit, if they dislike the alterations.)

In the golden days of Hollywood, most screenwriters worked under contract to the big studios. Today, most screenwriters and scriptwriters are freelancers. They may work on a project-by-project basis, trying to interest producers in ideas for series or one-shot programs. Or, they may work under short contracts—13 weeks is standard for most serial shows on television, such as soap operas or comedy/variety programs.

A beginner usually must write an entire script or screenplay before a producer will consider it for option. Writers with more experience and good track records may be commissioned on the basis of less—a "treatment" or "story," which is an outline. According to Guild rules, writers are paid for all work, even outlines and the polishing of someone else's work, though rates are less than if a writer does all the work alone. Not every producer, however, recognizes Guild agreements. It's not uncommon, especially for beginners, to work on speculation.

Most scriptwriters and screenwriters employ agents to help them find work and negotiate contracts. They may attend special screenings of pilots for new television shows, at which networks solicit script ideas. They may meet with production executives to discuss ideas, a process called "pitching" or "spitballing." Such a session can lead to an assignment for a treatment.

Scriptwriters and screenwriters often work in stages, with many projects never seeing completion. Some projects never go beyond treatments; others are killed after a first draft is written. Frequently other writers are called in to rewrite and polish someone else's work. Payments are negotiated for each step.

It's difficult to write full-time for the entertainment industry without living in its capital, Los Angeles. Day-to-day contacts and proximity to producers and studios are vitally important. Many writers also live in New York City.

Income Potential

Scriptwriters' and screenwriters' earnings vary widely. Some never sell anything. Others, especially if they author one hot script, can make a comfortable living even if they never get anything else produced. And some sell lots of scripts even if the first one turned into a terrible bomb of a movie.

The first step to selling a script is selling an option—the right to buy the script within a specific time period—to use the script, which generally pays the author 10 percent of the total fee. If the script is made into a production, they get the remaining 90 percent. After 18 months, the option generally expires. The script can be sold elsewhere or the option can be renewed for another 10 percent.

Some scriptwriters earn a comfortable living just selling options and never have a script produced. Others, if they author a screenplay or script that results in a successful production, receive additional money from the novelization of the script and television or videocassette presentations of the production.

Scriptwriters and screenwriters may also get a bonus if they receive credit on the final film. Because so many scripts are rewritten, receiving credit depends on how much rewriting occurs.

Income also varies according to the medium (TV, film, or radio), the length and type of script, and other services such as narrations, treatments, rewrites, and polishing. Income also depends on whether or not a writer is under contract to a network or studio to produce multiple scripts.

According to the Writers Guild of America's 1992 Theatrical and Television Basic Agreement, in the period effective from May of 1994 to May of 1995, some of the minimum pay ranges were as follows: screenplay with treatment—$33,362 to $62,039; rewrite of a screenplay—$12,509 to $19,069; polish of a screenplay—$6,257 to $9,534; 60-minute other than network prime-time teleplay and story—$13,676 to $14,223. In addition, writers receive additional pay for reruns and foreign sales.

Week-to-week and term employment for theatrical and television writers ranges from $1,950 to $4,642 per week, depending on the number of weeks employed in a given period of time.

Radio scriptwriters are paid according to the number and length of programs. For example, a writer earns a minimum of $162 for one five-minute program. The same writer earns progressively higher fees for successive five-minute programs up to a minimum of $536 for the sixth program. There is a minimum fee of $1,347 for a single 60-minute program. For a sixth 60-minute program the writer earns $3,555.

Work Prospects

In spite of the large number of films, television, cable TV, and radio programs produced every year, breaking into the business is very difficult—particularly in film or commercial television. An agent in Los Angeles is almost mandatory for most film and television work. Most scriptwriters and screenwriters live in Los Angeles or New York City. Steady work is unpredictable and highly competitive.

Most scriptwriters and screenwriters in the entertainment industry are white males; women far outnumber minorities. Since this is largely a freelance field, there are no affirmative-action policies. Opportunities depend on talent, contacts, and luck.

Education

Most scriptwriters and screenwriters have broad educations, such as undergraduate degrees in fine arts, English, or communications. Some have degrees in advertising and start their careers as ad copywriters.

Experience/Skills

It is possible for someone with little previous writing experience to write salable scripts and screenplays. Most scriptwriters and screenwriters have had seasoning in some medium, such as print or broadcast. Experience matters less than talent, creativity, and ability to write good dialogue. Good scriptwriters and screenwriters have an ear for how people talk. They also understand the visual aspects of their work—how their ideas will translate to the screen.

Unions/Associations

Writers who work for most major film studios and television networks are required to join the Writers Guild of America. Salaried writers for radio and television stations may belong to the WGA; American Federation of Radio and Television Artists; or National Association of Broadcast Employees and Technicians. Scriptwriters and screenwriters may belong to other professional writing groups as well.

PLAYWRIGHT

CAREER PROFILE

Duties: Write dramatic and comedic scripts for public performance

Alternate Title(s):   Dramatist

Income Potential: Quite variable, ranging from a percentage of the gross receipts, a small fee per performance plus royalties and a percentage of the receipts, to $1,000 and up per performance plus royalties and a percentage of the receipts

Work Prospects: Fair to poor

Prerequisites:

Education—Undergraduate degree in drama, writing, English, communications, or other liberal or fine arts; advanced course work in drama and writing beneficial

Experience—None necessary to break in; acting experience considered a must by some

Special Skills—Excellent command of English; writing skills, particularly in dialogue; self-motivation; ability to withstand repeated rejection before finally achieving success

Position Description

Like working on a novel, writing a play is a labor of love. Unless commissioned to create a particular story, playwrights usually develop their plays in their spare time. Few can devote all their energies to playwriting unless receiving income from another source. Writing a play may be something that many writers dream of doing, but it is more hard work than glamour.

Formerly, a playwright knew the audience: a congregation of interested (he or she hoped) individuals enjoying the action at the time it was performed. The playwright received instant feedback about the play's success or failure. Now, however, playwrights may write initially for the stage, but the play may also appear as a TV movie, a miniseries, a film, or even on radio.

A play written for the stage is much less susceptible to change by directors, actors, or producers. If the playwright's work is covered by a contract approved by industry organizations such as the Dramatists Guild, no changes at all may be made in the script without the author's consent. He or she, along with the producer, also have approval of cast and director, full ownership of copyright and all other rights, and the right to formulate contracts for all other uses of the play. Works for

TV or the movies may be rewritten, according to the dictates of commercial and moral standards.

On radio, playwrights must create "movies" of the imagination and are expected to be familiar with sound effects, music, narration, and dialogue. As on the stage, the power of the author's written word is so important that few producers choose to change it.

In addition, playwrights may be called upon to:

- act as agent to sell the play;
- perform in the production, either on stage or behind the scenes;
- represent the play at industry functions and be responsible for talking with the press.

Income Potential

Since writing a play is quite different from regular employment, payment is not so much a salary as consideration for a finished work. Radio scripts can bring from $75 to $900 for a half-hour, and from $1,000 to $2,000 for a full hour. Regional theater groups may pay a playwright a flat $500 to $2,000 for a play, or negotiate a variety of payment schedules. Some theaters pay $50 a week against a percentage of the box office receipts;

some offer $35 for the first performance and $15 for every performance thereafter; some offer a percentage of the receipts only; and some generously pay a flat rate, a percentage, and travel and/or living expenses for the playwright. Payment depends entirely on the size of the theater company, the support of the community, and the previous success or "bankability" of the playwright.

Work Prospects

Playwrights do not apply for jobs in the same manner as magazine editors, although there are established channels for getting a play published and performed. Contrary to popular belief, publishers and theater groups are seeking new works all the time; the best chances are with small and regional theaters. Another "given" that is no longer true: Playwrights do not have to live in New York (or Los Angeles).

The prospects of making a career out of playwriting can be quite good if the playwright enjoys a successful first play—or better yet, a successful second or third effort. Advancement is based on luck and skill; there is no established career path.

Education

While an undergraduate degree in English, drama, writing, or other liberal or fine arts field is preferable, there is no set educational requirement for playwriting. Course work in writing or acting is a plus. Sometimes education in the "school of hard knocks" gives a playwright as much fodder for drama as college might.

Experience/Skills

It is difficult to pinpoint exactly what experience a playwright should possess. Some authorities feel that work as an actor is almost a necessity in order to know how actors transmit words to an audience. Others merely want proof that the playwright can write plays—sort of a chicken-and-the-egg situation, but usually borne out by work for small, regional theaters or academic productions. A good knowledge of English is essential; so is the ability to write dialogue and visualize how the actor will express the playwright's words. One successful play does not guarantee a playwright a career in drama, but it does make him or her more likely to receive attention upon completion of the second effort.

Unions/Associations

Playwrights for radio join the Writers Guild of America—the union for TV, motion picture, and radio writers—upon selling a script. There is no union for stage dramatists, but most usually join the Dramatists Guild to protect their rights to a play, to stay informed of standard business practices, and to learn who's looking for scripts. Guild membership also offers members use of the Members' Hotline for emergency problems, access to health insurance, subscriptions to Guild publications, and participation in Guild workshops and symposia. The Dramatists Guild is part of the Authors League of America. Playwrights may also join the National Writers Union.

LYRICIST/JINGLE WRITER

CAREER PROFILE

Duties: Write lyrics for musical compositions, whether for popular distribution or as commercial advertising vehicles

Alternate Title(s):   Songwriter

Income Potential: $0 to no limit

Work Prospects: Fair to poor

Prerequisites:

Education—An undergraduate degree in music, writing, English, or other liberal or fine arts field is preferable but not required; knowledge of music theory, harmony, counterpoint, standard, and popular songs is necessary

Experience—Previous work as a lyricist; no experience necessarily required

Special Skills—Ability to write "singable" words; skill to take a commercial idea or motto and create singing verse around it; attentiveness; ability to take directions and compromise; business and public-relations skills; self-discipline; versatility; feel for current trends; poise and stamina

Position Description

As with playwright, employment as a lyricist or jingle writer is not quite definable. Fitting words to music is not a science or learned skill so much as a talent. Lyricists are employed by stage producers, record producers, movie companies, and struggling composers.

The life-style is anything but "normal." Lyricists keep no regular hours, have little or no job security, and can count on night and weekend work. Few lyricists become famous, but some achieve modest recognition after receiving industry awards.

For jingle writing, the important thing is to make sure the product's name and motto or slogan are incorporated prominently into the song. Being able to write jingles or little songs quickly is definitely a plus, as advertisers may request almost immediate turnaround.

Most jingle writers work for music production houses, although some may work for advertising agencies. Some freelance. Jingle writing is considered less "important" work than writing legitimate lyrics, yet a jingle is heard instantly by millions on television and may accompany a really catchy tune. Some jingles become part of American popular culture, such as "Join the Pepsi generation," "Have it your way," or "It's the real thing."

Most jingle writers also write song lyrics, and some see their jingles expanded into full-length songs. Many lyricists began their careers as jingle writers. Once a lyricist has sold a song lyric successfully, he or she is more likely to be called upon to write the words for other pieces of music. Occasionally a composer and lyricist work so well together that they collaborate on all future work.

Income Potential

Lyricists can sell songs for one-time flat fees, or on a royalty basis. The average advance against royalties is $5,000 to $6,500. According to the American Guild of Authors and Composers, a good minimum contract should pay the songwriter 50 percent of the gross receipts earned from mechanical reproduction (royalties from sale of records, tapes, or sheet music), electrical transcriptions, and synchronization.

The three performing-rights organizations—American Society of Composers, Authors and Playwrights (ASCAP); Broadcast Music Inc. (BMI); and SESAC Inc.—monitor the performances of all members' music and handle payment of royalties. ASCAP uses a formula based on the number of performances within each media group (radio, TV, concert, restaurant music, etc.) and weights the performance by factors accounting for that medium's share of income among all media and the possibility of performances not accounted for. This formula yields "credits," which are then multiplied by a standard figure. ASCAP then distributes the member lyricist's royalties based on the fee negotiated in his contract. Both BMI, which is the largest performing-arts organization in America, and SESAC, which is the smallest, operate similarly.

If the lyricist is not the composer, his or her 50-percent share will be divided between the two songwriting partners. The more popular and successful a lyricist becomes, the higher a percentage he or she may negotiate, and the more money he or she earns. Successful songwriters earn $500,000 or more a year. A few earn more than $1 million a year.

Work Prospects

Breaking into the field is quite difficult. Many people want to write song lyrics. The field is highly competitive, but there are opportunities for talented people. As more television and film projects use music, whether for title songs or as background, the need for lyricists will grow. Check the business trade weekly magazines and newspapers such as Songwriter magazine, for the names of publishers interested in songs.

Becoming a jingle writer is most likely an intermediate stop for a serious lyricist; the best opportunities are in New York or Los Angeles, with the major advertising and music production companies. Getting your foot in the door usually works best through personal connections, individual contractors, studios, music reps, and your own sterling reputation. Other opportunities exist as staff writers for music publishing companies, or lyricists for TV or movie soundtracks.

There is no set career path. Once a lyricist has had success with a producer or advertiser, he or she is likely to continue. Good jingle writers can count on more and more work as companies put catchy words and tunes on television. Industry recognition, such as a Clio award in advertising, an Oscar, an Emmy, or a Grammy, help assure the lyricist of continued success and financial reward.

Education

There are no educational prerequisites for work as a lyricist or jingle writer, but a background in music or writing is definitely a plus. Undergraduate degrees in music, English, or other liberal or fine arts are the norm. One source believes that jingle writers must have a complete musical education, with a working knowledge of theory, harmony, and counterpoint. Talent alone is not quite enough. It is also important for any lyricist or jingle writer to remain familiar with the old standards and keep abreast of current pop tunes.

Experience/Skills

As with playwriting, success at writing song lyrics depends on the success of earlier efforts, but the trick is getting the first one accepted. Most producers of songs, movies, and television shows prefer previous work on other songs or productions. Spending time in a music or recording studio as an observer will give you a good grounding in how the system operates.

The best skills to have for this business are the abilities to write clearly, to work well with the music's composer, and to be willing to compromise. Jingle writers often begin with copy provided by the advertising agency or client, so he or she needs to be flexible. The ability to work fast, sometimes producing immediate turnaround, is also important. Business and public-relations skills, self-discipline, versatility, stamina, and poise help as well.

Unions/Associations

Most lyricists join one of the performing-rights organizations—ASCAP, BMI and SESAC—and/or guilds. Both the American Guild of Authors and Composers/the songwriters' guild and the Dramatists Guild are open to lyricists. Guild membership entitles members to review of contracts, health insurance, and participation in seminars and workshops. Membership in a performing-rights organization provides the lyricist with a valid tally of performances and distribution of royalties. Other groups include the National Association of Composers, USA, and Songwriters Resources and Services.

POET

CAREER PROFILE

Duties: Compose various forms of verse and poems for magazines and books

Alternate Title(s):   None

Income Potential: Up to $2.00 per line, sometimes more

Work Prospects: Poor

Prerequisites:

  Education—Undergraduate degree in English or liberal arts
  Experience—Background in creative writing helpful
  Special Skills—Thorough understanding of grammar and English language; knowledge of disciplines of poetry

Position Description

Poetry is an artistic form of expression of emotions, ideas, and visual images. There are three basic types of poetry: dramatic, which is action-oriented; narrative, which tells a story; and lyric, which describes first-person emotions and also includes verses for songs. Each of those types is broken down into specific forms. Free verse, for example, follows no meter but allows the poet to compose in lines of any length. A haiku poem has a rigid form of three lines with five, seven, and five syllables per line, respectively.

Many persons write poetry as a hobby. Professional poets publish their work in literary, academic, and a few general-circulation magazines, and occasionally in books, such as poetry anthologies.

Some write traditional, humorous, and inspirational verses for greeting-card publishers, while still others take their talent to music, writing lyrics for songs and plays (see "Lyricist," page 106). Whatever market is sought, a poet should be thoroughly familiar with the work being published and produced.

Most poets earn their livings teaching English, literature, creative writing, or poetry, or by freelance writing.

Income Potential

All but a handful of poets earn little or nothing for their work. Literary and academic magazines, even small book presses, often pay in free copies rather than money. Some magazines pay from $1 to $15 per poem, while others pay per line. A good rate range is $1 to $1.50 per line. Prestigious magazines pay up to $10 a line.

Books of poems do not sell well—a few hundred copies is considered excellent. Advances are negligible, perhaps several hundred dollars, or nonexistent. Many poets resort to self-publishing in order to see their works in print, or enter into cooperative arrangements with publishers to share production and distribution costs.

Typical advance pay for the lyrics to a song ranges from several hundred dollars to $1,000, plus royalties. Many music publishers pay no advance but will underwrite the costs of a demonstration tape.

Some poets can obtain foundation grants to subsidize their work.

Work Prospects

Selling poetry is hard work. Markets include literary and academic magazines, as well as general interest magazines and some newspapers. Poets in search of a book publisher will find their best chances with small presses or in self-publishing.

Songwriting and selling poems, gags, and ideas to greeting-card publishers are more lucrative areas for the poet but very competitive.

Education

Most accomplished poets have had extensive educations in English, poetry, literature, and creative writing. An undergraduate degree in English or liberal arts is good preparation. Graduate degrees—preferably a Ph.D.—are required for college-level teaching positions. Lyricists should have an educational background in music.

Experience/Skills

Many poets begin by joining writing groups and reading their work aloud for critiques. Command of the English language—a good vocabulary and grammar skills—is essential.

Unions/Associations

The American Guild of Authors and Composers and the American Society of Composers, Authors and Publishers represent music publishers, composers, and lyricists. Other associations for poets include the Academy of American Poets; P.E.N. American Center; Poetry Society of America; and National Writers Union. The National Society of State Poetry Associations can provide contacts for state poetry affiliates. The National Association of Greeting Card Publishers has an industry market list for artists and writers.

GREETING CARD WRITER

CAREER PROFILE

Duties: Write verse and sentiments for greeting cards

Alternative Title(s): None

Income Potential: $25 to $300 per sentiment, depending on size of the company and whether artwork is included

Work Prospects: Poor

Prerequisites:

    Education—Undergraduate degree in English or liberal arts

    Experience—Background in creative writing helpful

    Special Skills—Understanding of what attracts a sender to a card; ability to be witty and innovative

Position Description

Greeting card writers compose verse and sentiments for inclusion in a wide variety of types of cards. Some bear traditional rhymed poems, others inspirational verse, others clever sayings or humorous phrases.

A good greeting card will attract the sender to the card. It expresses a universal sentiment but makes the sender think of the person who will receive it. Greeting card writers are constantly coming up with new ways to say "I love you" and "Happy Birthday."

While larger greeting card companies hire their own stable of writers, many buy freelance ideas for cards.

Card lines are being developed to reflect demographic changes, according to the Greeting Card Association. Trends in card design include cards for seniors, cards targeted at working women, cards about health and fitness, and cards about divorce, separation, terminal illness, and friendship.

Of the holidays, Christmas is the one that results in the most card sales. Next is Valentine's Day, followed by Easter and Mother's Day.

Some companies that buy free-lance require illustrations to be submitted with card ideas. Others prefer to provide their own illustrations, although suggestions for artwork may be welcome.

Income Potential

The greeting card industry is very competitive. Some companies prefer to receive a resume, business card, and client list along with card ideas; others like to get individual card ideas on index cards. Freelancers should contact the greeting card company first to see what their submission procedures require.

Most companies pay per idea; only a few pay royalties. Pay can be $50 to $250 per idea, depending on the company. Some companies maintain large writing staffs and do not purchase much freelance material.

Most greeting card writers, unless they are on staff, do other kinds of free-lancing or have other jobs.

Work Prospects

About one idea in 10 ends up being purchased at most companies. Odds might be better at companies where cards are primarily freelanced.

Education

If your ideas are good, many companies are not interested in your background. However, most freelancers have undergraduate degrees in liberal arts, communications, journalism, or creative writing. Some companies ask for a resume.

Experience/Skills

Good command of the English language is essential. An ability to express an old sentiment in a fresh and new way is also important.

Unions/Associations

The National Greeting Card Association has an industry market list for artists and writers.

BUSINESS COMMUNICATIONS AND PUBLIC RELATIONS

PUBLIC-RELATIONS ASSISTANT

CAREER PROFILE

Duties: Assist public-relations manager, director, editor, and others with public-relations activities

Alternate Title(s):   Editorial Assistant; Publicity Assistant

Salary Range: Under $20,000 to $25,000

Employment Prospects: Good

Advancement Prospects: Good

Prerequisites:

Education—Undergraduate degree in communications, journalism, liberal arts, or English

Experience—School journalism experience helpful

Special Skills—Good writing and editing skills; knowledge of graphics; ability to work as part of team and independently; outgoing personality; secretarial skills

CAREER LADDER

```
┌─────────────────────────────────┐
│   Communications Specialist     │
└─────────────────────────────────┘

┌─────────────────────────────────┐
│   Public-Relations Assistant    │
└─────────────────────────────────┘

┌─────────────────────────────────┐
│      College; Journalist        │
└─────────────────────────────────┘
```

Position Description

The role of the public-relations professional is to present a favorable image of the employer to its audience, which could include the general public, the investment community, lawmakers, or clients.

Public relations encompasses many image-building tasks, and the public-relations assistant gets exposure to all or nearly all of them. The job is entry-level and can be found in private business and industry, government, nonprofit associations, and education. Many of the job duties are menial, such as typing, filing, running errands, and taking telephone calls. Most public-relations assistants get opportunities to work in a variety of public-relations functions. For example, they may contribute short articles to an internal newsletter or magazine, called the "house organ," or write and distribute bulletin board notices and paycheck stuffers.

They may also help develop and update mailing lists for news releases, write simple news releases for executive approval, assemble press kits, and stuff envelopes. They may handle certain media queries themselves.

In addition, a public-relations assistant may:

- update biographies of key company executives and photo files;
- help arrange speaking engagements;
- assist in community activities and fundraising drives; assist internal publication editors on production work.

Salaries

Salaries for public relations graduates employed full-time in 1992 were generally higher than for other recent journalism school graduates. Those starting out at public relations firms or departments earned a median salary of $21,000. New graduates employed by daily newspapers earned a median of $19,600 in 1992.

Salaries in public relations can range from under $17,000 up to the mid-$20,000s at the assistant level.

These salaries experienced growth in the late 1980s, but stalled in the early 1990s. The median public relations salary in 1993 was $46,204, a slight drop from 1992, according to a survey by the *Public Relations Journal.*

According to the federal government, the median salary for public relations specialists was $32,000 in

1992, with the middle 50 percent earning from $24,000 to $51,000.

Women make less than men with comparable experience in public relations, but a recent salary survey showed the gap closing a little.

Salaries vary according to employer; account executives and other non-management employees (including assistants) at public relations firms earned a median of $29,016; at corporations, similar jobs brought median salaries of $35,715; in non-profit organizations, health care and government, the median was $29,677, according to a survey done by the *Public Relations Journal.* Men not in management earned a median of $33,908; women, $30,036, according to the survey.

The median 1993 salary for public relations employees in media and communications was $49,473; in government, $44,019; in advertising agencies, $41,066; and in education, $41,008. The overall median was $46,204.

Employment Prospects

More graduates of journalism schools in the last six years majored in public relations than in print journalism. Nationwide, 16,750 students majored in print reporting in the fall of 1992, while 18,220 majored in public relations.

This does not mean that job prospects are better in public relations. The top 10 public relations companies cut their payrolls by an average of 7.5 percent in 1993; a survey found that public relations as a major offered the weakest match between journalism school specialty of study and job found.

That didn't stop the popularity of public relations as a major from surging in the mid-1980s. The publicist's role evolved from a primarily behind-the-scenes one to a high-profile, glamorous, "spin doctor" job.

Public relations seems to have captured the imaginations of students raised on media images, and demand for good public relations specialists should continue as business grows more competitive.

Advancement Prospects

Public-relations assistants who perform well can expect good chances of advancement. The exposure to a wide range of activities is helpful for targeting a career path.

Education

Entry level jobs generally require a college degree in communications, public relations, journalism, advertis-

ing, or liberal arts. In addition, some organizations have their own formal training programs for new employees.

Journalism school graduates are also combining specialties, leaving them qualified for more specialized public relations jobs.

A 1992 survey of graduates done at Ohio State University showed that 32 percent of journalism students listed "other" as their major; an analysis of those responses showed students were combining majors—advertising and public relations, for example, or public relations and print journalism.

Jobs that might use such combinations include public-relations assistant positions at newspapers, where the best opportunities might be within chains such as Gannett; at magazines, where planning press and trade parties can be part of the duties; at television stations; in advertising agencies, which often offer public-relations services to clients and maintain staff to provide them; in the federal government, where projecting public reaction to policies may be an important part of the job; or at non-profit institutions, where lobbying in the state capital or Washington on behalf of the institution might be needed, in addition to the basic public-relations functions.

Experience/Skills

Public relations firms and departments once recruited former journalists. Now increasing numbers of journalism school graduates are going directly into public relations. While no experience may be necessary for entry-level jobs, the field is increasingly competitive. Internships or college newspaper experience are advantageous.

Public-relations professionals should be creative, outgoing, and able to motivate and persuade others. They should be good writers and editors, understand the needs of the media, and be knowledgeable in graphics and layout. Experience with video display terminals is helpful.

Unions/Associations

Major professional associations include the International Association Of Business Communicators; the Public Relations Society of America, Inc.; and Women In Communications, Inc.

INTERNAL PUBLICATIONS EDITOR

CAREER PROFILE

Duties: Write, edit, and produce employee magazine or newsletter

Alternate Title(s): Communications Specialist; Editor

Salary Range: $25,000 to $45,000+

Employment Prospects: Good

Advancement Prospects: Good

Prerequisites:

Education—Undergraduate degree in communications, journalism, public relations, liberal arts, or English

Experience—Background as news reporter or editor helpful

Special Skills—Good writing and editing ability; photography and graphics skills; self-motivation; organizational skills

CAREER LADDER

```
┌─────────────────────────────────┐
│  Manager of Editorial Services  │
└─────────────────────────────────┘

┌─────────────────────────────────┐
│  Internal Publications Editor   │
└─────────────────────────────────┘

┌─────────────────────────────────┐
│    Journalist; News Editor;     │
│ Public-Relations Assistant; College │
└─────────────────────────────────┘
```

Position Description

Rare is the company, association, or organization that does not produce and distribute an employee newsletter or magazine. Management views internal publications as a pipeline for communication and a means to foster goodwill and boost morale. A publication may be a mere two-sided single sheet of paper or a slick, four-color magazine. Many employers have more than one internal publication; a slick magazine may come out quarterly, supplemented by monthly newsletters. Most publications, however, are monthly magazines.

The job of internal publications editor encompasses planning, writing, editing, editorial decision-making, photography, layout, and production. Most editors are able to put their personal stamp on their publications.

The editors usually work under the supervision of communications coordinators or managers of editorial services. The editors must plan issues in advance and submit outlines for managerial review and approval, then arrange for interviews and photographs. Editors must be able to meet deadlines and stay within their production budgets.

Some editors produce a publication alone, doing all the work or hiring freelancers to assist them. Some may have an assistant, and others may have a staff.

Editors are responsible for clearing all material for publication through management channels. They also spec type (decide typeface style and point size), do page layouts, or work with graphic artists. In addition, they instruct typesetters and printers.

Content depends on the nature of the publication. Articles usually include profiles of employees or departments; new hires and promotions; messages from senior executives; community projects; and other news and features.

In addition, an internal publications editor may write occasional press releases and speeches, or produce slide shows and films for internal audiences.

Salaries

An entry-level internal publications editor is generally paid between $25,000 and $45,000.

Employment Prospects

The job of internal publications editor is one of the most common public-relations positions, and is often the easiest way to break into a public-relations department. Turnover in this type of job is steady.

Advancement Prospects

An employee publication provides a good showcase for talent, skill, and visibility. Prospects for advancement to higher-level positions are good.

Education

The minimum requirement is an undergraduate degree in communications, journalism, public relations, liberal arts, or English.

Experience/Skills

Some internal-publications-editor positions are entry-level, filled by college graduates. Others require several years of experience, preferably as a news reporter or editor, or in another aspect of public relations.

Excellent writing and editing skills plus leadership qualities are essential for any editing job. Editors should have good news judgment and organizational skills as well. They also must be able to work well with others and be able to take direction. Corporate editors have much less latitude than news media editors in determining content. Corporate interests are served first, and negative news is often downplayed or ignored.

Unions/Associations

Major professional associations include the Public Relations Society of America, Inc.; International Association of Business Communicators; and Women In Communications, Inc.

EXTERNAL PUBLICATIONS EDITOR

CAREER PROFILE

Duties: Write news releases, articles, informational brochures, speeches, slide scripts, and letters for an external audience

Alternate Title(s): Communications Specialist; Communications Associate; Information Representative; Public Information Officer

Salary Range: $25,000 to $45,000+

Employment Prospects: Good

Advancement Prospects: Good

Prerequisites:
  Education—Undergraduate degree in public relations, communications, journalism, liberal arts, or English

  Experience—Background in news reporting helpful

  Special Skills—Strong newswriting ability; organizational and analytic skills

CAREER LADDER

```
┌─────────────────────────────────┐
│   Communications Coordinator;   │
│    Public-Relations Manager     │
└─────────────────────────────────┘

┌─────────────────────────────────┐
│   External Publications Editor  │
└─────────────────────────────────┘

┌─────────────────────────────────┐
│   Public-Relations Assistant;   │
│    Journalist; News Editor      │
└─────────────────────────────────┘
```

Position Description

External publications editor is a job that specializes in promoting the interests of the employer with the general public, media, or special-interest groups. In some cases, particularly small companies and organizations, job duties may be combined with others for more generalized job descriptions.

The external publications editor is responsible for educating and informing external audiences, such as the general public, stockholders, the news media, or special-interest groups. The job involves producing news releases, feature articles for the business and trade press, brochures, slide scripts, and speeches.

The communications could concern the announcement of new products; how ongoing programs are benefiting the economy or community; or the appointment of new executives. Feature articles are written for trade, industry, and professional publications. For example, a bank may describe a program to serve customers more quickly at teller windows, or a trucking firm might put together an article about how a computerized maintenance system has cut repair bills by a significant percentage.

External publications editors may also develop informational material, such as booklets that answer common questions for stockholders, or pamphlets that tell the histories of their companies or organizations.

In addition, external publications editors may write articles for internal publications and write community-relations letters for an executive officer's signature.

Salaries

An external publications editor with some experience either in public relations or journalism can expect to earn about $25,000 to $45,000 a year. Salaries can go as high as $50,000—and more—after several years of experience, depending on the level of the job.

Employment Prospects

Job opportunities in public relations are expected to be good throughout the 1990s, though the profession is subject to cutbacks in economic downturns and recessions.

Advancement Prospects

External publications editors are in good positions to move into managerial jobs. They often work directly with upper management, which gives them visibility that helps them move through the ranks.

Education

An undergraduate degree in communications, public relations, journalism, liberal arts, or English is the minimum requirement. Degrees in finance or business can advantageous, as can be advanced degrees.

Experience/Skills

A journalism background is the best preparation for this type of public-relations work. An external publications editor must be able to write not only many types of material but for different audiences as well.

Good writing and editing skills are important, as is an understanding of the needs of the news media. A background in graphics is useful.

Unions/Associations

Major professional associations include the Public Relations Society of America, Inc.; International Association Of Business Communicators; and Women In Communications, Inc.

PUBLIC INFORMATION OFFICER

CAREER PROFILE

Duties: Handle media relations for company or organization; write and distribute news releases; place articles in news media

Alternate Title(s): Public-Relations Manager; Public Affairs Practitioner

Salary Range: $25,000 to $50,000+

Employment Prospects: Good

Advancement Prospects: Good

Prerequisites:

  Education—Undergraduate degree in communications, journalism, English, or liberal arts

  Experience—Newswriting, wire service, or previous communications experience essential

  Special Skills—Newswriting; organizational ability; outgoing personality

CAREER LADDER

```
┌─────────────────────────────────┐
│                                 │
│    Director of Communications   │
│                                 │
└─────────────────────────────────┘

┌─────────────────────────────────┐
│                                 │
│    Public Information Officer    │
│                                 │
└─────────────────────────────────┘

┌─────────────────────────────────┐
│                                 │
│   Communications Coordinator     │
│                                 │
└─────────────────────────────────┘
```

Position Description

Public information officers act as liaison between the news media and the company or organization they represent. They answer questions from the news media; generate favorable news stories about the company or organization, then try to place these stories in newspapers, with the wire services, or on television and radio; keep management informed of issues that might result in media inquiries; and prepare in advance management's responses to anticipated questions.

A large part of the public information officer's job is to maintain regular contact and establish a relationship of trust with the news media. Trust is very important in getting a message or image across to the public. The public information officer also must be able to answer press questions immediately or within a set deadline. Other duties include coaching company executives on how to handle media interviews.

Public information officers must stay informed of all news developments that affect their employers so that they can act quickly to shield executives from unfavorable publicity or seize opportunities for favorable pub-

licity. They may be responsible for providing daily news digests and clips to management.

Most supervise a staff or one or more assistants; some may have only secretarial help. Depending on the employer, the public-information-officer position can be a mid-level position or a top position.

In addition, a public information officer may write speeches and slide show scripts or produce informational brochures.

Salaries

Salaries vary greatly according to professional experience, geographic location, type of employer, and where the public information officer fits into the hierarchy. Average salaries are in the thirties; nearly half of the professionals earn more than $45,000, depending on their expertise, special skills and employer.

Employment Prospects

Public information officers have become increasingly important in recent years to many businesses, organizations, and government agencies, due largely to more aggressive reporting by the news media. Job opportunities are expected to be good throughout the 1990s, especially in private industry. Job openings in education—school districts, colleges and universities—will be limited due to staff cutbacks.

Advancement Prospects

The public information officer is a front-line position with high visibility. Chances are good for promotion to higher-level, more responsible positions.

Education

Most public information officers have undergraduate degrees in communications, journalism, English, or liberal arts. Some have undergraduate or graduate degrees in business, economics, or political science.

Experience/Skills

Public information officers generally have previous experience working in the news media as well as in other public-relations positions. Some employers may require several years' experience.

Public information officers should have sound news judgement, as well as good writing and editing skills. They should be outgoing and able to mix well with a wide variety of people. In addition, they should be well organized and responsive to requests made on deadline.

Unions/Associations

Major professional associations include the Public Relations Society of America, Inc.; International Association of Business Communicators; American Business Communication Association; and Women In Communications, Inc.

GOVERNMENT AFFAIRS SPECIALIST

CAREER PROFILE

Duties: Monitor government and public-affairs issues of concern to employer; prepare position papers for management; oversee company's political action committee

Alternate Title(s): Public Affairs Specialist

Salary Range: $30,000 to $60,000

Employment Prospects: Good

Advancement Prospects: Good

Prerequisites:

Education—Undergraduate degree in communications, journalism, public relations, liberal arts, political science, or history; graduate degree helpful

Experience—Background in journalism, politics, or public relations essential

Special Skills—Strong analytical skills; good organizational ability; understanding of political process; speaking ability; salesmanship

CAREER LADDER

```
┌─────────────────────────────────────┐
│                                      │
│    Manager of Government Affairs     │
│                                      │
└─────────────────────────────────────┘

┌─────────────────────────────────────┐
│                                      │
│    Government Affairs Specialist     │
│                                      │
└─────────────────────────────────────┘

┌─────────────────────────────────────┐
│                                      │
│      Communications Specialist       │
│                                      │
└─────────────────────────────────────┘
```

Position Description

The government affairs specialist plays a very important role in many large companies and corporations, by monitoring the activities of various local, state, and federal government bodies and agencies whose activities might affect a company's business and operations. He or she may be part of a large public-relations department and assigned specific areas of responsibility, or else be the company's sole legislative watchdog.

Government affairs specialists keep track of such things as tax legislation, labor regulations, consumer rights regulations and legislation, and other related issues. They keep management apprised of pending issues that are of immediate or long-term concern. They often prepare position papers outlining the effect of proposed laws or regulations on a company's business.

Government affairs specialists also act as spokespersons for their companies when the media calls for information about their companies' stands on certain issues, such as proposed tax increase or regulations governing minority hiring. Occasionally, they testify on behalf of their employers at government hearings; they may also lobby lawmakers and members of government agencies.

A government affairs specialist may also coordinate a company's political action committee, or PAC—the arm of the company that is allowed to contribute to political campaigns. As part of the job, a government affairs specialist may develop dossiers on various candidates for public office, evaluating which deserve support by his or her company; write letters or prepare newsletters for other PAC members to update them on pending issues; and answer queries from governmental agencies seeking information to help them formulate legislation or regulations.

In addition, a government affairs specialist may prepare speeches or testimony for management on a variety of issues.

Salaries

A government affairs position carries a great deal of responsibility in most companies and is not an entry-level job. Salaries typically begin in the low thirties and climb according to a person's experience and the size of the employer. According to the *Public Relations Journal* 1992 Annual Salary Survey, the median salary in this field is about $52,000.

Employment Prospects

This is a crucial position for many companies because of the proliferation of governmental agencies, the activities of which need to be monitored, as well as ever-changing and complex regulations. Employment prospects are good for qualified individuals.

Advancement Prospects

A government affairs specialist has a high-visibility job and often works closely with upper management, which enhances opportunities for advancement.

Education

An undergraduate degree in communications, journalism, public relations, liberal arts, political science, or history is the best preparation for this type of work. Advanced degrees may be advantageous.

Experience/Skills

Experience as political journalists or legislative assistants or aides on the state or federal level are ideal backgrounds for government affairs specialists. A background in public-relations work is also good.

Government affairs specialists must be able to analyze complex information and explain it clearly to others. They should be well organized, personable, and outgoing. In addition, they should be persuasive and comfortable making speeches.

Unions/Associations

Major professional associations include the Public Relations Society of America, Inc.; International Association of Business Communicators; and Women In Communications, Inc.

SPEECHWRITER

CAREER PROFILE

Duties: Write speeches for company executives on a variety of topics and for a variety of audiences

Alternate Title(s): Management Communications Specialist

Salary Range: $30,000 to $100,000+

Employment Prospects: Good

Advancement Prospects: Good

Prerequisites:

Education—Undergraduate degree in communications, journalism, liberal arts, English, or business

Experience—Background in journalism or public relations essential

Special Skills—Excellent writing ability; creativity; good research and organizational skills; persuasiveness

CAREER LADDER

```
┌─────────────────────────────┐
│                             │
│   Director of Management     │
│      Communications          │
│                             │
└─────────────────────────────┘

┌─────────────────────────────┐
│                             │
│       Speechwriter           │
│                             │
└─────────────────────────────┘

┌─────────────────────────────┐
│                             │
│  Public Information Officer;  │
│     Publications Editor       │
│                             │
└─────────────────────────────┘
```

Position Description

Speechwriting jobs are found mainly in larger corporations with highly structured communications staffs and in companies whose executives make frequent public appearances. Speechwriters are responsible for developing speeches for corporate executives on a wide range of subjects and for a wide range of audiences. For example, an executive might address a group of Wall Street analysts one week and a community-fundraising organization the next.

Some executives work closely with speechwriters to develop content and tone, but in many cases, the speechwriter must research and write alone. Before beginning a draft, the speechwriter usually meets with the executive or his or her assistant to get preliminary information: the audience, topic, length of speech, and general content; whether anyone from the company has addressed this audience before and on what topic; who else is on the roster; whether the speeches will be before or after a meal; whether or not questions will be allowed; and the possibility of media coverage.

In some cases, the speechwriter may be able to rewrite or update a previously delivered speech. In most cases, he or she will write from scratch, going through many drafts and revisions. There is little pride in authorship in speechwriting.

The speechwriter does extensive reading to stay abreast of news and trends that relate to his or her employer.

In addition, a speechwriter may write slide scripts and video tape presentations or write articles for industry or business publications, which will carry an executive byline.

Salaries

Speechwriters are paid according to experience and talent. A beginning speechwriter can expect to earn about $30,000; experience can bring salaries up to $100,000 or more. Some freelance speechwriters earn well over $200,000 a year.

Employment Prospects

Speechwriters are always in demand. The profession is noted for its high turnover, because of the pressure of the job and also because speechwriters tend to move from company to company. The best job opportunities are in private industry and business.

Advancement Prospects

Speechwriter is a highly visible position, and those who do well in the job have a good chance of being promoted to management.

Education

An undergraduate degree in communications, journalism, English, or liberal arts is essential. Some speechwriters have undergraduate or advanced degrees in business, economics, or political science.

Experience/Skills

Speechwriters come from all backgrounds. Many started in the news business; others have come from other public-relations jobs.

Speechwriters should have a flair for writing the spoken word. They should be able to easily mimic an individual's style of speaking. In addition, they need strong research skills and patience in dealing with extensive revisions.

Unions/Associations

Major professional associations include the Public Relations Society of America, Inc.; International Association of Business Communicators; and Women In Communications, Inc.

COMMUNICATIONS COORDINATOR

CAREER PROFILE

Duties: Coordinate internal/external public and community-relations activities

Alternate Title(s): Public-Relations Specialist; Communications Specialist

Salary Range: $20,000 to $45,000

Employment Prospects: Good

Advancement Prospects: Good

Prerequisites:
  Education—Undergraduate degree in public relations, communications, journalism, liberal arts, or English

  Experience—Background in public relations or journalism essential

  Special Skills—Strong writing and organizational skills; creativity; administrative ability

CAREER LADDER

```
┌─────────────────────────────────┐
│                                 │
│     Public-Relations Manager    │
│                                 │
└─────────────────────────────────┘

┌─────────────────────────────────┐
│                                 │
│   Communications Coordinator    │
│                                 │
└─────────────────────────────────┘

┌─────────────────────────────────┐
│                                 │
│   Internal Publications Editor; │
│           Journalist            │
│                                 │
└─────────────────────────────────┘
```

Position Description

Communications coordinator is a position usually found in a company or organization with three to four communications professionals reporting to a manager or director. The coordinator generally has decision-making authority and may supervise lower level employees, such as public-relations assistants or publications editors.

The communications coordinator has a broad range of responsibilities, almost all of which are writing-related. Duties fall into three categories: internal communications; external communications; and community relations.

Internal communications account for the greatest share of the communications coordinator's workload. He or she might be responsible for editing or supervising the editing and production of the employer's newsletter, magazine, company notices for the bulletin board or paycheck stuffers, and/or informational brochures on company benefits and programs. Other internal responsibilities might include managing an employee feedback program or assisting the personnel department in a recruiting program.

External communications include quarterly and annual stockholder reports; financial statements for the federal government; mailings to stockholders and the public; and all press materials and inquiries.

Community-relations activities might include coordinating a speakers' bureau or representing the company on communications committees of allied industry groups or trade associations.

In addition, a communications coordinator may write speeches for executives or write or supervise the writing and production of scripts for slide shows and films.

Salaries

This is not an entry-level position in most companies. Depending on previous experience, employer, and geographic location, salaries can range from $20,000 to $45,000 or more.

Employment Prospects

Employment opportunities for all public-relations jobs are expected to be good throughout the 1990s, according to the federal government. The best prospects for communications coordinator are in private business and industry, especially with large corporations that have big public-relations departments.

Advancement Prospects

A communications coordinator has a good chance of advancing to a higher managerial or supervisory position within the communications department.

Education

Most public-relations workers have undergraduate degrees in public relations, communications, journalism, liberal arts, or English. A degree or advanced degree in business or economics may be advantageous for employment and advancement.

Experience/Skills

A background in public-relations work is desirable for communications coordinator, though some persons may come directly from a journalism background.

Strong writing skills are a must, as is the ability to handle a diverse number of projects simultaneously with minimum supervision. Communications coordinators should be creative and able to direct and motivate others.

Unions/Associations

Major professional associations include the Public Relations Society of America, Inc.; International Association Of Business Communicators; and Women In Communications, Inc.

PUBLIC-RELATIONS ACCOUNT EXECUTIVE

CAREER PROFILE

Duties: Perform public-relations functions for and advise clients

Alternate Title(s): Consultant

Salary Range: $18,000 to $40,000

Employment Prospects: Good

Advancement Prospects: Good

Prerequisites:

Education—Undergraduate degree in communications, public relations, journalism, liberal arts, or English

Experience—Three to five years in public relations, journalism, or as assistant account executive

Special Skills—Outgoing personality; salesmanship; good writing and organizational skills

CAREER LADDER

```
┌─────────────────────────────┐
│    Account Supervisor       │
└─────────────────────────────┘

┌─────────────────────────────┐
│    Account Executive        │
└─────────────────────────────┘

┌─────────────────────────────┐
│  Assistant Account Executive;│
│   Journalist; News Editor;   │
│  Public-Relations Professional│
└─────────────────────────────┘
```

Position Description

A large percentage of public-relations professionals work for agencies or consulting firms. These businesses function the same way as advertising agencies—they perform public-relations services for clients, create publicity campaigns and strategies, and advise clients on public-relations matters, for all of which they charge fees or commissions. Some clients have little or no public-relations staff, while others use agencies to handle projects that would be too big or time-consuming for their own staff.

The account executive is the liaison between the agency and client. He or she works under the supervision of an accounts supervisor or senior consultant. Beginners are usually called assistant account executives, and they perform mostly routine tasks.

Duties depend on the types of services requested by the client. These may include preparing and mailing press kits; conducting press conferences; arranging media interviews and tours for client executives; placing favorable news or feature stories in the media; handling arrangements for promotional luncheons and dinners as well as trade shows; and conducting opinion surveys.

Advisory duties concern planning publicity campaigns; setting up a public-relations department or program; evaluating such a program; and establishing a lobbying platform. Account executives are likely to coordinate their work with advertising and marketing activities.

Many agencies or consultants specialize in certain areas, such as entertainment or government regulations.

In addition, public-relations account executives may canvass for new clients and write reports for senior staff.

Salaries

Salaried public relations specialists working full-time earned a median salary of $32,000 in 1992, according to the federal government. The middle 50 percent earned from $24,000 to $51,000 annually.

According to a salary survey done by the *Public Relations Journal,* account executives working for a public relations firm earned a median of $29,016; those working in corporations earned a median of $35,715; and those working for the government, health care organizations, or non-profit organizations earned $29,677. Men earned a median of $33,908 while women earned a median of $30,036.

The median overall salary, including managers, was $46,204, according to that survey.

A salary survey done by Women In Communications, Inc., reflected similar findings. That survey found an average salary of $32,500 for public relations specialists working for corporations; $27,500 for those working for non-profit agencies; and an average of $35,000 for those working for public relations agencies.

Employment Prospects

Public relations specialists held about 98,000 jobs in 1992, according to the federal government. Employment prospects are best in large cities where communications facilities are based and businesses and trade associations have their headquarters. Cities such as New York, Los Angeles, Chicago, and Washington, D.C., house many public relations firms.

This field is expected to remain competitive, with more people applying for jobs than there are job openings. Employment is expected to increase about as fast as average for all occupations in the upcoming decade. An increased awareness of the need for public relations should feed growth; corporate downsizing, however, could eliminate some jobs.

Advancement Prospects

The account executive is in a good position for advancement, either in the agency or by moving to a corporation or association. Some account executives become self-employed consultants.

Education

An undergraduate degree in communications, journalism, public relations, liberal arts, or English is the minimum requirement. For consulting, a graduate degree in business or finance is advantageous.

Experience/Skills

Most account executives have backgrounds in public-relations work or in the news media—as journalists or news editors. Skills include ability to work well with others; salesmanship; good writing; creativity; and self-motivation.

Unions/Associations

Major professional associations include the Public Relations Society of America, Inc.; International Association of Business Communicators; and Women In Communications, Inc.

TECHNICAL COMMUNICATOR

CAREER PROFILE

Duties: Write and/or edit technical materials for technical and lay audiences

Alternate Title(s): Technical Writer; Technical Editor

Salary Range: $20,000 to $70,000+

Employment Prospects: Excellent

Advancement Prospects: Fair

Prerequisites:

Education—Undergraduate degree in English, technical communications, science, engineering, computer science, journalism, liberal arts

Experience—Previous work as writer or in some capacity in a technical or scientific field advantageous

Special Skills—Comprehension of field being served; ability to work with engineers, technicians and scientists; ability to rewrite technical material for lay audiences

CAREER LADDER

```
┌─────────────────────────────────┐
│   Technical Communications or   │
│      Publications Manager       │
└─────────────────────────────────┘

┌─────────────────────────────────┐
│                                 │
│     Technical Communicator      │
│                                 │
└─────────────────────────────────┘

┌─────────────────────────────────┐
│                                 │
│            Writer               │
│                                 │
└─────────────────────────────────┘
```

Position Description

Technical communicators write and edit a wide range of technical material for a variety of audiences. Depending on the industry in which they work, they might write software manuals for the lay computer user; technical manuals for the computer programmer; sales materials that will be aimed at engineers and technicians; repair manuals; inhouse communications; specifications sheets; inserts for pharmaceutical products; speeches for industry conferences and meetings; scripts for slides and films, etc.

Their duties may extend into production, for which they work with graphic artists and oversee galleys, proofs, and mechanicals. They may supervise other writers, assistants, and freelancers. Some technical communicators work in education, preparing information and training materials.

Technical communicators often have prior experience in journalism or corporate communications, or in technical fields.

They typical member of the Society for Technical Communications (STC), the leading professional organization, has seven years' experience, lives in a major metropolitan area, works for the computer industry, and is female. About 70 percent are writers or editors.

Members also report a high level of job satisfaction. About 83 percent said they were satisfied with their jobs. Ninety-four percent said job satisfaction was very important to them; 80 percent cited adequate salary; 79 percent said creative opportunity was very important; 76 percent listed freedom as very important.

Salary Range

The 1994 median salary of technical writers and editors was $40,000. Female writers and editors earned 93 cents to the dollar earned by their male counterparts, compared to 74 cents earned by other female full-time employees. Women make up 62 percent of the membership of the Society for Technical Communications (STC).

Pay was also influenced by experience, job responsibilities, industry, and geographic location. Pay was highest on the coasts and lowest in the Midwest.

Those with bachelor's degrees only earned a median of about $39,000 to $40,000; those with master's degrees earned a median of $42,000; and those with doctorates earned a median of $48,000. Those in the computer industry earned a median of about $40,500; those in other industries earned a median of about $38,500.

The top salary reported in the Technical Communicator 1994 Salary Survey was $70,000 for an employee with a doctorate, with 90 percent of those responding to the survey reporting lower salaries and 10 percent higher. The lowest, $20,500, was for entry-level jobs, with 10 percent of survey respondents earning less and 90 percent earning more.

Employment Prospects

Demand for technical writers is expected to increase because of the continued expansion of scientific and technical information and the continued need to communicate it. Although many people are attracted to writing and editing jobs, technical writers and editors enjoy better opportunities than most because of the limited number of people who can handle technical material.

Advancement Prospects

About 20 percent of the members of the STC have managerial responsibilities. However, a survey of members showed that only 24 percent feel that managerial responsibility is very important. The majority valued job satisfaction, adequate salary, creative opportunity, freedom, professional development, and job security.

Education

Ninety-one percent of STC members graduated from a four-year college; a third hold master's degrees or higher. A third majored in English; 18 percent majored in technical writing. A majority of members were hired for their communications skills. Many technical writers picked up specialized knowledge on the job.

Degrees in science, engineering, computer science, graphic arts, mathematics, or economics can also be helpful when combined with good writing ability.

Experience/Skills

Many technical writers transfer to the field from jobs as scientists or engineers. Others start out in lower-level assistant or trainee jobs within a technical information department, learn about the technology, and assume writing jobs.

Technical communicators have to be able to cut through jargon to explain technical points or offer instruction in everyday language. Some jobs may require a technical background or degree. Attention to detail, precision, creativity, organization, and self-discipline are important attributes for these jobs.

Unions/Associations

The Society for Technical Communication is the primary professional association. Technical communicators also may belong to organizations in their areas of expertise, such as the American Medical Writers Association and National Association of Science Writers, Inc.

ADVERTISING

ASSISTANT ACCOUNT EXECUTIVE

CAREER PROFILE

Duties: Research and prepare materials pertaining to advertising agency account management

Alternate Title(s):   Account Executive Trainee

Salary Range: $16,000 to $45,000

Employment Prospects: Fair

Advancement Prospects: Good

Prerequisites:
   Education—Undergraduate degree in advertising, liberal arts, journalism, business

   Experience—None

   Special Skills—Grasp of advertising and marketing; organization; salesmanship

CAREER LADDER

```
┌─────────────────────────────────┐
│                                 │
│       Account Executive         │
│                                 │
└─────────────────────────────────┘

┌─────────────────────────────────┐
│                                 │
│    Assistant Account Executive  │
│                                 │
└─────────────────────────────────┘

┌─────────────────────────────────┐
│                                 │
│        Trainee; College         │
│                                 │
└─────────────────────────────────┘
```

Position Description

Assistant account executive is generally an entry-level position, though in some agencies it may be a step up from trainee, which is essentially a clerical and secretarial job.

Assistant account executives learn the advertising business by performing routine and low-level tasks for the account service department. They may work for one account executive on one or two accounts, or they may work for an entire department of account executives. In the process, they learn how to look after a client's interests, coordinate creative and production work, plan campaigns, and do market analyses.

Duties include research for client proposals and advertising campaigns; assistance in preparing reports and proposals, including writing and graphics; typing; proofreading; and errands. Assistant account executives may occasionally take part in meetings with clients or in presentations.

Assistant account executives often shoulder the bulk of the legwork on projects but share very little of the credit. Work hours are regular business hours, but overtime is not uncommon, especially on short notice.

Some public-relations agencies may also employ assistant account executives to work on public relations and publicity campaigns.

Salaries

According to a 1994 salary survey conducted by *Adweek,* the average salary for assistants or junior-level employees of all types in advertising agencies was $33,600. Women earned less than men, averaging around $32,700.

Survey respondents reported that raises were scant and benefits had been trimmed. The best raises went to those who changed jobs. Most increases were around 5 to 10 percent.

Younger employees with less experience were most concerned about pay levels, particularly those working in New York, where the cost of living eats up low pay. Those under 30 averaged $27,100 in assistant or junior-level jobs.

Employment Prospects

Mergers and consolidations of agencies make the field very competitive (see Introduction).

Advancement Prospects

An assistant account executive who is willing to work hard has a good chance of being promoted to a full-fledged account executive. Often promotion comes through turnover, which is high in the advertising industry.

Education

Assistant account executives generally have undergraduate degrees in advertising, business, journalism, or liberal arts. The work is marketing- and sales-oriented, so an educational emphasis on business and economic studies is helpful. Advanced degrees in business or advertising can give job candidates the competitive edge with many employers.

Experience/Skills

Some assistant account executives begin their careers as trainees, little more than clerical and secretarial as-sistants. Others come straight from college or from entry-level work in a related field, such as sales, public relations, or journalism. Writing and selling experience is helpful.

Skills include a flair for making favorable impressions and getting along well with others; clear writing ability; salesmanship; good organization; persistence.

Unions/Associations

Major associations for advertising professionals include the American Advertising Federation; Business/Professional Advertising Association; American Marketing Association; and Women In Communications, Inc.

ACCOUNT EXECUTIVE

Duties: Coordinate all advertising activities for advertising agency clients; maintain good client relations

Alternate Title(s):   None

Salary Range: $25,000 to $65,000+

Employment Prospects: Fair

Advancement Prospects: Fair

Prerequisites:

Education—Undergraduate degree in advertising, business, liberal arts, journalism, or communications

Experience—One to three years as trainee or assistant account executive helpful

Special Skills—Leadership and salesmanship; copy judgment; knowledge of graphics, media, and marketing

```
┌─────────────────────────────────────┐
│                                     │
│      Accounts Manager; Accounts     │
│             Supervisor              │
│                                     │
└─────────────────────────────────────┘

┌─────────────────────────────────────┐
│                                     │
│          Account Executive          │
│                                     │
└─────────────────────────────────────┘

┌─────────────────────────────────────┐
│                                     │
│   Assistant Account Executive; Trainee  │
│                                     │
└─────────────────────────────────────┘
```

Position Description

Most account executives work for advertising agencies; others work in the advertising or sales departments of businesses and media. The account executive is in charge of the advertising for one or more of an ad agency's clients (usually one large account or several small accounts). He or she determines and plans the nature of the advertising to be produced, relaying the client's expectations and needs to the agency's creative and media buying departments. The account executive coordinates the agency's activities and reviews the creative work produced before presenting it to the client. He or she is the agency's liaison with clients, and must work to maintain good communication and a good relationship.

Account executives must have a thorough knowledge of all operations within an agency, and understand their clients' businesses, marketing, and competition. They must be able to judge whether or not creative copy and proposed ad campaigns are on target. They must be able to understand market analyses and have a thorough understanding of all media, in order to plan the most effective ad campaigns. When campaigns are developed, account executives make formal presentations to the clients or management.

Account executives report to an account supervisor or account manager, who in turn reports to a director or vice president of account services. In large agencies, account executives may delegate research and clerical functions to assistants; in small agencies, they may do everything themselves.

Public-relations agencies also employ account executives, who are responsible for publicity campaigns and press relations.

Additionally, account executives may participate in campaigns and presentations to win new clients, and coordinate publicity and promotional activities along with advertising.

Salaries

The average salary for a senior ad agency employee without supervisory responsibilities was $48,100, according to a 1994 salary survey by *Adweek*. The average salary in account services departments was $76,700.

Women made less than men, averaging $62,500 in account services to the average male salary of $92,200.

The average senior employee salary for women was $41,300, while men earned an average of $55,400. Supervisors earned an average of $54,200.

A big salary jump occurs between those under 30 and those over 30. Those under 30 working in account services average $37,600; those over 30 average $78,100.

Those who change jobs more frequently may gain bigger raises. Many survey respondents reported no cecent raises or raises in the 5 to 10 percent range; 20 percent reported changing jobs in the previous year.

Employment Prospects

The recession of the late 1980s and early 1990s slowed salary growth and limited job prospects. Salary reviews, normally annual, were stretched out to 18–month intervals at some advertising agencies. Changes from the 1980s, the consolidation of large agencies and a new emphasis on global marketing, continue to affect job opportunities. Competition is keen and starting salaries remain low.

Employment in advertising is projected to increase at a fast rate during the next 10 years, however. Competition between businesses will require greater marketing and promotional efforts, according to the federal government.

Advancement Prospects

Account executives who excel at their jobs can advance rapidly in responsibility and pay. The top execu-tives of most advertising agencies came up through the ranks of account executives. Competition is fierce, how-ever, and job security is low—it is not uncommon to be fired if an agency loses an account or if the economy is in recession.

Education

Most account executives have undergraduate degrees in advertising, business, liberal arts, or journalism. A graduate degree in advertising, business, or economics is not necessary but works to the candidate's advantage.

Experience/Skills

In most cases, account executives work as assistant account executives or trainees before being given full responsibility for clients. Some account executives have worked previously as journalists or in advertising sales.

Account executives must understand all aspects of an advertising campaign, from judging creative copy to coordinating the purchase of media space and time. Since they have highly visible positions as their agen-cies' representatives, they must be skilled in salesman-ship and demonstrate leadership.

Unions/Associations

Associations include the American Advertising Fed-eration; Business/Professional Advertising Associa-tion; and Women In Communications, Inc.

ASSISTANT COPYWRITER

CAREER PROFILE

Duties: Assist in development and execution of creative ad copy; clerical tasks

Alternate Title(s): None

Salary Range: $16,000 to $35,000

Employment Prospects: Fair

Advancement Prospects: Good

Prerequisites:

Education—Undergraduate degree in advertising, liberal arts, journalism, communications, or art

Experience—None

Special Skills—Imagination; creativity; command of English

CAREER LADDER

```
┌─────────────────────────────┐
│         Copywriter          │
└─────────────────────────────┘

┌─────────────────────────────┐
│     Assistant Copywriter    │
└─────────────────────────────┘

┌─────────────────────────────┐
│       Trainee; College      │
└─────────────────────────────┘
```

Position Description

Assistant copywriter is an entry-level position, usually at an advertising agency, sometimes in the advertising or marketing department of a business. An assistant copywriter may be fresh out of college or may still be enrolled, working during summers or through class internships.

The position involves routine work assisting copywriters, as well as limited opportunities to handle creative projects. Routine work includes researching a client, product, service, or industry that will be used by the copywriter in developing an ad; proofreading copy; trafficking copy among departments; and running errands.

Assistant copywriters also may be assigned creative projects of their own. They work under the supervision of a copywriter or senior copywriter, sometimes the copy supervisor. Their position may enable them to receive career counseling or training. Opportunities to learn other aspects of the advertising business, such as production, media buying, or account services, may be offered them.

Salaries

According to a 1994 salary survey done by *Adweek*, assistants of all kinds in advertising agencies averaged $33,600. Employees in creative departments earned more than those in account services or media, averaging $85,900. Women assistants averaged $32,700, while men averaged $41,100 in junior or assistant positions.

A 1992 survey of recent journalism school graduates, however, reported an average starting salary of $20,000 for those working in advertising agencies or departments.

Job-jumpers fared better with raises in 1994. Most *Adweek* survey respondents reported raises in the 5 to 10 percent range; raises of 20 percent or more were primarily reported by those who changed jobs.

Employment Prospects

Employment slowed and competition for jobs in advertising grew in the late 1980's and early 1990's as agencies consolidated. But government projections show employment in advertising growing at a fast rate during the next 10 years. Growth will be spurred by increased competition between businesses, which will then need to promote their products and services more vigorously.

Advancement Prospects

Once hired, advancement opportunities in the creative department can be good for those with talent and initiative. New and fresh ideas are always encouraged, and successful ideas are well rewarded in salary, bonuses, and other peaks.

Education

An undergraduate degree in advertising, liberal arts, communications, or art is the minimum requirement. Education should include courses in writing and creative writing. Advanced degrees are not all that helpful for the creative side of the advertising business.

Experience/Skills

Any kind of writing experience, especially advertising-related, is advantageous for copywriting jobs. Aspiring copywriters should work on school publications, community projects, or for agencies or the media part-time. Some journalists make the transition to advertising copywriting.

Copywriters should excel in command of English and have a flair for persuasion. They should be able to write for different media.

Unions/Associations

Associations open to advertising professionals include the American Advertising Federation; Direct Marketing Creative Guild; American Marketing Association; Business/Professional Advertising Association; and Women In Communication, Inc. The Writers Guild of America, a union, includes many copywriters who also write scripts and screenplays for television and film.

COPYWRITER

CAREER PROFILE

Duties: Develop ideas and write ad copy and scripts for media, sales campaigns and direct marketing

Alternate Title(s): None

Salary Range: $25,000 to $70,000+

Employment Prospects: Fair

Advancement Prospects: Fair

Prerequisites:

Education—Undergraduate degree in communications, liberal arts, art, advertising, or business

Experience—Background as a professional writer or journalist helpful

Special Skills—Creativity, imagination, salesmanship, command of English

CAREER LADDER

```
┌─────────────────────────────────┐
│                                 │
│         Copy Supervisor         │
│                                 │
└─────────────────────────────────┘

┌─────────────────────────────────┐
│                                 │
│           Copywriter            │
│                                 │
└─────────────────────────────────┘

┌─────────────────────────────────┐
│                                 │
│  Assistant Copywriter; Journalist; │
│             College             │
│                                 │
└─────────────────────────────────┘
```

Position Description

Copywriters write the text of print ads for radio and television ads, as well as text for promotional material, sales campaigns, and direct marketing campaigns.

Many copywriters work for advertising agencies, while others work for the in-house advertising departments or marketing departments of companies and corporations. Their jobs are highly demanding, because the success of the advertising depends greatly on the creativity and sales stimulus of the copy. Working hours generally are regular weekday hours, but overtime is often required to meet deadline pressures.

In a large agency or department, copywriters report to a senior copywriter or copy supervisor, who in turn reports to a creative director or advertising director. In a smaller environment, copywriters may report directly to the creative or advertising director.

The creation of an advertising campaign is a team effort. The creative staff works with the account service or marketing staff to execute an overall strategy or theme that will accomplish the client's goals. Any combination of media may be used: print, broadcast, point-of-sale, direct mail, billboards, transit, or specialty (giveaway premiums imprinted with the client's name).

In a small agency or department, one copywriter may do all the media copy for a particular client; in a large agency, the client's work may be divided among several copywriters who each specialize in one or two media, such as billboards or broadcast. Copy and scripts must convey information and persuade others to buy products or services, or accept ideas. Radio and television scripts must also include instructions for voice-overs and special effects.

In addition, copywriters may research information for ads, edit and rewrite copy, and be responsible for production and distribution of ad materials.

Salaries

Employees in creative departments of advertising agencies can expect to make slightly more than those in other departments. While senior employees overall make an average of $48,100, creative department employees average $85,900.

A big salary jump takes place between those under 30 and those over 30. Creative department employees under 30 average $39,100; those over 30 average $77,100. Women, however, average about $35,000 less than male employees of creative departments.

Salaries in the early 1990's were frozen or supplemented by small raises. Those who received larger raises of 20 percent or more generally had changed jobs.

Employment Prospects

Employment in advertising in the late 1980's and early 1990's became very competitive as agencies consolidated.

The job outlook for the next 10 years seems brighter, however. Government projections predict fast growth in advertising as businesses compete vigorously to promote their products and services.

Advancement Prospects

Advertising is a highly competitive field, but those with initiative, fresh ideas, and talent advance rapidly and are well rewarded. Good copywriters are given increasing supervisory responsibility and more prestigious accounts. Advertising is characterized by high turnover, and advancement often comes by moving to another agency or company.

Education

The minimum requirement is an undergraduate degree in communications, liberal arts, art, business, or advertising. Advanced degrees are of less value for copywriting than for account service. Education should include courses in copywriting or creative writing.

Experience/Skills

Education should be supplemented with writing experience, such as working on school or community publications. Part-time advertising jobs or advertising-related extracurricular work is helpful. Previous experience in journalism also is useful for copywriting.

The copywriter must have an excellent command of language and be able to visualize ad ideas. One should have a good knowledge of production, including typography and layout. Above all, he or she should be inventive and willing to experiment with unusual approaches or ideas.

Unions/Associations

The American Advertising Federation, Direct Marketing Creative Guild, and American Marketing Association are principal associations of interest to copywriters. Many women in the field belong to Women In Communications, Inc. Some copywriters are members of the Writers Guild of America, a union for television, film, and radio scriptwriters and screenwriters.

FEDERAL GOVERNMENT

EDITORIAL ASSISTANT AND CLERK

CAREER PROFILE

Duties: Edit and handle production of manuscripts; secretarial tasks

Alternate Title(s): None

Salary Range: $17,000 to $28,000

Employment Prospects: Fair

Advancement Prospects: Good

Prerequisites:

Education—High school diploma minimum

Experience—General office, clerical, or editorial support work required

Special Skills—Knowledge of grammar, editorial production; clerical skills

CAREER LADDER

```
┌─────────────────────────────────────┐
│  Supervisory Editorial Assistant or  │
│               Clerk                  │
└─────────────────────────────────────┘

┌─────────────────────────────────────┐
│      Editorial Assistant or Clerk    │
└─────────────────────────────────────┘

┌─────────────────────────────────────┐
│         High School or College       │
└─────────────────────────────────────┘
```

Position Description

Editorial clerks and assistants perform a wide range of clerical and editorial support work, in preparing manuscripts for publication and in verifying information in copy. Basic duties include proofreading final copy, galleys, and page proofs against the original manuscripts; specifying formats, type, and styles; editing for basic grammatical accuracy and structural clarity; and verifying references, footnotes, and tabular material.

Specific duties vary according to federal agency and grade level. Some editorial clerks and assistants work in groups under the direction of a supervisory editorial clerk or assistant. Others work directly for writers, editors, or subject matter specialists. Regardless of the work setting, editorial clerks and assistants usually all perform the same types of work. Most of their editing jobs concern accuracy and grammar, though they may suggest to editors changes to reorganize material.

They prepare the layout, including placement of graphics, and give typesetting and printing instructions.

High-level clerks and assistants may perform more writing, as well as substantive editing tasks similar to those expected of writers and editors.

Special knowledge of subject matter isn't necessary, except for certain specialized and technical subjects. Editorial clerks and assistants should be thoroughly familiar with grammatical rules and production procedures.

Employees frequently work under rigid deadlines, high pressure, and last-minute rushes. Accuracy is all-important. The editorial assistant/clerk also must have the ability to handle a high volume of work independently, follow detailed instructions, and interpret policies and regulations.

Salaries

Editorial assistant and clerk positions are among the few in the federal government in which women tend to earn more than men. Overall, salaries can range from $17,000 to $28,000. Most positions fall within the G54 to G57 range, around $20,000.

Employment Prospects

Federal jobs are highly competitive. Growth in new positions has been slow and is expected to remain so due to budget cutbacks. Nearly 80 percent of all federal employees work outside of Washington, D.C., throughout the United States.

Advancement Prospects

Advancement by grade level brings additional responsibilities and pay. Editorial clerks and assistants may also move up to writer or editor positions, or other posts in communications.

Education

A high school diploma is the minimum education requirement for editorial assistant and clerk positions.

Experience/Skills

Two to five years of clerical or editorial support experience is considered minimal. College education may be substituted for experience in order to qualify. Experience includes responsibilities for grammatical editing, reviewing, and screening; fact-checking; research; proofreading; and editorial production.

Because of the detail of their work, editorial assistants and clerks must be meticulous, dependable, and accurate to a very high degree. The work also requires an unusual degree of patience and a liking for close and exacting work.

Unions/Associations

Major unions and associations that represent federal white collar employees are the National Association of Government Employees; American Federation of Government Employees; National Federation of Federal Employees; National Association of Government Communicators; American Federation of State, County and Municipal Employees; and Federally Employed Women, Inc. Editorial assistants and clerks may also belong to related professional associations outside of government.

WRITER AND EDITOR

CAREER PROFILE

Duties: Write and edit articles, news releases, publications, and scripts

Alternate Title(s):   None

Salary Range: $19,000 to $65,000

Employment Prospects: Fair

Advancement Prospects: Good

Prerequisites:

Education—High school diploma minimum; college degree preferred

Experience—Two to six years' writing or editing experience for most positions

Special Skills—Good writing, editing skills; originality; initiative

CAREER LADDER

```
┌─────────────────────────────────────┐
│                                     │
│   Supervisory Writer or Editor      │
│                                     │
└─────────────────────────────────────┘

┌─────────────────────────────────────┐
│                                     │
│         Writer or Editor            │
│                                     │
└─────────────────────────────────────┘

┌─────────────────────────────────────┐
│  Editorial Assistant or Clerk; High │
│         School or College           │
│                                     │
└─────────────────────────────────────┘
```

Position Description

Writers and editors communicate information for several purposes: to report research and investigations carried on by federal agencies; to explain laws and regulations, as well as changes in them; and to make public reports on the activities and plans of agencies. The forms of communication include articles, press releases, pamphlets, brochures, speeches, and radio, television, and film scripts.

Some writing and editing positions do not require substantial subject-matter knowledge; all positions, however, require the ability to adapt information to a particular style, format, or audience. Most positions do not involve formulating the policy or philosophy behind the content of the information.

Writers collect information through library research, reading, and interviewing subject specialists, policy officials, and others. They turn their manuscripts over to editors, who review, rewrite, and edit as necessary and in consultation with writers. Editors may supervise editorial assistants and clerks to do routine checking and editing.

Most positions are either wholly writing or editing, but some combine the two functions. Those employees are called writer-editors. Writers and editors may specialize according to media, working predominantly in print, radio, film, or television.

The overall scope of a writer or editor's responsibilities depends on the grade level of the job. At lower grade levels, assignments are specific, and detailed instructions cover scope and content. There is limited opportunity for creativity. At higher levels, the writer or editor has greater opportunity to influence the scope of the assignment.

Salaries

Salaries for federally employed writers and editors depend on the job grade and years of experience. Most fall between the pay scales GS5 and GS12 or GS13, with pay ranging from $19,000 at entry level to $65,000 at the top. The highest-paying positions may require ten or more years of experience. The average salary for writers and editars in the federal government in 1992 was $39,077.

Employment Prospects

The chances of getting a federal writing or editing job are only fair, due to budget cutbacks and lack of growth.

Advancement Prospects

Writers and editors have a good chance of advancing to more responsible grade classification positions or to supervisory jobs. Other communications jobs exist outside of writing and editing.

Education

The minimum requirement is a high school diploma. Undergraduate degrees in English, journalism, or communications may be preferred for many higher level posts. College study may be substituted for job experience in meeting minimum hiring qualifications.

Experience/Skills

Persons without college degrees must be experienced in professional, administrative, technical, or other work that requires the ability to analyze information and present it in written form. Specialized experience in writing or editing jobs in a particular medium may also be required.

Basic skills include researching, analyzing, and organizing information; good writing and knowledge of grammar; editing ability; self-motivation; and the ability to work independently and, at times, under deadline pressure.

Unions/Associations

The National Association of Government Employees; National Association of Government Communicators; American Federation of Government Employees; National Federation of Federal Employees; American Federation of State, County and Municipal Employees; and Federally Employed Women, Inc., are the major unions and associations for federal white collar workers. Employees may also belong to related professional organizations outside of federal government.

TECHNICAL WRITER AND EDITOR

CAREER PROFILE

Duties: Write and edit technical manuals, specifications, and publications for federal agencies

Alternate Title(s): Technical Publications Writer or Editor; Technical Manuals Writer or Editor; Specifications Writer or Editor

Salary Range: $19,000 to $65,000

Employment Prospects: Poor

Advancement Prospects: Fair

Prerequisites:
   Education—Undergraduate college degree preferred

   Experience—Two to six years' writing or degree with courses in science, engineering, or computer science

   Special Skills—Understanding of and ability to explain technical subjects; writing and editing skills; self-motivation

CAREER LADDER

```
┌─────────────────────────────────┐
│  Supervisory Technical Writer or │
│             Editor               │
└─────────────────────────────────┘

┌─────────────────────────────────┐
│    Technical Writer or Editor    │
└─────────────────────────────────┘

┌─────────────────────────────────┐
│  College; Other Technical Writing or │
│          Editing Job             │
└─────────────────────────────────┘
```

Position Description

There are three general categories of technical writers and editors in the federal government: publications, specifications, and manuals.

Technical publications writers and editors are involved in government activities that carry on programs of research, investigations, or operation in natural and social sciences, engineering, medicine, law, and the like. They are responsible for disseminating findings and information to the general public as well as to scientific and administrative communities. Their work involves preparation of papers, articles, reports, summaries, and digests based on interviews, research reports, and their own reading.

Many agencies combine technical writing and editing assignments. Some editors may be assigned to groups or committees, and be responsible for assembling individual reports into a single document reflecting the total viewpoint of the group.

Both technical manual and specifications positions are found in federal activities that carry on programs of applied scientific research and development of weapons, communications systems, equipment, and devices. Job duties include writing, editing, and disseminating basic instruction materials, maintenance and operation instructions, design information, and training guides. Equipment specifications are used for purchasing and inventory control.

Most technical writing and editing jobs require substantial knowledge of a particular subject or field. Those technical writers and editors who have educations or specializations in journalism or English usually have had additional training or education in technical subjects.

About three-fourths of the technical writers and editors work for the Department of Defense, writing manuals on weapons and instruments for military personnel. The departments of Agriculture, Interior, and Health and Human Services, as well as the National Aeronautics and Space Administration, also employ many technical writers and editors.

Salaries

Beginning technical writers with undergraduate degrees, including 15 semester hours in science, engineering, or computer science, earn about $19,000; those with superior academic records or a year of experience may start at a higher salary.

In 1992, the average salary for a technical writer or editor in the federal government was $40,669.

Employment Prospects

Few federal job openings are expected through the 1990s. Most vacancies will occur due to retirements or transfers to other jobs.

Advancement Prospects

Chances of advancement are limited, due to the small number of openings that occur every year. Rising in job grade classification levels brings increasing responsibilities and salaries. Other advancement may be possible by moving to related communications jobs.

Education

Job candidates should have undergraduate degrees, preferably in a science. Those with nonscience degrees should have had studies in science, engineering, or computer science. In this field, a graduate degree in a science is likely to be very advantageous.

Experience/Skills

Job experience is not necessary for some entry-level positions; a year or more of experience can qualify a candidate for a higher level job with more pay.

Technical writers and editors must be able to understand complex subjects and be able to write clearly about them. They are often required to write for different audiences, explaining the same topic to a sophisticated professional group and to the general public, for example. Their job requires accuracy and an orientation to detail. Editing, production, and supervisory skills may be necessary for many positions.

Unions/Associations

Major unions and associations include the American Federation of Government Employees; National Association of Government Communicators; National Association of Government Employees; American Federation of State, County and Municipal Employees; National Federation of Federal Employees; and Federally Employed Women, Inc. Technical writers and editors may also belong to the Society for Technical Communications, as well as to related writing or scientific professional associations.

PRESS SECRETARY

CAREER PROFILE

Duties: Respond to press inquiries; write press releases; ghostwrite speeches, newspaper columns, letters to constituents and other materials for legislators; arrange press conferences; write and produce material for radio shows and release to radio reporters; stay abreast of news developments and try to anticipate their impact

Alternate Title(s): Public Affairs Specialist

Salary Range: $20,000 to $90,000+

Employment Prospects: Fair

Advancement Prospects: Fair

Prerequisites:
Education—Bachelor's degree

Experience—Several years working in news (print, radio, or television); familiarity with media in legislator or political figure's home state, if working for an individual

Special Skills—Ability to imitate employer's writing style; ability to anticipate what issues or news events will prompt questions from the media; good organizational skills

CAREER LADDER

```
┌─────────────────────────────────────┐
│   Private industry; Press Secretary at │
│          Federal Agency             │
└─────────────────────────────────────┘

┌─────────────────────────────────────┐
│          Press Secretary            │
└─────────────────────────────────────┘

┌─────────────────────────────────────┐
│           Journalist                │
└─────────────────────────────────────┘
```

Position Description

Press secretaries perform a wide range of duties, depending on how much emphasis their employers place on media visibility and whether they work for a legislative committee or political figure.

Some politicians do not like to write, and rely heavily on their press secretaries to compose speeches, letters, newspaper columns, and other written material in addition to press releases. While press releases are generally straightforward and written like news, other materials may require the press secretary to know how his or her boss thinks and speaks to be able to ghostwrite in that style.

A press secretary must also monitor the news — television shows, newspapers, wire services, and magazines — and anticipate what impact events may have upon the policies and public stances of his or her employer. Responses to anticipated questions from the media need to be assembled and information gathered.

Some press secretaries may also act as chiefs of staff or administrative assistants, making personnel decisions or influencing a politician's legislative agenda.

While most press secretaries confine their work to Washington, almost all of them visit the legislator's home district from time to time. It is important for press secretaries to meet with the reporters back home who will be reading the releases and calling with questions.

Press secretaries also sometimes produce short radio programs, during which they ask the congressman five or six questions, in the House recording studio. Tapes and scripts are then sent out to radio stations.

Part of the job also involves getting publicity for the legislator's pet projects and bills he or she may be sponsoring.

Workdays can be long. During times of heavy political activity, or if a particular issue of concern to the employer comes to the fore, 12-hour days are not uncommon. As in the news business, events often dictate the workload. Press secretaries for high-profile figures may also have heavier workloads.

Salaries

Salaries vary widely according to the priorities of each legislator. Each congressman and senator receives a budget for his or her office staff to spend as he or she sees fit.

A high-profile politician may hire a press secretary with impressive credentials for a higher salary, and cut back on staff in some other area. Some highly paid press secretaries also double as the administrative assistant, who oversees the office staff and is in charge of hiring and firing. Legislative committees and sub-committees employ press secretaries and have more money at their disposal to hire staff.

Public affairs positions within government agencies range from about $17,000 to $65,000. The average press secretary in the House makes about $38,200. The average salary for a press secretary to a senator is $54,000.

Employment Prospects

Prospects are best in Washington, D.C., where there might be a dozen press secretary openings at any given time. Jobs turn over regularly, either due to the defeat of incumbents at the polls or because seasoned press secretaries leave for less pressured jobs.

However, competition is stiff, and many legislators prefer to hire people with a familiarity with the media in their home state rather than those versed in the mores of Washington power politics.

Related positions, public affairs jobs in federal agencies, account for the highest number of communications-related jobs in the federal government, and many press secretaries cross over into these jobs.

Advancement Prospects

The wide range of public affairs-related jobs within the federal government makes for good advancement prospects. Press secretaries can become chiefs of staff or administrative assistants, take jobs with higher-profile legislators or ones they get along with better, work for legislative committees or federal agencies.

Most press secretaries work in the legislature for a few years and then move on to less-pressured, more stable jobs, either with government agencies or in the private sector.

Education

Most press secretaries have undergraduate degrees in communications, journalism, English, or liberal arts.

Experience/Skills

A background in one of the news media or public relations is generally required, although there is no one unifying characteristic among press secretaries. A familiarity with news organizations in a legislator's home state is very helpful.

Creativity, intelligence, the ability to analyze information and to communicate clearly are also key attributes of successful press secretaries.

Unions/Associations

Each political party has its own professional organization for public affairs specialists and press secretaries in Washington, D.C., such as the Republican Communicators Association. In addition, press secretaries may also belong to the Public Relations Society of America, Inc., or Women In Communications, Inc.

Some also belong to the National Association of Government Communicators; the National Association of Government Employees; American Federation of Government Employees; National Federation of Federal Employees; American Federation of State, County and Municipal Employees and Federally Employed Women, Inc. Many find it advantageous to belong to the National Press Club.

POLITICAL SPEECHWRITER

CAREER PROFILE

Duties: Research, draft, and edit speeches for political figures or bodies

Alternate Title(s):   Special Assistant for Communications

Salary Range: $20,000 to $100,000

Employment Prospects: Fair

Advancement Prospects: Fair

Prerequisites:

Education—Bachelor's degree in liberal arts, communications, or journalism; some jobs may require a law degree or other advanced degree

Experience—Experience varies; can include backgrounds in law, journalism, public relations, legislative research, political campaigning, public policy

Special Skills—Must be able to know where to find information; must understand the substance of the speech and whom it is targeting; must be able to work under pressure and imitate style of person who will be delivering the speech

CAREER LADDER

```
┌─────────────────────────────────┐
│   Director of Communications    │
└─────────────────────────────────┘

┌─────────────────────────────────┐
│         Speechwriter            │
└─────────────────────────────────┘

┌─────────────────────────────────┐
│  Public Information Officer; Press │
│  Secretary; Legislative Director │
└─────────────────────────────────┘
```

Position Description

Political speechwriters are generally people interested in politics who have had some other contact with political life. Often they are hired for their expertise in a specific area and frequently write speeches on related topics. In some offices, speechwriters divide up the workload according to topic; sometimes the division can be as broad as foreign and domestic policy.

In smaller offices, speechwriting duties may be handled by a press secretary or legislative director. The work is often high-pressure with little advance warning. Speeches often have to be prepared in response to news events, and information has to be gathered quickly.

Speeches also have to be prepared for a wide range of audiences. The speechwriter needs to know if questions from the media and the audience will be allowed, how long the speech should be, the topic, and general content.

Speechwriters may also be moved between staff jobs and campaign jobs. A staff speechwriter cannot work on his boss's campaign; a campaign speechwriter must be paid from campaign funds.

Salaries

Because speechwriting is such a visible job, experienced and talented speechwriters can earn $100,000 or more. Those hired with little experience to work for a low-profile legislator or committee may only make $20,000; others may find speechwriting just one of a number of public relations duties within an office.

Employment Prospects

Demand for speechwriters is growing as more professional speechwriting is being used both by politicians and private businesses. Within the federal government, political offices, committees, and federal agencies hire speechwriters.

Advancement Prospects

Just as people come to speechwriting from all kinds of backgrounds, they move into all different types of careers from speechwriting. Some move into private-sector speechwriting, drafting speeches for company executives. Others become newspaper columnists, bookwriters or political consultants.

Speechwriters may move from less-visible offices to those of higher-profile political figures or agencies. They may become press secretaries or legislative directors.

Education

An undergraduate degree in communications, journalism, English, or liberal arts is essential. An advanced degree in political science, government, public policy, law, or journalism is a plus.

Experience/Skills

A wide variety of backgrounds can be found among speechwriters. Public policy, campaigning, legislative research, journalism, or public relations are generally good preparation for this field.

Speechwriters should have an ear for the spoken word and an ability to mimic the style of the person who will deliver the speech. Strong research skills, an ability to work under pressure, and a tolerance for revisions are also important attributes.

Unions/Associations

Major professional associations include the Public Relations Society of America, Inc. and Women in Communications, Inc. Some speechwriters may also belong to unions for federal employees.

SCHOLASTIC, ACADEMIC, AND NONPROFIT INSTITUTIONS

JOURNALISM TEACHER

CAREER PROFILE

Duties: Teach secondary-school classes in journalism, creative writing, and English; advise student publications

Alternate Title(s): None

Salary Range: $15,000 to $40,000+

Employment Prospects: Fair

Advancement Prospects: Fair

Prerequisites:

    Education—Undergraduate degree in communications, journalism, education, liberal arts; graduate degree preferred

    Experience—None to several years

    Special Skills—Ability to help and motivate others; organization; speaking skills; ability to handle problems

CAREER LADDER

```
┌─────────────────────────┐
│                         │
│      Administrator       │
│                         │
└─────────────────────────┘

┌─────────────────────────┐
│                         │
│        Teacher           │
│                         │
└─────────────────────────┘

┌─────────────────────────┐
│                         │
│        College           │
│                         │
└─────────────────────────┘
```

Position Description

A journalism teacher in a junior or senior high school usually has a wide range of responsibilities. Only one or two classes may be devoted to teaching news gathering, writing, and editing, or work on student publications. The teacher may also conduct classes in English and creative writing, plus supervise study hall, homeroom, or lunch periods.

Journalism teachers are responsible for all or most student publications, such as newspapers, creative writing magazines, and yearbooks. They advise the student staffs on content and layout, and give final approval to the finished product before it is published.

Disciplinary problems must be handled with sensitivity and tact. Classroom presentations must be designed to meet the individual needs and abilities of students. Instructional materials can include films, slides, and computer terminals, as well as books. Teachers may bring in journalism and editorial professionals as guest speakers, as well as arrange field trips to visit local newspapers, magazines, or printing companies.

In addition to developing and teaching regular classes, teachers supervise extracurricular activities,

meet after hours with students and parents, and are expected to participate regularly in classes and workshops, to stay current in their field. Most teachers work more than 40 hours a week, but have at least two months off during summer break.

Salaries

Public secondary school teachers averaged about $36,000 a year in 1992–1993. Beginners often earn less; graduate degrees bring higher pay. Earnings in private schools are generally lower.

Employment Prospects

Overall job prospects at the secondary school level are expected to increase through the next decade due to the corresponding growth in the population of 14- to 17-year-olds.

Advancement Prospects

Experienced teachers with additional preparation may move into positions as school librarians, reading specialists, curriculum specialists, or guidance counselors. Teachers may also move into administrative or supervisory jobs. In some schools, experienced teachers may become senior or mentor teachers, helping less experienced teachers while continuing to teach.

Advancement opportunities may be improved as the high school age population grows; however, pressure from taxpayers to limit spending on education could reduce advancement opportunities.

Education

An undergraduate degree, preferably in English, liberal arts, communications, or journalism, is the minimum educational requirement. Approximately half the states in the nation require graduate degrees. In addition, teachers must be certified by state boards of education.

Experience/Skills

Beginning teachers start right after graduation from college. Previous work as a journalist or editor is helpful for specializing as a journalism teacher. Teachers should be comfortable speaking to groups, able to organize class content, materials, and tests, and interested in helping and instructing others.

Unions/Associations

The National Education Association and American Federation of Teachers are the major professional and wage-bargaining unions for secondary-school teachers. The AFT is affiliated with the AFL-CIO. Teachers may also subscribe to the AFL-CIO's Academic Corrective Bargaining Information Service.

ASSISTANT PROFESSOR

CAREER PROFILE

Duties: Teach college-level classes in all or various aspects of communications

Alternate Title(s):   None

Salary Range: $27,000 to $40,000+

Employment Prospects: Good

Advancement Prospects: Fair

Prerequisites:
  Education—Ph.D. usually required

  Experience—Four to five years working in the field

  Special Skills—Skill in instructing and helping others; speaking ability; organization

CAREER LADDER

```
┌─────────────────────────────┐
│                             │
│     Associate Professor     │
│                             │
└─────────────────────────────┘

┌─────────────────────────────┐
│                             │
│     Assistant Professor     │
│                             │
└─────────────────────────────┘

┌─────────────────────────────┐
│                             │
│         Instructor          │
│                             │
└─────────────────────────────┘
```

Position Description

Assistant professor is an entry-level untenured teaching position in colleges and universities. Candidates have worked several years as journalists or advertising or public-relations professionals, and have earned graduate degrees, usually Ph.D.s.

Assistant professors teach undergraduate courses, many of them large lecture classes of several hundred students. They may specialize in certain areas of communications, such as print or broadcast journalism, advertising, or public relations. Their courses may include introductions to mass communications and mass-communications law and theory, as well as practical instruction in news or copy writing, editing, composition, and layout. They may coordinate course materials and lectures with other faculty members. Teaching loads average 9 to 12 hours a week. Besides lecturing, assistant professors make reading and writing assignments, and develop and grade exams.

Assistant professors, as well as their colleagues, are expected to stay abreast of developments in the field and to write and publish articles or books. They may also supervise or help supervise intern programs and have advisory roles on student publications.

Assistant professors should enjoy instructing and helping others in their career preparation. Their schedules are flexible and change from one quarter or semester to another. Their days can be long, from morning classes to night ones. In addition, they maintain office hours for consultations with students.

Salaries

In 1992–1993, assistant professors on nine-month contracts averaged $36,800. Faculty in four-year institutions earn higher salaries in general than at two-year institutions.

Employment Prospects

Employment of college and university faculty is expected to increase through the next decade due to increased college enrollments and faculty retirements.

Advancement Prospects

Assistant professorship is an untenured position. Tenure-continued employment and freedom from dismissal without cause may be granted after several years of employment and a review of an assistant professor's teaching and research record. During the probationary period, usually seven years, assistant professors work under term contracts. Failure to receive tenure generally means they must leave the institution.

Tenure is required to become an associate and full professor.

Education

Assistant professors must have earned graduate degrees, preferably in communications, English, or liberal arts. Doctorates are usually preferred for most positions.

Experience/Skills

In addition to advanced degrees, assistant professors must have had four to five years working in the field as journalists, editors, or advertising or public-relations professionals. Knowledge of video display technology is essential.

Skills include the abilities to organize course direction and materials, to instruct and help others, and to speak to large audiences.

Unions/Associations

Associations and unions include the American Association of University Professors and National Education Association.

ALUMNI COMMUNICATIONS SPECIALIST

CAREER PROFILE

Duties: Prepare fliers, newsletters, letters, invitations and other materials for distribution to alumni

Alternative Title(s): Donor Relations Specialist; Gift Recognition Specialist; Information Officer

Salary Range: $20,000 to $35,000

Employment Prospects: Good

Advancement Prospects: Good

Prerequisites:

   Education—Undergraduate degree in communications, liberal arts, journalism

   Experience—Knowledge of word processing, desktop publishing, and professional writing experience all helpful

   Special Skills—Ability to write and edit well very important

CAREER LADDER

```
┌─────────────────────────────────┐
│     Alumni Office Director       │
└─────────────────────────────────┘

┌─────────────────────────────────┐
│ Alumni Communications Specialist │
└─────────────────────────────────┘

┌─────────────────────────────────┐
│            College               │
└─────────────────────────────────┘
```

Position Description

Alumni communications require many of the same skills needed for public relations work. A person in this job must promote the university and its activities to alumni and also solicit donations to support university programs.

Jobs in alumni communications take on a variety of forms. Some involve helping local alumni clubs plan events and contacting members with newsletters, fliers, and invitations. Others in alumni communications write thank-you letters to alumni who have made gifts to the university or write letters soliciting donations.

The alumni office also promotes educational programs for alumni, generally cruises or other trips that feature one of the university's professors. A person in this job would not be involved with continuing education, which is generally a separate department, but rather serve as a liaison between the faculty and alumni.

The alumni office may also plan speaking engagements and graduation activities. It attempts to make contact with recent graduates and to track the whereabouts of all graduates.

Salaries

A beginner with no experience can expect a salary close to, or perhaps even below, $20,000. Salaries range up to about $35,000.

Employment Prospects

Because turnover in alumni offices can be high, the prospect of getting a job is good. In addition, because alumni donations provide significant revenue to the university, this job might be less susceptible to cutbacks in a bad economy.

Advancement Prospects

A communications specialist who performs well can expect good chances at advancement within the alumni office, although many staffs are small. A person in this field may also be able to move into public relations, performing similar functions at a public relations agency or working in private industry.

Education

A bachelor's degree is essential to this job. In addition, if the school has a specialized program, a degree in that subject might be required. A person working in the alumni office of a particular school does not necessarily need to be an alumni of that school. A degree from a comparable school should be sufficient. A journalism degree, with a specialization in public relations, might also be appropriate.

Experience/Skills

No experience is necessary for an entry-level job. For a more advanced position, knowledge of desktop publishing and word processing systems may be needed. A person in an alumni office should also be creative and outgoing, and be able to write well.

Unions/Associations

Alumni Communications Specialists can receive career development information from the Council for the Advancement and Support of Education.

In addition, many of them belong to the same groups that serve other public relations professionals, including the Public Relations Society of America, Inc. and Women in Communications, Inc.

ALUMNI MAGAZINE EDITOR

CAREER PROFILE

Duties: Supervise magazine preparation; manage staff; rewrite and edit

Alternate Title(s): Alumni Magazine Editor-in-Chief; Editorial Director

Salary Range: $35,000 to $80,000+

Employment Prospects: Fair

Advancement Prospects: Poor

Prerequisites:

Education—Undergraduate degree in liberal arts, journalism, or communications (does not have to be from institution issuing the magazine)

Experience—Background as an editor, journalist, or writer essential

Special Skills—Ability to identify different readership groups and be sensitive to their concerns; tactful handling of controversial subjects without compromising the magazine's editorial integrity

CAREER LADDER

```
┌─────────────────────────────┐
│                             │
│          Editor             │
│                             │
└─────────────────────────────┘

┌─────────────────────────────┐
│                             │
│       Managing Editor       │
│                             │
└─────────────────────────────┘

┌─────────────────────────────┐
│                             │
│       Associate Editor      │
│                             │
└─────────────────────────────┘
```

Position Description

The editor has complete responsibility for the editorial content and production of the magazine. He or she assigns stories, oversees the budget, and may perform day-to-day editing and production tasks.

At smaller alumni magazines, the editor may have other responsibilities as well, handling some public relations functions. However, the best magazines maintain an editorial integrity separate from public relations and do not see themselves as a promotional vehicle for the college but a forum for information.

Duties are similar to those for a mainstream magazine, but with the additional task of remaining sensitive to the concerns of alumni, faculty, administration, students, parents of students and other magazine readers. An alumni magazine might choose to do a story on a controversial professor but must be aware of the possible reaction of different groups to such a story. These points of view should be sensitively represented.

Editorial integrity must also be closely guarded so university groups know the magazine's policies and respect them. Those who question why the magazine might choose to do a story should have their point of view represented, but should not have the power to censor the magazine.

The magazine editor plans issues, assigns photographs and stories, and edits manuscripts. He or she also hires and fires employees, answers letters from readers, and oversees placement of articles within the magazine.

He or she also has to operate within the magazine's budget. The magazine may rely solely on advertising revenue, donations from alumni, or a combination of the two, plus a sum allocated by the university.

Salaries

Editors earn between $35,000 and $80,000, depending on the size of the magazine. Prestigious colleges with larger endowments may pay more.

Employment Prospects

Alumni magazines provide opportunities away from New York, where many business and consumer magazines are based. Employment prospects are fair, but the field is competitive. Some editors and writers who have worked in New York or other large cities are attracted to alumni magazines in order to live in college communities.

Advancement Prospects

Editor is the top position at many alumni magazines. Advancement can be made by going on to larger magazines, either mainstream publications or at larger colleges.

Education

A bachelor's degree in liberal arts, communications, or journalism is required. Most alumni magazines do not require the degree to come from the employing college. If the college is highly specialized, such as an engineering or scientific school, some graduate level education may be required.

Experience/Skills

The amount of experience required to be editor varies with the publication. Three to five years may be necessary for some jobs; ten years or more for others. Experience can include news reporting, reporting jobs at magazines, and other magazine experience.

Unions/Associations

Major professional associations that serve the magazine industry in general are the American Society of Journalists and Authors, Inc.; American Society of Magazine Editors; and Women In Communications, Inc. Other writer associations as well as trade and industry groups are open to magazine editors.

In addition, alumni magazine editors can receive career development information from the Council for the Advancement and Support of Education.

LIBRARIAN

CAREER PROFILE

Duties: Acquire, catalog, and maintain collections of books, records, and other sources of information

Alternate Title(s): Information Specialist; Information Scientist; Information Manager

Salary Range: $11,000 to $90,000+

Employment Prospects: Fair to good

Advancement Prospects: Fair

Prerequisites:
    Education—Graduate degree in library science

    Experience—None to several years for entry-level jobs

    Special Skills—Knowledge of book publishing and computer data bases; attention to detail; good organization

CAREER LADDER

```
┌─────────────────────────────┐
│      Senior Librarian       │
└─────────────────────────────┘

┌─────────────────────────────┐
│         Librarian           │
└─────────────────────────────┘

┌─────────────────────────────┐
│   Library Assistant/Clerk   │
└─────────────────────────────┘
```

Position Description

Librarians perform a vital role of information management. They acquire, catalog, maintain, and provide access to collections of information, either to the general public or to business, scientific, and technical professionals. In addition, they may develop media and educational programs.

Most librarians work either in schools, colleges, and universities, or in public or special libraries. A growing number work in business and industry, managing computerized data bases of highly specialized information.

Tasks are varied. Some librarians specialize in certain areas, such as acquisitions or media development, but most handle a wide range of responsibilities.

After materials are acquired, they must be cataloged, indexed, and shelved or filed. Much information is transferred to microfilm. Librarians must be able to handle many requests to locate specific information. They may assist teachers in developing educational programs, or compile bibliographies for researchers. They may prepare computer abstracts for scientists and engineers. Librarians also may develop community programs and speakers' forums on issues and topics of

interest. They often develop their own publicity materials.

Most librarians work a five-day week of 35 to 40 hours, including evenings and weekends for public and college libraries.

Salaries

The average beginning salary of full-time professional librarians was $26,666 in 1992, according to *Library Journal*. That was a 6.5 percent increase from 1991. Highest pay on average was in either school libraries, where many of a librarian's duties are similar to those of school teachers, or in special libraries.

Those in special libraries averaged $28,257; those working for public libraries averaged $24,652; those working in school libraries averaged $28,227; and those working in college libraries averaged $26,484.

The more specialized the job, the better the pay. Librarians working for the federal government average $44,500. Those in special libraries averaged $29,200 with one to two years of experience and $31,800 with three to five years of experience.

Employment Prospects

Specialties or concentrations that might increase opportunities for library school graduates include chemistry, engineering, sciences, math, foreign languages, music, cataloging, medicine, computer science, and information systems.

Of the placements of new library school graduates in special libraries, about half went to audio-visual and media centers or to youth services. Law, non-library information services, medicine, rare books, and business were the next most popular choices.

According to the federal government, employment of librarians is expected to lag behind other jobs in growth during the next 10 years. Opportunities are expected to be best in nontraditional settings, including information brokerages, private corporations, and consulting firms. Companies need librarians to do research and organize information. Familiarity with on-line computer databases and computer-assisted research could be especially valuable in the job market.

Many librarians working in non-traditional settings are known by other job titles such as systems analysts, data base specialists, managers, and researchers.

Job prospects may also be better for those willing to relocate. Due to the closing of several accredited library school programs, there are fewer graduates of library science. Large areas of the country have no accredited library school programs. According to a *Library Journal* survey of the placement of library school graduates, in 1992 three-quarters of the graduates took jobs in the same state where they attended school. This may result in a glut of librarians in some areas of the country, depressing salaries there, the magazine reported.

Advancement Prospects

Advancement to senior librarian, manager, and director depends heavily on the area of work. Business and technical fields offer the best opportunities for promotion.

Education

Education should include an undergraduate degree in liberal arts, English, social sciences, or business, plus at least a master's degree in library science (M.L.S.) The M.L.S. includes advanced courses in cataloging, indexing, computer automation, abstracting, and library administration. A Ph.D. is advantageous for teaching or academic administration. Specialized technical or research work requires additional education.

Experience/Skills

For entry-level positions, experience or internships as a library assistant are helpful. In some localities where jobs are few and applicants many, several years' experience is required for entry-level positions. Public librarians must be state-certified, and requirements vary widely in each state.

Skills include attention to detail; knowledge of publishing, current events, or specialized subjects; and ability to work with the public. Knowledge of computer data bases is becoming increasingly important in all types of librarian jobs.

Unions/Associations

The American Library Association, American Society for Information Science, and Special Libraries Association are major support groups serving the profession. Specialized associations and groups serve educational, technical, music, medical, and other library fields.

NEWS DIRECTOR

CAREER PROFILE

Duties: Distribute news about the college to newspapers, faculty, and staff members

Alternate Title(s): None

Salary Range: $20,000 to $80,000

Employment Prospects: Good

Advancement Prospects: Good

Prerequisites:
  Education—Undergraduate degree in liberal arts, communications, journalism

  Experience—None for entry-level jobs at smaller colleges; several years at larger schools

  Special Skills—Ability to identify different groups to which the school disseminates information and develop a specific approach to each

CAREER LADDER

```
┌─────────────────────────────────┐
│                                 │
│   Director of Public Relations  │
│                                 │
└─────────────────────────────────┘

┌─────────────────────────────────┐
│                                 │
│         News Director           │
│                                 │
└─────────────────────────────────┘

┌─────────────────────────────────┐
│                                 │
│  Assistant News Director; Reporter; │
│            College               │
│                                 │
└─────────────────────────────────┘
```

Position Description

College news directors distribute information about the college to the public through news releases. They also provide information about newsworthy campus events to the school's faculty, staff, and students.

To do this effectively, news directors need to identify what the college is all about and how it wants to be perceived. Messages to different groups can be adjusted to help promote the college.

News directors also need to be aware of how the different groups view them and their role. Who is in each group and what information they need helps determine the messages the news director sends.

Salaries

Salaries vary widely, depending upon the size of the institution and the amount of money allocated for the news office. Some schools prefer to put more money into admissions or fundraising. Others hire experienced professionals to serve as news directors and pay top dollar.

The range can be from $20,000 at an entry-level job requiring no experience to $80,000 at a prestigious school interested in promoting itself effectively.

Employment Prospects

The need for public relations professionals is expected to grow throughout the next decade.

Advancement Prospects

Advancement prospects are good. Advancement could be by moving up within the college to director of public relations or director of development or by moving to a larger college to take a similar job.

Education

An undergraduate degree in liberal arts, communications, or journalism is required.

Experience/Skills

Experience required varies with the job market and the institution. None may be required, or several years as a newspaper reporter or a public relations professional may be necessary. Additionally, a college news director must be sensitive to how the college wants to present itself to the public and the college community, and tailor the news accordingly for each group.

Unions/Associations

Many college news directors belong to the same groups other public relations professionals join: the Public Relations Society of America, Inc.; Women In Communications, Inc. They also may belong to the Council for the Advancement and Support of Education.

FREELANCE SERVICES
AND SELF-PUBLISHING

FREELANCE WRITER

Duties: Write nonfiction articles for magazines and businesses, or publicity, promotion, and ad copy

Alternate Title(s):   Writer

Income Potential: $12 to $100 per hour+; $200 to $2,000 per 2,000-word magazine article; $40 to $500 for a feature article for a daily newspaper; $15 to $25 per hour for small associations and up to $85 per hour for larger groups; $20 to $35 per hour for a brief annual report for a business; various flat fees for projects

Work Prospects: Excellent

Prerequisites:

   Education—No minimum education required; undergraduate degree in journalism, communications, or liberal arts preferred

   Experience—Background as a journalist helpful

   Special Skills—Good writing ability; persistence; self-motivation; salesmanship

---

Position Description

Freelance writing is a difficult way to make a living, but the rewards are great for those who succeed: the satisfaction of bylines and credits, ongoing relationships with editors, perhaps even retainers, and increasing income as one's reputation is established.

Most freelance writers begin their freelancing part-time while holding full- or part-time jobs. They send queries and manuscripts to magazines, or write brochures or slide show scripts for businesses. Eventually, business builds to a point where the writer is able to begin freelancing full-time.

General-interest magazines are a very tough market to crack, and many rejection slips may be collected before a sale is made. Freelancers who approach magazines with ideas for articles must first study a publication for its content, style, and slant. With the exception of a very few publications, most magazines do not pay well for the time a writer invests in researching, writing, and revising an article.

Trade and special-interest magazines that cover such topics as home computing, advertising, and business often are easier to break into than general-interest magazines, but they require that the writer have a background in the subject area.

Many freelancers rely heavily on business writing for regular income, which pays much better than most magazines. Business writing for corporations includes press and publicity material, trade stories, speeches, film scripts and slide shows, and internal newsletters and magazines. Some freelancers are able to work on retainers for businesses—a flat monthly fee in exchange for a specified amount of work, such as production of a newsletter. Many advertising and public-relations agencies also rely on freelancers.

Freelance writers must be highly self-disciplined to work on their own. Most put in long hours, and work tends to come unevenly, bringing frequent deadline pressures at the same time. Writers usually have many projects going concurrently in various stages of development—queries or proposals sent out for consideration, researching and interviewing for assignments, writing, and revising. It is essential to maintain a constant pursuit of assignments, because writers never know how long it will take to sell a particular idea. It could sell to the first magazine queried, or it could sell to the tenth after many months.

Many freelance writers find steady work contributing to textbooks, encyclopedias, and other reference books. This work usually is "work for hire," that is, the writer receives a flat fee from the publisher in exchange for all rights. No royalties are paid.

Writers must keep their own business records. They bill clients and keep track of tax deductible expenses.

Additionally, freelance writers may:

- write fiction stories or novels;
- write plays or screenplays;
- work as public-relations consultants;
- edit manuscripts.

Income Potential

A freelance writer's income depends on his or her geographic location and type of projects. Major cities, where more business, magazine, and publishing headquarters are located, offer more fruitful hunting grounds. Yet many freelance writers earn a fair amount of money by sending manuscripts through the mail to distant publications.

Many successful freelance writers earn $20,000 or more, and some who work mostly for businesses and industries earn $40,000 and up.

Pay for trade and general-interest magazine articles can range from $50 to $3,000; top-rated freelancers who work for prestigious publications can command more.

Many freelancers, especially those serving corporate clients, charge by the hour or by day; rates vary according to the job. Typical day rates range from $200 to $800, and hourly rates range from $10 to $100. In 1992, the median gross income of members of the Editorial Freelancers Association was $25,000. Two-thirds of members fell within the $10,001 and $40,000 range; a quarter earned under $10,000; one in seven earned between $40,001 and $100,000; and only five earned over $100,000. The association draws most of its members from the New York City area.

Work Prospects

Thousands of trade and general-interest periodicals and businesses rely on freelance writers, yet competition remains stiff, especially for the premium markets. The best bet for beginners is to look to small publications or businesses with which to build the experience and credentials sought by larger markets. It usually takes a freelance writer several years to become established and build a fairly steady income.

Education

Most freelance writers have undergraduate degrees in liberal arts, journalism, or communications. Specialized fields may require certain educational or work credentials. In general, however, a magazine editor looks for good ideas and good writing, not for degrees.

Experience/Skills

Many freelance writers start with no experience other than school writing courses. Others begin freelancing after spending several years as journalists, public-relations writers, or editors. To succeed against the competition, freelancers must be good writers and deliver on time. They must be persistent in selling themselves and should not be easily discouraged by rejections. Freelancers must have a strong entrepreneurial drive.

Unions/Associations

Major national associations include the Authors Guild; American Society of Journalists and Authors, Inc.; Associated Business Writers of America; National Writers Club, Inc.; Public Relations Society of America, Inc.; and Women In Communications, Inc. The Writers Guild of America is a union that represents scriptwriters for radio, television, and film; the National Writers Union represents writers and authors.

TECHNICAL WRITER

Duties: Interpret technical and scientific information for technical and nontechnical audiences; research and write a wide variety of material

Alternate Title(s): Publications Engineer; Staff Writer; Communications Specialist; Communicator; Industrial Writer; Instructional Materials Developer

Income Potential: $35 per manuscript page or $35 to $75 per hour, depending on the complexity of the topic and the type of audience

Work Prospects: Excellent

Prerequisites:

Education—Undergraduate degree in technical communications, science, engineering, computer science, journalism, liberal arts

Experience—Previous work as a technician, scientist, engineer, or writer is helpful

Special Skills—Understanding of complex technical subjects; logic; good writing and layout skills; curiosity

Position Description

Technical writing is a highly specialized field that combines technical, scientific, or engineering backgrounds with the ability to write. Technical writers use their specialized knowledge to translate complex information into readily understandable terms. Their audience may or may not have technical backgrounds.

Technical writing covers a wide variety of tasks. Technical writers prepare instruction manuals for equipment or computer software programs; catalogs and other materials used by industrial sales representatives; equipment specifications and instruction manuals for persons who assemble, operate, or repair machinery; or training aids. They write printed materials or scripts for films, film strips, or cassettes, and also write books.

Technical writers also prepare reports on scientific research; write papers and speeches for scientists and engineers; draft articles for technical publications; and write news releases, advertising copy, promotional brochures, and corporate annual reports. They also prepare exhibits for museums and trade shows.

Technical writers usually work closely with scientists and engineers. They research their subject by studying blueprints; diagrams; technical documents, studies, and journals; and the actual products. They become thoroughly familiar with their subject before writing about it.

Once they collect sufficient information, they prepare a draft for review by technical professionals—computer programmers, engineers, or scientists. A technical editor oversees changes and coordinates artwork and production.

Most technical writers do not begin work in the profession directly out of college. First they gain experience in their area of expertise, or as writers or research assistants. Those with writing ability gradually move into technical writing jobs, first by doing library research and drafts for established technical writers.

Technical writers are concentrated in the electronics, computer manufacturing and software development, aircraft, and chemical and pharmaceutical manufacturing industries. Many freelance for research laboratories and hospitals. Others work for the federal government, technical publications, pharmacological and health-related industries, academic institutions, advertising and public-relations agencies, and technical publishing firms.

Income Potential

Freelance technical writers typically are paid by the hour. Some charge day rates. Hour rates are generally about $35 to $75, depending on the writer's credentials, the project, and the employer. Businesses generally pay more than publishers.

Work Prospects

Freelance opportunities for technical writers are expected to be strong throughout the 1990s, particularly in the electronics, computer, pharmaceutical, and health-related industries, and in research and development. The Society of Technical Communicators reports that the number of freelancers and consultants has been increasing significantly since 1985. Most work opportunities are in major metropolitan areas.

Education

Most technical writers have undergraduate degrees in science, engineering, technical communications, journalism, or liberal arts. Some have advanced degrees. Most employers prefer thorough technical backgrounds.

Experience/Skills

Many employers look for freelance technical writers who have gained experience working in jobs related to their profession.

Technical writers should be curious, well-organized, and able to explain complicated information. They must be consistently accurate. Technical writers should have the patience and persistence to work long hours sifting through great quantities of details. They should be able to work well as part of a team and on their own.

Unions/Associations

The Society for Technical Communications represents technical writers, editors, scientists, engineers, educators, and others. Other major professional groups include the National Association of Science Writers, Inc., and American Medical Writers Association.

TECHNICAL EDITOR

CAREER PROFILE

Duties: Supervise preparation of technical information material; coordinate artwork; supervise production

Alternate Title(s): Technical Information Editor; Technical Communications Editor; Publications Editor; Instructional Materials Editor

Income Potential: $15 to $60/hour or more

Work Prospects: Excellent

Prerequisites:

Education—Undergraduate degree in science, computer science, technical communications, engineering, journalism, communications, or liberal arts

Experience—Several years' experience as technical writer

Special Skills—Ability to translate technical material into understandable terms; sense of layout and graphics; copy-editing skills; supervisory ability

Position Description

Technical editors are responsible for the content, accuracy, and production of a wide range of technical information materials. Many such editors freelance for technical and scientific journals and book publishers. Other technical editors work for businesses, industries, health professions, or the federal government, producing instruction manuals, sales and promotion literature, advertising copy, books, news releases, speeches, films, film scripts, and cassettes.

Freelance technical editors edit the work of technical writers. They may proofread galleys. Their work requires adherence to production schedules and deadlines.

Technical editors work closely with scientific and technical professionals, who review their material.

Technical editors must have thorough backgrounds in their specific areas. Many begin their careers as engineers, scientists, or other technical professionals before becoming technical writers and editors.

Income Potential

Freelance/technical editors generally are paid between $15 and $60 or more an hour, depending on their expertise and the assignment.

Work Prospects

The demand for technical editors is expected to be strong throughout the 1990s, especially in major metropolitan areas. Major growth areas include computer manufacturing and software development, health professions, electronics, and pharmaceutical manufacturing. Research and development organizations also should provide good opportunities.

Education

While there are no rigid requirements for technical writing and editing, most technical editors have at least an undergraduate degree in science, engineering, or computer science, or in English, liberal arts, or journalism. Many have undergraduate degrees in science or engineering, and graduate degrees in journalism or English. A degree in almost any field is often acceptable with a good technical background and writing skills.

Experience/Skills

A professional background as a technician, scientist, engineer, or programmer is helpful for technical writing and editing. Most editors have had several years' additional experience as technical writers.

Creativity and interest in problem-solving are important traits of technical editors. They must be able to supervise others and work as part of a team. They must always be conscious of deadlines, production schedules, and budgets. They should be good editors as well as writers, and be knowledgeable in graphics and layout.

Unions/Associations

The Society for Technical Communication is the professional association for this profession. The National Association of Science Writers, Inc., and American Medical Writers Association are two other organizations to which many technical editors belong.

COPY EDITOR

Duties: Edit manuscripts and copy for book and periodical publishers, trade and industry publications, and corporate communications and publications

Alternate Title(s): None

Income Potential: $10 to $40 per hour for books, magazines and newspapers; $12 to $50 per hour for editing book content; $25 to $500 per day for general magazine editing; business copyediting, $20 to $50 per manuscript page; copyediting for nonprofit organizations, $15 to $30 per hour; copyediting for advertising, $25 per hour

Employment Prospects: Good

Prerequisites:

Education—Undergraduate degree; graduate degree may be preferred for technical subjects

Experience—Background and previous employment in communications helpful

Special Skills—Grammar, spelling and style skills; knowledge of subject areas helpful or may be required

Position Description

Freelance copy editors edit a wide range of copy for grammar, style, spelling, punctuation, consistency and clarity. They work within the house style guidelines provided by the employer. They improve awkwardly written sentences, correct spelling, and flag suspected errors or inconsistencies in numbers, dates, context and content for double-checking by the author. Their work requires them to be familiar with numerous standard reference works, which they consult frequently when verifying facts.

Copy editors are hired to review book manuscripts (including appendices, indices, and bibliographies), periodical articles, newsletters, and copy for manuals, advertisements, press kits, in-house communications and more. They work primarily from manuscripts or typeset galleys or proofs and mark corrections directly on the pages. With the increase in electronic text preparation, some copy editors edit online or with a disk.

Income Potential

Freelance copyediting fees usually are based on an hourly rate. Freelancers set their own rates for various types of jobs, but generally are limited to going rates established by industry or employer. The average rate range in book publishing, magazines, journals and packaging ranges from about $10 to $40 per hour. Copy editors who work in advertising, public relations, and corporate communications command up to $100 an hour or more.

Employment Prospects

Work prospects for freelance copy editors are consistently good, for employers can cut staff costs by contracting work out. Good copy editors can build ongoing relationships for steady work.

Education

Copy editors should have an undergraduate degree, preferably in English or communications. Advanced degrees may be preferred or required for technical and scientific work.

Experience/Skills

Previous employment as an editor, copy editor, proofreader or writer is desirable, or may be required, for freelance copyediting work. Technical or scientific backgrounds may be required for specialized work (see Technical Communicator).

Copyeditors are meticulous, good at detail work, and have a good command of grammatical rules and spelling. They are versed in production symbols and language and use them in editing. They are quick to grasp content and to spot weaknesses, errors, and inconsistencies. They use good judgment and do not impose their own prejudices on the writing. They are diplomatic in pointing out errors and inconsistencies. Copy editors frequently must work under great deadline pressure.

Unions/Associations

Editorial Freelancers Association is open to freelance copy editors. Those who also are writers may belong to a variety of writers' organizations, such as the American Society for Journalists and Authors and National Writers Union.

PROOFREADER

CAREER PROFILE

Duties: Check typeset galleys, page proofs, mechanicals, and blue lines for errors prior to printing

Alternate Title(s): None

Income Potential: Proofreading books and magazines, $12 to $30 per hour; proofreading business publications, $15 to $50 per hour

Work Prospects: Fair to good

Prerequisites:

Education—Undergraduate degree in communications or other field; technical or scientific study for work in these areas

Experience—Prior work as writer, editorial assistant, editor, production assistant helpful

Special Skills—Good command of grammar and style; eye for detail

---

Position Description

The proofreader provides the final check for errors before copy and text of all kinds—from books to periodicals to annual reports to brochures to advertisements—are sent to the printer. Thus, the proofreader carries a great deal of responsibility.

Proofreaders may be called in at different or multiple production stages: when copy is typeset in galleys; when typeset galleys have been arranged into pages; when copy and art are pasted onto boards (mechanicals); or when a dummy is printed (typically in blue ink, hence the name "blue line" or "blues"). They check the typeset copy against the corrected manuscript or corrected galleys to make sure that all changes have been executed as marked. They also look for typographical errors, unevenness in printed lines, and other typesetting or printing imperfections. In addition to text, proofreaders make sure that captions, tables, etc. are correct, and that all pieces of art are in the right places. They mark all corrections on their proofs using printer's symbols. Proofreaders also may find inconsistencies or factual errors, which they bring to the attention of the editor.

Freelance proofreaders usually are writers and editors who perform other services, of which proofreading may be a part. Proofreading may be done on an employer's premises or out of a freelancer's home or office.

Income Potential

Proofreaders usually charge an hourly rate that varies according to industry and the type of material being proofed. Book and magazine publishers typically pay the lowest rates, from about $8 to $30 an hour. Corporations and advertising and public relations agencies pay up to $50 or more an hour. If proofreading is part of an overall job done by a freelancer, especially for a corporation, the work may be billed at much higher rates.

Work Prospects

Freelancers have fair to good chances of frequent or steady proofreading work, especially in business and industry, where much communications production work is contracted out. Publishing work opportunities are greatest in the East, but exist wherever there are book and periodical publishers.

Education

Proofreaders usually are communications professionals who hold undergraduate degrees in communications or other fields. Scientific and technical employers may require graduate degrees.

Experience/Skills

Proofreaders must be careful readers and be meticulous in attention to detail. They should have a thorough knowledge of the rules of grammar, punctuation, and style. Since they may work directly with typesetters and printers, they should be versed in production procedures.

Proofreading is largely clerical in nature and can be tedious work. Proofreaders should be careful not to move through type too quickly or cut corners, as they may miss errors.

Unions/Associations

Depending on other communications services provided, proofreaders may belong to a variety of organizations, such as Editorial Freelancers Association, American Society of Journalists and Authors; Women in Communications, Inc.; National Writers Union, etc.

FACT CHECKER

Duties: Check the accuracy of manuscripts prior to publication

Alternate Title(s): Researcher

Income Potential: $17 to $30 per hour

Employment Prospects: Fair

Prerequisites:

Education—Undergraduate degree in journalism, mass communications or other field

Experience—None required, but prior work as writer or researcher helpful

Special Skills—Attention to details, knowledge of how to use library and reference works

Position Description

The publishers of articles, reports, and books rely heavily upon the author's accuracy, but many pass manuscripts on to fact checkers to doublecheck for errors. The depth of fact checking varies from verification of dates and spellings of names, titles, and places to verification of nearly every detail.

Fact checkers work from a copy of the manuscript and may be given all the author's original notes and tapes. They make heavy use of libraries and reference works. For example, if a writer states that a battle took place on a certain date and at a certain place, a fact checker would look it up, perhaps in an encyclopedia, to verify the information. Fact checkers also call persons interviewed to verify the accuracy of their quotes and statements, and research topics to ascertain whether or not the statements and claims in a manuscript can be validated. They may query the author to find out the sources of certain facts. They report their findings back to the editor.

Fact checking carries a great deal of responsibility but can be tedious work.

Income Potential

Freelance fact checkers typically earn $17 to $25 per hour. Some may work on a flat fee basis, or on retainer.

Employment Prospects

Work opportunities are fair at book publishing houses and magazines. However, fact checking is seen as expendable by many publishers, who are constantly looking for ways to cut costs. Increasingly, publishers rely on authors' statements that information in their manuscripts is accurate. Fact checking is still rigorously pursued at some publications, such as *Reader's Digest,* which has fact checkers on staff who immerse themselves in every article the *Digest* seeks to publish. Articles that do not stand up to fact checking are killed. Other publishers check only selected manuscripts.

Education

There are no specific educational requirements for fact checking. An undergraduate degree in journalism, mass communications, English, or other field is desirable.

Experience/Skills

Prior experience as a writer, editor, researcher, or librarian's assistant is advantageous to obtaining freelance fact checking work.

Fact checkers must be diligent in their search for verifications and unwilling to let minor discrepancies go by. Their attention to detail is required to catch inconsistencies. They must be polite and sensitive in dealing with sources. In some cases, knowledge of the subject at hand is advantageous.

Unions/Associations

There is no professional association of fact checkers, but freelancers who offer this service usually provide other communications services, and may qualify for membership in the Editorial Freelancers Association; American Society of Journalists and Authors; Society for Technical Communications; or Women In Communications, Inc., among others.

INDEXER

Duties: Compile indices to books, newspapers, periodicals, journals, databases, maps, and software

Alternate Title(s): None

Income Potential: $10 to $50 per hour, with higher rates charged if using computer indexing software programs that take fewer hours; $1.50 to $6.00 per printed book page; 40 cents to 70 cents per line of index; or flat fee of $250 to $500 per book, depending on length

Employment Prospects: Fair to good

Prerequisites:

Education—Undergraduate degree in humanities, social science, or liberal arts; graduate degree in library science or in scientific or technical areas may be required

Experience—Background in scholarly research or as librarian helpful

Special Skills—Organization, grammar, detail, logic, accuracy, reading skills, perception, ability to make connections, predictive ability

Position Description

Indices are the road maps of information—they guide a reader in a direct manner to a logical sequence of information and help the reader discover new information. Without indices, it would be difficult, if not impossible, to conduct research efficiently, and vast quantities of information would go unexplored and unused.

There is a misconception that indexing is clerical work and can be done with little or no experience. On the contrary, indices are complex constructions that require skill and training to produce. A poor index that confuses the reader is worse than no index at all.

Indices are compiled by professional indexers, many of them freelancers, who work for libraries, publishers, databases, and corporations. They are familiar with the different formats of indices and with international style standards. Rules and practices are in constant change, and professional indexers must stay abreast of them.

Prior to beginning work on an index, an indexer finds out the job requirements. The length and depth of the index is determined by the number of pages allotted, the number of columns per page, the type size, and the

format and style rules to be followed. Ideally, the length of the index should be between 1/50 and 1/20 the length of the text. Large reference works such as encyclopedias require the most complex indices, with up to 100,000 or so entries. A short and simple index, on the other hand, may have fewer than 1,000 entries. The more complex the index, the greater the skill required on the part of the indexer, who must cross-reference and spot associations that will lead readers to specific information.

Once the job requirements are known, the indexer carefully reads the entire text and begins compiling entries. The indexer keeps track by marking the text, by keeping alphabetical lists manually, or by using a computer software program. Numerous changes are made as work progresses and the indexer gets new ideas for referencing the information. In the final edit, the indexer checks the index to make sure that all entries lead the reader to the right information, and that the length fits the publisher's requirements. Sometimes indexers can obtain more space for an index by convincing the publisher to increase the number of pages or, more likely, to decrease the type size and leading (space between lines).

Indexers also provide a valuable service by spotting inconsistencies and errors in the writing and typographical errors overlooked by editors.

The average book index is compiled in two to four weeks. Large reference works may take months of work. Indexers often work under a great deal of pressure, as they are called in at the last minute to provide an index as quickly as possible.

With the proliferation of personal computers and software programs, many indexers now compile indices electronically. Some, however, still prefer to work manually, constructing indices with a stack of 35-inch cards and a shoebox, and typing the final copy. In fact, there are some opinions among indexers that any index with fewer than 9,000 entries need not be done on computer. Increasingly, however, publishers are requiring indices to be submitted on disk or transferred electronically via modem.

In addition to indexing, some indexers provide other services, such as researching, abstract writing, updating databases, writing, editing, and proofreading.

Income Potential

Earnings depend on the type of indexing and one's expertise. Technical and scientific work pay more than consumer work. Freelance fees are negotiated according to the project, the employer's pay scales and the indexer's scale of fees. Indexers may be paid by each line in an index, by the manuscript page indexed, by the hour, or by a flat fee. The average consumer book brings a fee of $250 to $500. Some indexers work on retainer and give that employer first priority. Court rulings on work-for-hire have enabled many indexers to retain rights to their work, and thus to earn additional monies for new editions, reprints, and foreign translations.

Employment Prospects

There is an increasing need for indexers due to the proliferation of information and the need to organize and manage it. More and more, people want speedy access to information and do not want to wade through texts in search of facts. In book publishing, some publishers still forego an index as an optional expense, but book reviewers are paying more attention not only to the inclusion of indices, but their quality as well. Databases, libraries, corporations, newspapers, and periodicals require indexes to keep track of their collections.

Education

In addition to an undergraduate degree, many indexers have graduate degrees in library science. Some also have advanced degrees in technical or scientific areas. Graduate degrees, especially in library science, may be required for highly complex indexing work.

Experience/Skills

A background in library science and information management is helpful to a freelance career as an indexer. Indexing is precise work and should not be undertaken without some training. Graduate schools of library science may offer non-credit or credit seminars, workshops, and courses for the novice indexer.

Indexers bring a wide range of skills to the job. They must be careful readers who get a quick grasp of material. They must be able to anticipate how a reader might look for a specific piece of information. Though indices are logical, the reader does not always approach them logically. Indexers also must be knowledgeable on the latest rules and practices concerning index formats and grammatical style. In addition, indexers are good at seeing patterns, organizing information, paying attention to detail and accuracy, and working under pressure.

Unions/Associations

The American Society of Indexers, Inc. is the only professional association in the U.S. devoted to the advancement of indexing; it is affiliated with professional indexing societies in Canada, the United Kingdom, and Australia. Membership is open to anyone interested in the field. Indexers who provide other freelance communications services may belong to societies for authors, writers, editors, technical writers and editors, public relations professionals, etc.

STRINGER

Duties: Provide frequent copy to newspapers and/or magazines

Alternate Title(s):   Correspondent; Contributing Writer; Contributing Editor

Income Potential: Sometimes flat fee of $20 to $35 to cover a meeting and write an article

Work Prospects: Fair

Prerequisites:

    Education—Undergraduate degree in communications, journalism, English, or liberal arts, or at least a high school diploma

    Experience—Background as a journalist helpful

    Special Skills—Ability to work independently and meet deadlines; good writing; sense for news

Position Description

Many newspapers and magazines cover broad geographic areas but are not able to maintain writing staff to monitor far-flung events. Instead, they rely on stringers or correspondents, writers who are expected to monitor local news of interest to the publication and provide timely, frequent stories. Some magazines pay writers to provide copy on specialized topics for columns and departments, such as computer technology or personal health. These writers are usually called contributing writers or contributing editors.

Stringers are expected to keep abreast of news developments and inform their editors of important or special events, or ideas for in-depth or feature stories. Their duties may include reporting on local government and school-board meetings, providing local material for roundup stories and reader surveys, and filing reports on conventions, exhibits, and conferences.

Deadlines depend on publication frequency. A newspaper stringer may be expected to cover an evening meeting and then dictate a story over the telephone. Some transmit copy by telecopier or other facsimile device, and others may only be required to mail articles. A stringer may be required to submit a certain number of stories a week or month, or just report on an as-needed basis. Assignments are given by home-base editors.

If a disaster strikes, such as a flood or tornado, stringers may be called on short notice to provide news coverage. Occasionally they may be asked to travel.

Stringers may hold writing or reporting jobs on other, noncompetitive publications, or they may be part- or full-time freelancers. Their editors depend on them the same way they depend on their immediate reporting or writing staff.

Income Potential

Most stringers do not earn a great deal of money, but the pay can be steady and can lead to other work. Major national news magazines pay hourly rates to stringers, from about $10 to $35 an hour, or daily rates of about $150 to $250 plus expenses. Other publications pay per story, $25 and up, and some pay by the published inch, usually $1 to $5. Some stringers can earn flat monthly retainer fees of $50 to $500 and up, depending on the publication and the work involved.

Work Prospects

Publications covering broad areas, particularly newspapers, and weekly trade and news magazines, are the best bets for stringing.

Education

Most stringers, like other journalists and writers, have undergraduate degrees in communications, journalism, or liberal arts. Those who specialize may have advanced degrees.

Experience/Skills

Stringers generally are established writers, either freelance or employed by another, noncompetitive publication, with several years' experience as journalists. They must be dependable, accurate, and self-motivated.

Unions/Associations

Major national associations include the Society of Professional Journalists, Sigma Delta Chi; American Society of Journalists and Authors, Inc.; National Writers Union; National Association of Black Journalists; National Association of Media Women; National Federation of Press Women, Inc.; and Women in Communications, Inc.

BOOK REVIEWER

CAREER PROFILE

Duties: Write book reviews for newspapers, periodicals, and newsletters

Alternate Title(s): Columnist

Income Potential: For a byline and the book only at small newspapers; $35 to $200 at larger publications; $50 to $300 for magazines

Work Prospects: Poor

Prerequisites:

Education—Undergraduate degree in communications, English, liberal arts, or in area of specific expertise; graduate degree may be preferred in some cases

Experience—Recognition as expert in subject areas or in literature; knowledge of other and current books

Special Skills—Good writing ability, criticism skills

Position Description

Book reviewers help readers choose books by providing summaries of their contents, plot synopses (without giving away surprises and endings), and opinions on their merits and flaws.

Reviewing books can provide a small but often steady source of income for freelance writers and authors. Most newspapers, consumer and trade periodicals, and industry newsletters carry book review columns in each issue; many rely on freelancers to provide the reviews. The column itself may be produced on a regular basis by a freelancer, or an editor may assign reviews to a variety of writers. Since the majority of publications are specialized and thus limit reviews to books of specific interest to their audiences, expertise in a subject area is often required of book reviewers. Some writers work regularly or often as reviewers, while others write occasional reviews upon invitation by publications.

Unless a writer is given responsibility for developing a book review column and generating his or her own material, a publication will ask a writer to review a certain book. The writer is given the book as well as instructions on length and format, and a deadline.

There are several types of review, which depend upon the publication and the importance of the book. Straight descriptive reviews are short and give the reader the title, author, publisher, price, and a brief description of the contents with no evaluation. Short reviews of several paragraphs provide the pertinent information with a brief evaluation. Essay reviews can be up to one or two thousand words in length and include comparisons of the book to previous works by the same author and similar works by other authors, and an evaluation on the part of the reviewer. Critique reviews are even broader in scope, discussing an entire genre or literary movement.

Income Potential

Most writers are paid small fees for individual book reviews—$10 to $25 are typical fees. In some cases, a free book and a byline are the sole compensation. Large and prestigious consumer publications pay up to several hundred dollars for essay and critique reviews, but rely primarily upon well-known writers and experts.

Work Prospects

Many book reviews are assigned on the basis of the reviewer's credentials, expertise, and sometimes name recognition. The best prospects for regular work as a reviewer are in local markets, and through establishing a relationship with a publication by writing articles first. Aspiring reviewers also can query publications with a letter outlining credentials and expertise and, if available, sample review clips.

Education

No education is required to become a book reviewer. Most writers have an undergraduate degree in communications, liberal arts, English, or other subjects. Graduate degrees may be preferred for certain specialized areas or publications.

Experience/Skills

Book reviewers should be knowledgeable about the subjects covered in a book, if nonfiction, or the genre, if fiction. One need not be an expert to write straight descriptive and short reviews, but expertise enhances the prospects for higher-paying reviews. Reviewers should be objective, fair, and sensitive and have good criticsm skills.

Unions/Associations

There are no associations specifically for book reviewers. Those who are writers may belong to one or more writers' organizations, such as the Authors Guild; American Society for Journalists and Authors; Mystery Writers of America; Poets, Essayists and Novelists (P.E.N.); National Writers Union; etc.

CONTRIBUTING EDITOR

CAREER PROFILE

Duties: Suggest and write articles for periodicals

Alternate Title(s):   Contributing Writer; Correspondent

Income Potential: Up to $50,000+

Work Prospects: Poor

Prerequisites:

> **Education**—Undergraduate degree preferred; graduate degree
> may be preferred or required for specialized areas
>
> **Experience**—Extensive published credits or name recognition
> with audience; thorough knowledge of subject areas
>
> **Special Skills**   —Excellent writing; dependability;
> self-discipline

Position Description

Contributing editors are hired by periodicals to write an article for every issue, or a certain number of articles per year. They generally are not part of the periodical's staff, but work on a freelance, contract basis. Pay is set per article or annually, depending on the contributing editor's responsibilities.

Contributing editors usually have extensive experience as writers. They have an established expertise and a reputation for dependability. They are invited to become contributing editors by writing regularly for periodicals. Some well-known or celebrity writers may be invited by a periodical to become contributing editors in order to draw readers. Many small periodicals use contributing editors as a way of stretching their staffs, particularly if they require coverage of far-away areas.

Contributing editors may be responsible for providing coverage of certain topics or geographic areas, or may be roving. They suggest their own ideas and are given assignments by their superior editors. Duties can range from writing articles, reviews, and columns to attending staff meetings to supervising other writers. (Distant contributing editors usually are not expected to attend staff meetings.)

A contributing editorship usually is but one of several sources of income for a writer.

Income Potential

Earnings depend on the size and nature of publication, the responsibilities of the position, and the contributing editor's credentials and reputation. Contributing editors can earn as little as a few thousand dollars a year to $40,000 a year or more at prestigious publications. Celebrity writers may earn more.

Work Prospects

A solid track record of published credits and a good reputation as a writer usually are required to become a contributing editor at major periodicals. A writer may work into this position over time by writing regularly on a topic or for a periodical, and developing a good working relationship with the staff. However, small periodicals in need of dependable, freelance contributors may provide the best prospects for writers in the early stages of their careers.

Education

Most writers have an undergraduate degree in communications, liberal arts, English, or social sciences. Graduate degrees may be advantageous or required in technical and specialized areas.

Experience/Skills

Contributing editors usually have demonstrated their expertise over a period of years before becoming contributing editors. They must be creative, self-disciplined, reliable, knowledgeable about their areas, and good writers.

Unions/Associations

Contributing editors can belong to organizations for writers, such as the American Society of Journalists and Authors; the Society for Technical Communication; the National Writers Union and Women in Communications, Inc. They may also belong to trade or professional associations related to the areas and topics they cover.

SYNDICATED COLUMNIST

Duties: Write, self-edit, and deliver columns to client newspapers; prepare sales material; sell column

Alternate Title(s):   None

Income Potential: $5 to $10 each for weeklies; $10 to $25 per week for dailies, based on circulation

Work Prospects: Poor

Prerequisites:

   Education—Depends on need for expertise; most have undergraduate degrees

   Experience—Background as journalist or writer helpful; knowledge of subject area important

   Special Skills—Concise writing; self-editing; sales and entrepreneurial ability; self-discipline; perseverance

Position Description

All newspapers publish columns on a wide variety of subjects, including self-help pieces, feature articles, news analyses, and puzzles. Some of the columns are written by the newspaper's own staff, but most are purchased through syndication.

Writers who have ideas for columns can try to market them to syndicates—organizations that in turn sell to the newspapers-or market them directly to newspapers in self-syndication.

The proliferation of columns makes it appear deceptively easy to become syndicated. Almost anyone with a novel idea, it seems, can become wealthy and famous. In reality, syndication, by either route, is difficult and highly competitive work; few columnists become famous or wealthy.

A prospective columnist must be able to offer something new, or be able to write about a subject better than established columnists. The idea should be strong enough to generate interesting material at least once or twice a week over a long period of time. Syndicates and newspapers are not interested in fads. What's more, the columnist should have experience in writing and a background in the subject area.

Most columns are short, 500 to 1,000 words or so. They must be tightly written and deliver good information.

There are more than 60 major syndicates that handle all kinds of columns. A prospective columnist should submit to such syndicates at least six sample columns, along with a pitch letter that describes the writer's qualifications, the potential audience, and the column's appeal. Syndicates keep anywhere from 40 to 60 percent of the gross revenues of a column.

In addition to columns, syndicates also purchase single articles, called "one-shots," which have wide appeal and can be sold to newspapers for one-time use. A typical one-shot might be a feature story on a prominent person, or a topic or issue of great current interest. The author is usually paid a flat fee of about 20 to 50 cents a word.

Self-syndication is much costlier and more time consuming, but the writer keeps all of the profits. Sample columns and pitch letters are sent directly to newspaper editors and usually followed up by phone calls. Several hundred newspapers may have to be approached in order to net a few dozen clients. Some columnists start out by establishing themselves with one or two newspapers, and then expanding.

The self-syndicated columnist is responsible for writing, editing, and delivering the copy to all clients by their deadlines, and for billing them. Self-syndication can easily be a full-time job or more, requiring 40 to 80 hours of work per week.

Income Potential

Most columns are sold for $5 to $75 per piece to each client. Rates depend on the popularity of the column and writer. A few columnists earn over $100,000 a year, including Jack Anderson (well over $200,000), William Safire, Russell Baker, Art Buchwald, Abigail Van Buren (Dear Abby), Ann Landers, and others. A self-syndicated columnist who is published in about 60 or 70 newspapers and charges $10 per piece can clear about $30,000 a year. Most columnists earn far less than that.

Work Prospects

Syndicates and newspapers receive far more queries for columns than they can possibly use. Writers who can identify new and developing trends in popular interest have the best chances for successful sales. Self-syndication is an alternative for those willing to put in long hours to get established, a process that usually involves giving columns away on free trials. Most aspiring columnists will find their best bets in their own local markets, and among the nation's many small daily and weekly newspapers.

Education

Little attention is paid to education unless it is necessary to establish the columnist as an authority. However, an undergraduate degree in journalism or any subject is desirable.

Experience/Skills

Most columnists are already established writers or journalists with several to many years of experience. Regardless of previous writing experience, columnists must demonstrate good writing ability. They must be able to research and develop fresh, concisely written material on a regular schedule. Persistence and a flair for sales and promotion is helpful to self-syndicators.

Unions/Associations

There are no associations specifically for syndicated columnists. Related groups include the Society of Professional Journalists, Sigma Delta Chi; Women In Communications, Inc.; American Society of Journalists and Authors, Inc.; National Association of Media Women; and National Federation of Press Women.

COMMUNICATIONS CONSULTANT

Duties: Advise clients on ways to improve writing and communications skills, or editorial operations

Alternate Title(s):   Editorial Consultant

Income Potential: $250 per day plus expenses for nonprofit, social services, and religious organizations; $400 per day and up for others

Employment Prospects: Fair

Prerequisites:

Education—Undergraduate degree in communications, liberal arts, or related field; graduate degree advantageous

Experience—Sufficient background to provide expertise

Special Skills—Excellent written and oral communications skills; teaching ability; salesmanship; self-motivation

Position Description

Consulting is viewed as a highly glamorous, prestigious occupation. Consultants enjoy a reputation for high compensation relative to work performed, as well as complete independence. While it is true that consultants can earn high pay, most work very hard for it, putting in long hours searching for and pitching clients. Their work and reputation must be good enough to earn repeat clients, for it is virtually impossible to stay in business on one-shot efforts.

Consultants exist in just about every profession, discipline, and occupation. In communications, consultants perform a variety of services. They assist businesses, publications, and newspapers in special projects, in streamlining and improving editorial operations, and in launching new publications. They conduct research and studies of potential advertisers, markets, and subscribers. They help pinpoint weaknesses. They conduct seminars for staff on how to improve writing and editing skills, or training sessions on new technology. Consultants may also assume responsibility for such publications as corporate newsletters, handling the editing and production involved.

To be successful, consultants must have expertise and credentials to attract and satisfy clients. Such a reputation usually comes after years of work in the field as a writer, editor, or publishing executive. Some people enter consulting on a part-time basis, handling projects that are not conflicts of interest with their jobs. Part-time consulting allows for a base of clients and references to be built with a minimum of financial risk; however, it does limit the types of assignments that can be accepted. Part-time consulting can be built into a full-time occupation.

Most consultants have a strong desire to be self-employed and are highly motivated to succeed. Building a client base requires persistence and good sales skills. They must identify their target audience and develop direct-mail, telephone, and advertising campaigns to promote their particular skills and abilities.

Hours can be very long, especially in the beginning. Consultants spend a great deal of time prospecting for clients, by attending professional meetings and conferences, accepting speaking engagements, and soliciting on the telephone. Work loads are seldom spread evenly, which creates many deadline pressures. Some consultants travel extensively.

Income Potential

Consultants usually work on a per diem or project basis. Per diem rates range from $200 to $1,000 and up—some top consultants charge as much as $2,000 a day. Rates depend on experience and expertise; the average is about $550 per day. Flat fees for projects depend on the nature of the work and time spent.

Other common types of fees include: retainer fees (a flat monthly rate in exchange for a specified amount of time); percentage fees (a percent of the value of a product that is to be offered for sale); and equity fees (an interest in a business in lieu of cash).

Employment Prospects

Overall, there are some 50,000 full-time consultants in all fields, with an additional 2,000 persons setting up shop every year. The industry totals more than $32 billion a year. About half of all consultants are sole proprietorships.

In communications, the best employment prospects are among corporations, many of which use consultants regularly for ongoing staff education and training. Many newspapers also use consultants. In addition to editorial experience, many newspaper consultants also have some background in production, advertising, or circulation.

Education

High academic credentials carry weight in consulting. An undergraduate degree in communications, liberal arts, or a specialized area is the minimum requirement. A master's degree won't guarantee success, but it can help attract clients. A background in finance or accounting is advantageous in all areas of consulting.

Experience/Skills

Besides expertise, consultants should possess good problem-solving ability. They should be quick at grasping situations and in seeing solutions.

Excellent writing and speaking skills are a must for consultants. Pitch letters, proposals, reports, and studies must be well researched, organized, and written. Consultants do a great deal of public speaking, either in instruction to small groups or to larger audiences at conventions and professional meetings.

Sales skills also are essential to success. Consultants must sell themselves to potential clients, and sell their ideas and proposals to existing clients. Consultants must be well organized, ambitious individuals with a strong desire to succeed on their own.

Unions/Associations

Membership in professional associations and organizations is wise because of the contacts and referrals that can be made. Which organizations to join depends on the individual's area of expertise.

DESKTOP PUBLISHER

CAREER PROFILE

Duties: Produce or publish newsletters, magazines, brochures, reports, and other small publications

Alternate Title(s): Communications Consultant; Freelance Publisher

Income Potential: $1,000 and up per job

Work Prospects: Fair to good

Prerequisites:

Education—Undergraduate degree in mass communications, journalism, English, art, or graphics design
Experience—Prior work in writing, editing, and publications production essential
Special Skills—Good writing and editing skills; knowledge of desktop publishing software; management skills; organization; ability to meet deadlines; salesmanship

Position Description

Sophisticated computer technology has enabled the freelance writer and editor to expand in new directions and produce a finished product end to end. With an investment in the right computer hardware and desktop publishing (DTP) software, the freelancer becomes producer or publisher.

The desktop publisher works with businesses, associations, agencies, and organizations to produce publications that have a professionally published look. These usually are newsletters, magazines, and reports for either an inhouse or external audience.

Desktop publishers work with a staff editor or communications manager who provides specifications for the publication's content, design, size and length. The desktop publisher may be given the copy, produced in-house or by freelancers, or may have to generate it in accordance with an assignment list. If the copy is hard (printed on paper), it is keyed or scanned into the computer. Some copy may be provided on disk or transferred by modem. The copy is edited, and the pages are formatted on-screen to accommodate graphics and design. The pages can be printed out exactly as they appear on the screen. Art must be screened and added.

Simple documents such as a single-sheet newsletter can be printed in quantity directly on a high-quality printer (laserjet is preferred). The printer also can be used to produce proofs, which are mounted on mechanicals and sent to a printer. The desktop publisher either delivers the finished product or the mechanicals, sends the mechanicals to a printer, or sends the printer a computer disk.

Desktop publishers wear all hats—writer, editor, copy editor, designer, typesetter—or supervise others who perform those tasks. All facets of producing a publication must be coordinated in order to meet deadlines. The task involves periodic meetings with the in-house person in charge of the publication, to review progress, and get the necessary in-house approvals on content and design.

Some desktop publishers found their own newsletters and periodicals. The success of these ventures relies in the astute meeting of a market need and the marketing of the product to paying subscribers. Fulfillment—the management of mail lists and the mailing of the publication—is time-consuming, as is collecting money and keeping track of accounts. New publications may operate in the red for a considerable period of time. If successful, self-published newsletters can be rewarding in terms of income and creative satisfaction.

Income Potential

Desktop publishers set individual fees, usually by establishing a day rate and estimating the time required to complete a job. Certain expenses may be billed in addition to the fee. The production of even a simple quarterly newsletter can bring in several thousand dollars annually.

An initial investment in equipment and software is necessary, however. One needs a personal computer with sufficient built-in memory to handle DTP programs, a word processing program, a DTP program and a high quality printer that can handle different fonts.

Work Prospects

Opportunities for desktop publishers are fair to good and are increasing due to downsizing in the business world. Businesses are trimming their staffs or keeping them small, yet their need to communicate remains the same or increases. It's more economical for many businesses to hire freelance desktop publishers than to assign staff to produce certain publications. The DTPer is to business communications what the packager is to book publishing.

The best DTP opportunities are at corporations of all sizes, professional or trade organizations, and associations, and the nonprofit sector, though pay is lower at the latter.

Education

An under graduate degree in mass communications, journalism, English, art, or graphics design is desirable. Although some desktop publishers have no design background, with some training in design desktop publishers can produce a higher-quality, more professional-looking product.

Experience/Skills

Previous experience as a writer or editor, and knowledge of production, are essential. Though DTP programs do not require graphics design skill, some knowledge of layout and design is helpful, and may be essential for larger and more complex publications.

DTPers must be well organized and able to coordinate people and tasks to bring the pieces together into a whole. Personal interaction skills are important, as DTPers typically work with a variety of people who must provide material, art, or approvals. DTPers also must have good sales skills to sell their services.

Unions/Associations

DTPers may belong to a number of communications organizations, such as the International Association of Business Communicators; Public Relations Society of America; Women In Communications, Inc.; the American Society of Journalists and Authors; Editorial Freelancers Association, and more.

PACKAGER

Duties: Create books for publishers

Alternative Title(s):   Book producer

Income Potential: $0 to no limit

Work Prospects: Poor to fair

Prerequisites:

Education—Undergraduate degree in English, communications, liberal arts, humanities; publishing and marketing courses desirable

Experience—Prior work as author or editor essential

Special Skills—Creativity; innovation; ability to sense marketing opportunities; salesmanship; marketing and finance savvy; familiarity with production

Position Description

Packagers provide complete book preparation services to publishers, from the outline to the finished product. Some also provide marketing and distribution services. By offering package deals to publishers, packagers save publishers money and reduce staff time. Most publishers pay packagers according to a percentage of the book's retail price and the number of copies ordered. The usual percentage is 20 percent. Thus, a packager is paid $5 for a book that will sell to the public for $20. To make a profit, the packager must hold production costs to less than $5 per book. Mistakes can make the difference between profit or loss.

Packagers conceive ideas for books and then write proposals, which they use as sales tools to interest editors. The proposal includes a summary of the book's contents, sample material, market potential, and, if the packager provides the finished product, the production specifications (number of pages, trim size, type of paper, etc.). The editor and packager then negotiate a price. The packager must take into account anticipated production expenses and build in a profit margin.

Some packagers write, edit, and produce their own books. Others work with authors, whom they pay on a flat fee or royalty basis. Unless a packager has production equipment, work is subcontracted to typesetters and print shops. The services of a graphic artist or illustrator usually are necessary. The packager consults with the editor at numerous points along the way. Depending on the contract, the editor may have a significant voice in how the book is produced.

Packagers devise production schedules and must coordinate a variety of personnel and activities. They are familiar with production. Many packagers retain rights to their books, which they sell piecemeal to publishers, periodicals, and other outlets. Selling these rights is time-consuming and requires knowledge of the publishing marketplace. Some packagers have agents to help them sell proposals and rights.

Most packagers have had extensive prior experience as authors or editors. They know the business and have numerous contacts in the publishing world. They may opt to specialize in certain kinds of books, such as art books or lavishly illustrated coffee-table and gift books, or in serial fiction.

Packaging can provide the satisfaction of self-publishing without the distribution worries, unless the packager opts to provide marketing and distribution services. However, it can be difficult to get started, and vagaries in cash flow from typically slow-paying publishers can strain a tight budget.

Income Potential

Earnings depend on the type of books packaged, the end product provided (finished books fetch more money but consume more money to produce), and the success of books sold. Profit margins vary depending on individual negotiations. The profit from a book may be only a few thousand dollars. Big sellers can go on to earn hundreds of thousands of dollars over a period of time.

Packaging requires startup investment on the part of the packager. In a typical contract, a packager is paid in thirds by the publisher (one-third on signing, one-third on delivery, and one-third on publication) or in halves (half on signing, half on delivery). Payment from a publisher can come months after signing or delivery; meanwhile, work must be done on the book and suppliers and authors expect to be paid. Packagers who work out of an office must factor in rent and other office expenses.

Work Prospects

It is difficult to get started in packaging without personal contacts in the publishing world, but it can be done. Packagers can work anywhere, but the overwhelming majority are concentrated near New York City, where they can have easy access for face-to-face meetings with major publishers. A good-quality, professional product is paramount to success.

Education

Most packagers have an undergraduate degree in liberal arts, English, communications, humanities, or other area. They may have taken additional courses in publishing, business administration, marketing, advertising, and promotion.

Experience/Skills

Prior work as an author or editor is virtually essential to packaging. The packager functions almost as a publisher, and must be familiar with the market. The ability to make convincing proposals, both in writing and in person, is important. Packagers must manage cash flow, staff, and suppliers, and juggle tight deadlines.

Unions/Associations

The American Book Producers Association is the primary organization for packagers. Some may also belong to the Association of American Publishers, Inc., or various writers' organizations.

SELF-PUBLISHER

Duties: Write and publish one's own books, monographs, periodicals, etc.

Alternate Title(s):   Independent publisher, private publisher

Income Potential: $0 to no limit

Work Prospects: Fair

Prerequisites:

Education—Undergraduate degree in English or communications; courses in business and finance helpful

Experience—Work as writer and editor helpful; familiarity with production essential; sales experience, financial acumen desirable

Special Skills—Innovation; willingness to take risks; ability to predict trends and market opportunities; salesmanship and marketing skills; self-promotion; organization; financial planning; good records keeping

Position Description

In times past, self-publishing once carried a stigma—it was the mark of an author who failed to sell his or her work to a publisher. That stigma no longer exists. In fact, many a self-published author is considered a savvy businessperson, someone who retains total control over the product and stands poised to keep all the profits, not a small percentage of them.

Self-publishing became viable with the explosion in personal computing and desktop publishing software. For a moderate investment, an individual can purchase the equipment and programs needed to produce manuscript copy, galleys, and page mechanicals ready for the printer. At the same time, the consolidation of large publishing houses has left openings in the market to be filled by small presses (many of which began as self-publishing operations and expanded) and self-publishers. Self-publishing is not to be confused with vanity publishing, in which an author pays a publisher to publish a work.

Self-publishing requires a great deal of business planning and organization, for the self-publisher bears all the expenses of producing and marketing a book. The author wears many hats, and must plan and budget for every step along the way. Prior to writing the book, the self-publisher must try to estimate production costs and market potential. A marketing plan is drawn up. The book is then written, and then must be typeset, proofread and corrected, paginated, and made ready for mechanicals for the printer. The self-publisher must be familiar with production shop operations and able to work with those personnel. A cover must be designed, which may require hiring a graphic artist. If the text is illustrated, the art must be collected or commissioned and positioned in the text. Any legal questions must be resolved with the help of an attorney.

Once the book is produced, the self-publisher takes delivery and must be able to sell the copies through channels of distribution, which include book and specialty stores, catalogs, direct mail, and wholesale distributors. Orders are placed; prices and terms must be negotiated; books must be delivered and monies collected. In addition, publicity and reviews must be solicited and advertisements, if desired, placed. Many of these activities are time-consuming, and authors find themselves working more as business managers than as writers. Furthermore, not all markets are eager to do business with self-publishers, and it is at the point of distribution that many self-publishers fail and lose money.

Success, however, is a heady experience. Sufficient profits enable self-publishers to produce other books.

Once track records of sales are established, distribution becomes easier. Many authors who have been published by large publishing houses have found great satisfaction in self-publishing, even if profits are small or modest. They enjoy having complete control and in seeing immediate financial results, instead of waiting months to years to earn royalties.

Income Potential

A successful self-published book is one that earns at least enough income to cover production costs. Profits may range from several hundred dollars to several thousand dollars, depending on the profit margin per copy and the number of copies sold. Some very successful self-published books have made hundreds of thousands of dollars in profits. A trade paperback of about 155 pages with no illustrations and a simple cover might cost about 21¢ per copy to produce, and could sell for up to $9.95 or $10.95.

Minimum press runs typically are 1,000 or more copies. Depending on costs, the self-publisher must invest up front an average of $8,000–$12,000 or more for a typical book. Depending on how quickly a book sells, recovering costs and making a profit may take several months to years. Those who succeed have researched in advance the potential market for their books and potential distribution channels.

Additional income may come from the sale of subsidiary rights, such as foreign sales, audio tapes, condensations, serializations, film and television production, etc. Occasionally a successful self-published book is purchased for larger distribution rights by a major publisher.

Nonfiction self-published books, especially those that are self-help, guides, or subjects for specialty markets, are much more likely to succeed than fiction and poetry.

Work Prospects

The ranks of self-publishers have swelled since affordable desktop computing arrived in the early 1980s. Market opportunities depend upon trends and perceived needs as seen by the aspiring self-publisher. It is possible to get started in self-publishing on a part-time basis while one continues to work at a full-time job, though the time demands can be grueling. Successful self-publishing can lead to the establishment of a small press, which publishes several titles a year, including the works of others. Thousands of small presses operate in the U.S. alone.

Education

Most self-publishers are authors-turned-publishers and have undergraduate degrees in communications, English, liberal arts, and the humanities. Additional courses in business, marketing, and finance are recommended prior to launching a self-publishing venture.

Experience/Skills

Self-publishers are good writers who are creative and innovative. They are not afraid to take risks. Editing skills are advantageous, though self-publishers can always hire editors on a project basis. Self-publishers also have a working knowledge of production and printing requirements and procedures. Financial, sales, and promotion skills also are necessary. A great deal of advance business planning must be done in order to be successful.

Unions/Associations

The Committee of Small Magazine Editors and Publishers (COSMEP) is the leading association of independent book and periodical publishers. Many self-publishers also belong to the Publishers Marketing Association, a national nonprofit cooperative, and to various regional small-press associations. Self-publishers also may belong to local business organizations and writers' organizations, such as the American Society for Journalists and Authors; Authors Guild; National Writers Union; etc.

ADVERTISING COPYWRITER

CAREER PROFILE

Duties: Write advertising copy for advertising agencies, businesses, corporations, and design studios

Alternate Title(s):   None

Income Potential: $20 to $100 per hour, $250 and up per day, $500 and up per week, $1,000 to $2,000 as a monthly retainer; flat-fee-per-ad rates could range from $100 and up per page, depending on the client

Work Prospects: Excellent

Prerequisites:

Education—Undergraduate degree in communications, liberal arts, art, advertising, or business

Experience—Background as a professional writer or journalist helpful; proven track record as a copywriter required

Special Skills—Creativity, imagination, salesmanship, persistence, self-motivation, reliability

Position Description

Freelance copywriting can be frustrating, isolating, and erratic. It can also give you control over your own schedule and the satisfaction of running your own business.

To get started in the business, you must already have a strong portfolio of work. Clients hire freelancers to fill in when the in-house staff is swamped. As a consequence, freelancers are expected to come in and hit the ground running, delivering assignments of professional quality on time.

Freelancers are also expected to turn out assignments to meet deadline pressure, even if it means working over weekends or at night. An advertising agency in the middle of an important campaign may not call back if the freelancer turns down an emergency assignment.

A freelance copywriter must be able to manage time well, because he or she will most likely be handling several assignments at once. Assignments are best cultivated through contacts—repeat business from a former employer, word-of-mouth referrals, or networking within professional organizations. Some areas even have tip clubs—groups of people in different professions who meet and give one another leads.

Advertising agencies often need part-time help in busy seasons. Newspapers, radio, and television stations may also need copywriters for clients who do not have their own advertising agencies.

Advertising freelancers base their charges on hourly rates, but experienced freelancers can often estimate how long a job will take and quote a flat project rate or price range.

Doing business with repeat customers or referrals can also help cut down on problems receiving payment. A freelancer has to be prepared for uneven cash flow, sometimes waiting 90 days for checks. They also keep their own business records, bill clients, and keep track of tax-deductible expenses.

Income Potential

Hourly rates generally range from $35 to $75 and up. Daily rates are $250 and up per day; weekly, $500 and up. Monthly retainers can be from $1,000 to $2,000.

Many experienced copywriters base their fees on an hourly rate, but quote the client a flat project rate based on how much time they expect the job to take. Rates vary with the size and type of client.

Work Prospects

A copywriter with some business contacts and a reputation for doing good work on deadline has a good chance of building up a healthy client list. Getting established, however, could take some time.

Education

Most advertising copywriters have undergraduate degrees in communications, liberal arts, advertising, or business. Courses in copywriting or creative writing are also helpful.

Experience/Skills

A solid background in advertising is essential for someone trying to become a freelance copywriter. Reliability, professionalism, and creativity are key attributes of freelancers in this field.

Unions/Associations

The American Advertising Federation, Direct Marketing Creative Guild, and American Marketing Association are the major groups of interest to copywriters.

Other groups include Women in Communications, Inc. and The Writers Guild of America, a union representing scriptwriters for radio, television, and film.

APPENDIX I
EDUCATIONAL INSTITUTIONS

The minimum educational requirement for most salaried jobs featured in this guide is an undergraduate degree in communications, with emphasis in a particular sequence, such as print journalism, broadcasting, advertising/public relations, etc. The following is a list of some of the four-year colleges and universities that offer such undergraduate degrees; in addition, some offer courses in book publishing. The listings include addresses, telephone numbers, and the majors or sequences offered, in random order. In addition, the institutions whose programs have met the standards set by the Accrediting Council on Education in Journalism and Mass Communications (ACEJMC) have been marked with an asterisk (*). For more information about course descriptions, admissions requirements, and the availability of scholarships, call or write to the institutions of interest.

Many major professional associations have information on scholarships and internships; consult Appendix II. The Dow Jones Newspaper Fund publishes a comprehensive annual *Journalist's Road to Success* booklet, which contains information about journalism careers and scholarships. Copies can be obtained for $3 each from:

The Dow Jones Newspaper Fund
P.O. Box 300
Princeton, NJ 08543-0300
609-452-2820

ALABAMA

Alabama State University
Montgomery, AL 36101-0271
205-293-4493

Print journalism, radio-TV, public relations

Auburn University
Auburn, AL 36830
205-826-4607

News-editorial, public relations

Jacksonville State University
Jacksonville, AL 36265
205-782-5300

Communication, journalism

Samford University
Birmingham, AL 35229
205-870-2465

Broadcasting, print, public relations, advertising

Spring Hill College
Mobile, AL 36608
205-460-2392

Journalism, media writing, advertising and public relations, radio/TV

Troy State University
Troy, AL 36082
205-670-3289

Broadcasting, news-editorial

University of Alabama*
Tuscaloosa, AL 35487-0172
205-348-5520

Journalism, broadcast and film communications, advertising/public relations, speech communication, telecommunication
Courses in publishing

University of South Alabama
Mobile, AL 36688
205-380-2800

Broadcast news, communication studies, print journalism, organizational communication, public relations, radio-television-film

ALASKA

University of Alaska-Anchorage*
3211 Providence Drive
Anchorage, AK 99508
907-786-1506

News-editorial, photojournalism, public relations and advertising, telecommunications, general communications, photography

University of Alaska-Fairbanks*
18 Bunnell
Fairbanks, AK 99775-0940
907-474-7761

Broadcasting, news-editorial

ARIZONA

Arizona State University*
Tempe, AZ 85287-1305
602-965-5011

Journalism, broadcasting, photojournalism, public relations, journalism education

Northern Arizona University
Flagstaff, AZ 86011-5619
602-523-2232

Advertising, broadcast journalism, communication studies, electronic media management, electronic media production, family and interpersonal communication, journalism education, journalism-political science, mass communication, news-editorial, organizational communication, photography, photojournalism, pre-law, public relations, speech communication, speech communication education

University of Arizona[*]
Tucson, AZ 85721
602-621-7556

News-editorial (newspaper, magazine, public information, community journalism,), photojournalism
Courses in publishing

ARKANSAS

Arkansas State University[*]
State University, AR 72467
501-972-2468

Radio-television, broadcast news, radio-television production and performance, radio-television management and sales, cable and alternative technologies, news-editorial, community journalism, advertising, public relations, photojournalism, printing management, printing technology

Arkansas Tech University
Russellville, AR 72801
501-968-0640

Broadcast news, news-editorial, public relations

Harding University
Searcy, AR 72143
501-279-4445, ext. 445

Print journalism, radio/TV, advertising, and public relations

Henderson State University
Arkadelphia, AR 71999-0001
501-246-5511

News-editorial, secondary school, mass media, communications, theatre

John Brown University
Siloam Springs, AR 72761
501-524-3131

Broadcasting, news-editorial, public relations

University of Arkansas[*]
Fayetteville, AR 72701
501-575-3601

News-editorial, advertising, public relations, magazine journalism, broadcast journalism

University of Arkansas[*]
Little Rock, AR 72204
501-569-3250

News-editorial, broadcast journalism, professional and technical writing, public information

University of Central Arkansas
Conway, AR 72032
501-450-3162

Mass communications, news-editorial, magazine, photography, media ethics, law

CALIFORNIA

California Polytechnic State University
San Luis Obispo, CA 93407
805-756-2508

News-editorial, broadcast news, agricultural journalism, public relations

California State Polytechnic University
Pomona, CA 91768
714-869-3520

Public relations, telecommunications, journalism, organizational communications

California State University
Chico, CA 95929
916-895-4015

News-editorial, public relations, speech communication, organizational communication

California State University
Dominguez Hills
Carson, CA 90747
310-516-3313

Journalism, television studies, public relations, advertising

California State University[*]
Fresno, CA 93740-0010
209-278-2087

News-editorial, radio-TV news communications, photocommunications, advertising, public relations

California State University[*]
Fullerton, CA 92634-9480
714-773-3517

Journalism, public relations, advertising, photocommunications, TV-film

California State University
Hayward, CA 94542
510-881-3292

Mass communications, advertising, communication skills, photography

California State University[*]
Long Beach, CA 90840
301-985-4981

News-editorial, magazine journalism, broadcast journalism, public relations, journalism, photojournalism, secondary school teaching

California State University
Los Angeles, CA 90032
213-343-4200

Broadcast journalism, news-editorial, public relations, advertising

California State University[*]
Northridge, CA 91330
818-885-3135

News-editorial

California State University
Sacramento, CA 95819-2694
916-278-6353

Journalism, government-journalism

Humboldt State University[*]
Arcata, CA 95521
707-826-4475

News-editorial, public relations, broadcast news, media studies

Menlo College
1000 El Camino Real
Atherton, CA 94027-4185
415-323-6141

Corporate media, print and broadcast journalism, creative expression

Pacific Union College
Angwin, CA 94508
707-965-6437

News-editorial, communications, international communications, public relations, magazine, broadast

Pepperdine University Seaver College
Malibu, CA 90263
310-456-4211

Journalism (news-editorial), advertising, public relations, telecommunications (production, news and management), broadcast

Point Loma Nazarene College
San Diego, CA 92106
619-221-2200, 2260

Newspaper, magazine, broadcast journalism, linguistics, communications

Saint Mary's College of California
Moraga, CA 94575
510-631-4000

Communications theory, audio, video and print media

San Diego State University[*]
San Diego, CA 92182
619-265-6635

News-editorial, advertising, radio-TV news, public relations

San Francisco State University[*]
1600 Hollowsy Avenue
San Francisco, CA 94132
415-338-1689

News-editorial, photojournalism, magazine journalism

San Jose State University[*]
San Jose, CA 95192-0055
408-924-3240

Journalism, advertising, public relations (undergraduate), mass communications (graduate)

Santa Clara University
Santa Clara, CA 95053-2999
408-554-2798

News-editorial, broadcast production, communication

Stanford University
Stanford, CA 94305
415-723-1941

Communications (undergraduate), journalism (masters), documentary film production (masters), communications research (doctorate)
Courses in publishing

University of California[*]
121 North Gate Hall
Berkeley, CA 94720
510-642-3383

Graduate programs in news-editorial and television news, radio news

University of La Verne
La Verne, CA 91750
714-593-3511

Broadcast news, photography, news-editorial

University of the Pacific
Stockton, CA 95211
209-946-2505

Communication studies, public relations, and organizational communication and media studies

University of San Francisco
San Francisco, CA 94117-1080
415-666-6680

Broadcasting, news-editorial

University of Southern California[*]
University Park
Los Angeles, CA 90089-1695
213-740-3914

Broadcasting, print journalism, public relations

COLORADO

Adams State College
Alamosa, CO 81101
303-589-7427

News-editorial

Colorado State University[*]
Fort Collins, CO 80523
303-491-6310

News-editorial, public relations, electronic reporting, agricultural/natural resources journalism, technical-specialized

Mesa State College
Grand Junction, CO 81502
303-248-1687

Print media, news-editorial, public relations, radio/TV

Metropolitan State College of Denver
Box 173362
Denver, CO 80217-3362

Hands-on approach to reporting and editing; journalism department sponsors an internship newspaper that covers the Colorado legislature

University of Colorado[*]
Campus Box 287
Boulder, CO 80309
303-492-4364

News-editorial, advertising journalism, broadcast news, broadcast production management, radio-television

University of Denver
Denver, CO 80208
303-871-2166

Communications, journalism studies, mass communications

University of Northern Colorado
Greeley, CO 80639
303-351-2726

Telecommunications, news-editorial, advertising, public relations

University of Southern Colorado
Pueblo, CO 81001
719-549-2824, 2835

News-editorial, public relations, advertising, telecommunications

CONNECTICUT

Southern Connecticut State University
New Haven, CT 06515
203-397-4311

News-editorial, magazine, broadcast journalism, public relations

University of Bridgeport
Bridgeport, CT 06601
203-576-4128

News-editorial, advertising, communication studies

University of Connecticut
Storrs, CT 06268
203-486-4221

Journalism (news-editorial)
Courses in publishing

University of Hartford
West Hartford, CT 06117
203 768-4633

Communications, journalism, mass communications

University of New Haven
West Haven, CT 06516
203-932-7208

Journalism, public relations, managerial and organizational communications, international business, marketing, mass communications (TV, radio, film)

DELAWARE

University of Delaware
Newark, DE 19716
302-451-2361

News writing, opinion writing, and copy editing-layout courses; internships with newspapers, magazines, electronic media, and public relations offices

DISTRICT OF COLUMBIA

American University[*]
Washington, DC 20016-8017
202-885-2058

Print journalism, broadcast journalism, public communications, visual media

Graduate programs in journalism and public affairs (broadcast or print), film and video, public communications

George Washington University
Washington, DC 20052
202-994-6227

News-editorial

Howard University*
Washington, DC 20059
202-806-7855

Broadcast journalism, news-editorial, public relations, advertising

FLORIDA

Edward Waters College
Jacksonville, FL 32218
Radio/TV, journalism

Florida A&M University*
Tallahassee, FL 32307
904-599-3718

Newspaper journalism, broadcast journalism, magazine journalism, public relations, photography and graphic design, printing production, printing management

Florida International University*
North Miami, FL 33181
305-940-5625

Public relations, advertising, journalism (print and broadcast)

Florida Southern College
Lakeland, FL 33801-5698
813-680-4168

Journalism, public relations, advertising

Jacksonville University
Jacksonville, FL 32211
904-744-3950

Newspapers, magazine, public relations, advertising, radio/TV/film

University of Central Florida
Orlando, FL 32816
407-823-2681

News-editorial, radio-TV, advertising/public relations

University of Florida*
Gainesville, FL 32611-2084
904-392-0466

News-editorial, public relations, magazines, technical communications, photo-journalism, advertising, telecommunications

University of Miami*
Coral Gables, FL 33124-2030
305-284-2265

Advertising, public relations, journalism, motion pictures, video/film, speech communication, organizational communication, broadcasting

University of North Florida
Jacksonville, FL 32216
904-6446-2650

News-editorial, advertising, public relations, broadcasting, visual arts

University of South Florida*
Tampa, FL 33620
813-974-2591

Visual communications, public relations, news-editorial, advertising, magazine journalism, telecommunication

University of West Florida*
11000 University Parkway
Pensacola, FL 32514-5751
904-474-2874

News-editorial, public relations/advertising, broadcast journalism, radio-television-film, graduate program in mass communication

GEORGIA

Berry College
5022 Berry College
Mt. Berry, GA 30149-5022
404-232-5374

Journalism, public relations, speech-broadcasting

Brenau College
Gainesville, GA 30501
404-534-6179

Public relations, journalism, electronic media, business communications, broadcast news

Clark/Atlanta University
Atlanta, GA 30314
404-880-8304

Radio-film-TV, journalism, public relations

Georgia Southern College
Statesboro, GA 30460
912-681-5138

Public relations, journalism, broadcasting (radio-television-film), speech and theatre

Georgia Southern University
Statesboro, GA 30460
912-681-5138

Journalism, broadcasting, public relations, speech

Georgia State University
Atlanta, GA 30303
404-651-3200

Broadcast news, broadcast production, print, public relations, film and video, theater, speech

University of Georgia
Athens, GA 30602
706-542-1704

Advertising, public relations, journalism, telecommunications

HAWAII

University of Hawaii at Manoa*
Honolulu, HI 96822
808-956-8881

Public relations, news-editorial, broadcast journalism

IDAHO

Boise State University
Boise, ID 83725
208-385-3320

Mass communications (general), journalism (general)

Idaho State University
Pocatello, ID 83209
208-236-3295

Media studies, television, photography, journalism, advertising, public relations

University of Idaho
Moscow, ID 83844-1072
208-885-6458

News-editorial, advertising, public relations, radio-television news

ILLINOIS

Bradley University
Peoria, IL 61625
309-677-2354

Radio-video-photo, speech, public relations/advertising, news

College of Street Francis
Joliet, IL 60435
815-740-3696

News-editorial, advertising/public relations, broadcasting/graphic design

Columbia College Chicago
Chicago, IL 60605
312-633-1600

News-editorial, magazine editing, broadcast journalism

DePaul University
Chicago, Il 60614
312-362-6881

Journalism, radio, advertising, public relations, film studies

Eastern Illinois University[*]
Charleston, IL 61920
217-581-6003

News-editorial

Illinois State University
Normal, IL 61701
309-438-3671

Public relations, journalism, broadcasting, graphics, journalism education

Loyola University of Chicago
Chicago, IL 60611
312-915-6548

Journalism, mass communication

Northern Illinois University[*]
De Kalb, IL 60115
815-753-1925

Journalism (news-editorial, public relations, photojournalism, broadcast news)

Northwestern University[*]
Fisk Hall
Evanston, IL 60208
708-467-1882

News-editorial (undergraduate), magazine journalism, advertising, TV news, corporate public relations, direct marketing (graduate)

Roosevelt University
Chicago, IL 60605
312-341-3815

Broadcast journalism, news-editorial, public relations, marketing communications

Southern Illinois University[*]
Carbondale, IL 62901
618-536-3361

News-editorial, advertising

Southern Illinois University
Edwardsville, IL 62026
618-692-2230

Journalism, television and radio (general)

University of Illinois[*]
Urbana, IL 61801
217-333-2350

News-editorial, broadcast news, media studies, advertising

Western Illinois University
Macomb, IL 61455
309-298-1424

News-editorial, advertising, public relations

INDIANA

Anderson University
Anderson, IN 46012
317-641-4340

News-editorial, public relations, broadcasting

Ball State University[*]
Muncie, IN 47306
317-285-8200

Public relations, news-editorial, newspaper, photojournalism, magazine journalism, secondary school journalism

Butler University
Indianapolis, IN 46208
317-283-9357

News-editorial, public relations, advertising

Calumet College of Saint Joseph
Whiting, IN 46394
291-473 7770

News-editorial

De Pauw University
Greencastle, IN 46135
317-658-4473, 4495

Print journalism

Franklin College
Franklin, IN 46131
317-736-8200

News-editorial, broadcasting, advertising-public relations

Goshen College
Goshen, IN 46526-4798
219-535-7587

Broadcasting, journalism, public relations, photography, film

Indiana State University
Terre Haute, IN 47809
812-237-3217

News-editorial, photojournalism, magazine journalism

Indiana University[*]
Bloomington, IN 47405
812-855-9247

News-editorial, broadcast news, photojournalism, public relations, advertising, magazine journalism,

education, professional graduate, media management

Indiana University
Indianapolis, IN 46223
317-274-2773

News-editorial, magazine journalism, public relations, advertising

Purdue University
West Lafayette, IN 47907
317-494-3429

Mass communications, journalism, public relations, telecommunication, advertising, graduate program

Street Mary-of-the-Woods College
Street Mary-of-the-Woods, IN 47876
812-535-5209

News-editorial, public relations/advertising, secondary education

University of Evansille
Evansville, IN 47722
812-479-2377

News-editorial, advertising, public relations, telecommunications, broadcast journalism

Valparaiso University
Valparaiso, IN 46383
219-461 5271

Print journalism, public relations, broadcast journalism,

Vincennes University
Vincennes, IN 47591-5201
812-885-4551, 4554

News-editorial, print media advertising

IOWA

Drake University[*]
Des Moines, IA 50311
515-271-3194

News-editorial, broadcast sales and management, broadcast news, high school journalism teaching, radio-television, magazine journalism, public relations, advertising

Grand View College
Des Moines, IA 50316
515-263-2931

Journalism, radio-TV, mass communications

Iowa State University[*]
Ames, IA 50011
515-294-4340

News-editorial, advertising, magazine journalism, public relations, electronic media studies, corporate communications, science communication, visual communications

Marycrest College
Davenport, IA 52804
319-326-9343

Newspaper/magazine journalism, radio/television/public relations, advertising, organizational communications management, organizational communications

University of Iowa[*]
Iowa City, IA 52242
319-335-5821

News-editorial, mass communications laboratory, mass communications inquiry
Courses in publishing

KANSAS

Fort Hays State University
Hays, KS 67601
913-628-4411

Public relations/advertising, news-editorial, mass communications, photography, radio-television-film, desk top publishing

Kansas State University[*]
Manhattan, KS 66506
913-532-6890

News-editorial, advertising, public relations, radio-television

Pittsburg State University
PIttsburg, KS 66762
316-235-4715

Public relations, advertising, communication studies, communication education, radio and television, theatre, journalism

Street Mary-of-the-Plains College
Dodge City, KS 67801
316-225-4171

News-editorial, broadcasting

University of Kansas[*]
Lawrence, KS 66045
913-864-4755

News-editorial (community journalism, newspaper journalism, photojournalism, business communications, advertising, magazine journalism, radio-TV)
Courses in publishing

Washburn University
Topeka, KS 66621
913-295-6380

Electronic/print journalism, public relations, broadcasting, organizational communications
Courses in publishing

Wichita State University
Wichita, KS 67260
316-689-3185

Journalism, advertising-public relations, broadcasting, speech communications

KENTUCKY

Eastern Kentucky University
Richmond, KY 40475
606-622-1871

Broadcasting, news-editorial, public relations

Morehead State University
Morehead, KY 40351
606-783-2694

News-editorial, advertising-public relations, photojournalism, community newspapering, journalism education

Murray State University[*]
Box 2456
University Station
Murray, KY 42071
502-762-2387

News-editorial, public relations, radio-TV, advertising

Northern Kentucky University
Highland Heights, KY 41706
606-572-5435

News-editorial, organizational communications, radio/TV, advertising, public relations, photojournalism

University of Kentucky
Lexington, KY 40506
606-257-7811

General editorial, communications, advertising-public relations

Western Kentucky University[*]
Bowling Green, KY 42101
502-745-4143

News-editorial, advertising, public relations, photojournalism, journalism education

LOUISIANA

Grambling State University[*]
Grambling, LA 71245
318-247-2403

News-editorial, technical communication, visual

communications, public relations, broadcasting

Louisiana State University[*]
Baton Rouge, LA 70803-7202
504-388-2336

Journalism, political communication, public relations, advertising, telecommunication

Louisiana Tech University
Ruston, LA 71272
318-257-4427

News-editorial

Loyola University
New Orleans, LA 70118
504-865-3430

News-editorial, film studies, photojournalism, public relations, advertising, broadcasting (news, production), communications studies

Nicholls State University
Thibodaux, LA 70310
504-448-4586

Print journalism, broadcasting, public relations

Northeast Louisiana University
Monroe, LA 71209-0320
318-342-2144

News-editorial, public relations, photojournalism, broadcast news, filmmaking, radio-TV-film

Northwestern State University of Louisiana
Nachitoches, LA 71497
318-357-5213 or 357-6272

Broadcast journalism, news-editorial, public relations

Southeastern Louisiana University
Hammond, LA 70402
504-549-5021

Print journalism

University of Southwestern Louisiana
Lafayette, LA 70506-3650
318-231-6103

Print journalism, radio-TV, public relations, media advertising, interpersonal and public communications

MAINE

University of Maine
Orono, ME 04469-5743
207-581-1283

News-editorial, advertising, broadcast news, broadcasting, mass communication

MARYLAND

Bowie State University
Bowie, MD 20715
301-405-2379

News-editorial, advertising, public relations, broadcasting

University of Maryland*
College Park, MD 20742
301-405-2383

News-editorial (news, magazine, and public relations, advertising, broadcast news

MASSACHUSETTS

Boston University
Boston, MA 02215
617-353-3450

News-editorial, photojournalism, broadcast journalism, magazine, film, advertising/public relations, mass communications. Also. graduate studies

Emerson College
Boston, MA 02116
617-578-8800

Video, film, audio, print and broadcast journalism

Simmons College
Boston, MA 02115
617-521-2838

Communications, graphic design, advertising, public relations, writing for news media
Courses in publishing

Suffolk University
Boston, MA 02114
617-573-8000

Public relations, print media, broadcast media, film communications, law

University of Massachusetts
Amherst, MA 01003
413-545-1376

News-editorial

MICHIGAN

Central Michigan University
Mt. Pleasant, MI 48859
517-774-3196

Advertising, news-editorial, photojournalism, public relations

Eastern Michigan University
Ypsilanti, MI 48197-2210
313-591-7556

News-editorial, public relations, magazine, television, photography, advertising.

Madonna College
Livonia, MI 48150
313-591-5064

News-editorial, public relations, communications arts, video communications

Michigan State University*
East Lansing, MI 48824-1212
517-355-1520

News-editorial, public relations, radio-TV news, photojournalism, magazine

Oakland University
Rochester, MI 48309
313-3700-4120

News-editorial, public relations, advertising, broadcasting

University of Michigan
Ann Arbor, MI 48109-1285
313-764-0420

News editorial, newspapers, magazines, visual journalism, journalism education, broadcast news

Wayne State University
Detroit, MI 48202
313-577-2627

News-editorial, radio-TV, public relations-advertising

MINNESOTA

Bemidji State University
Bemidji, MN 56601-2699
218-755-2915

Broadcast, public relations, journalism

Mankato State University
Mankato, MN 56002-8400
507-389-6417

News-editorial, public relations

Moorhead State University
Moorhead, MN 56563
218-236-2983/2984

Advertising, broadcast journalism, print journalism, public relations, English/mass communications, photojournalism

Street Cloud State University*
Street Cloud, MN 56301
612-255-3293

Advertising, news-editorial, broadcasting, public relations

Street Mary's College
Winona, MN 55987
507-452-4430

Journalism, public relations, broadcasting

University of Minnesota*
Minneapolis, MN 55455-0418
612-625-9824

News-editorial, advertising, broadcast journalism, visual communications

Winona State University
Winona, MN 55987
507-457-5474

Advertising, broadcasting, journalism, photojournalism, public relations

MISSISSIPPI

Jackson State University*
Jackson, MS 39127
601-968-2151

News-editorial, news-editorial and public relations, advertising, broadcast production, broadcast journalism

Mississippi State University
Mississippi State, MS 38677
601-232-7147

Print journalism, radio-TV, public relations, magazine, advertising

Mississippi University for Women
Columbus, MS 39701
601-329-7249

Journalism (general), broadcasting, broadcast journalism

Rust College
Holly Springs, MS 38635-2328
601-252-4661

Journalism (general), mass communications (general), radio/TV, recording, public relations, advertising

Tougaloo College
Tougaloo, MS 39174
601-977-7747

Journalism (general)

University of Mississippi*
University, MS 38677
601-232-7147

Advertising, print, radio/TV, public relations, magazine .

University of Southern Mississippi*
Hattiesburg, MS 39406-5121
601-266-4258

News-editorial, public relations, photojournalism, advertising, broadcast journalism, film, radio/TV, speech communication, speech communication education, organizational communication

MISSOURI

Central Missouri State University
Warrensburg, MO 64093
816-543-4840

Broadcasting and film, journalism (news-editorial), mass communications, public relations

Culver-Stockton College
Canton, MO 63435
314-288-5221 ext. 382

Journalism (print), public relations, interpersonal communication

Evangel College
Springfield, MO 65802
417-865-2815

Broadcasting, journalism

Lincoln University
Jefferson City, MO 65101
314-681-5437

News-editorial, advertising/public relations, journalism

Lindenwood College
Street Charles, MO 63301
314-949-4835

Mass communications, (journalism, public relations, radio-TV), corporate communications

Northeast Missouri State University
Kirksville, MO 63501
816-785-4000 ext. 4481

Journalism, speech communication

Northwest Missouri State University
Maryville, MO 64468
816-562-1617

Broadcast journalism, media advertising, public relations, print journalism, mass media

Southeast Missouri State University
Cape Girardeau, MO 63701
314-651-2241

News-editorial, corporate video, radio, advertising, public relations, media studies, journalism education, community journalism

Stephens College
Columbia, MO 65215
314-872-7104

Broadcasting, public relations, journalism, communications studies

University of Missouri*
Columbia, MO 65205
314-882-4821

News-editorial, advertising, magazine, broadcast news, photojournalism, graduate professional program

Webster University
Webster Grove, MO 63119
314-986-6975

News-editorial, media communications, broadcast journalism, photography, public communications, video/film, media communications (graduate), print, photojournalism, audio recording, video, radio cable

MONTANA

University of Montana*
Missoula, MT 59812
406-243-4001

News-editorial, radio-TV (general)

NEBRASKA

Creighton State University
Omaha, NB 68178-0119
402-280-2825

News-editorial, broadcasting, advertising, public relations

Hastings College
Hastings, NB 68902
402-461-7460

Writing, news-editorial, advertising, public relations, theatre and film, speech, broadcasting, communications management

Midland Lutheran College
Fremont, NB 68025
402-721-5480 ext. 5078

News-editorial, photography, public relations/advertising, broadcasting

University of Nebraska*
Lincoln, NB 68588-0127
402-472-3044

Advertising, news-editorial, radio-TV (general), graduate professional program

University of Nebraska
Omaha, NB 68182
402-554-2600

News-editorial, broadcasting, public relations, advertising

University of Nebraska-Kearney
Kearney, NB 68849
308-234-8249

News-editorial, advertising, public relations, journalism education

NEVADA

University of Nevada
Las Vegas, NV 89154
702-895-3325

Broadcasting, communications theory, journalism, public relations, rhetoric, advertising, telecommunications

University of Nevada*
Reno, NV 89557-0040
702-784-6531

News-editorial, public relations, advertising, broadcast journalism

NEW HAMPSHIRE

Keene State College of the University System of New Hampshire
Keene, NH 03431
603-352-1909 ext. 224

Print journalism, broadcast media

NEW JERSEY

Glassboro State College
Glassboro, NJ 08028
609-863-7186 or 7187

News-editorial, advertising, public relations, radio/TV/film

Rider College
Lawrenceville, NJ 08648
609-896-5089

Journalism, public relations, communications, radio-TV, business and professional communications, news/editorial, public relations

Rutgers, The State University of New Jersey
New Brunswick, NJ 08903
908-932-8567

News-editorial, broadcast journalism, environmental and technical writing, mass media and government, advertising, magazine journalism

Rutgers, The State University of New Jersey
Newark, NJ 07102
201-648-5431 or 648-1107

Print journalism, photo journalism, public relations, broadcast journalism

Seton Hall University
South Orange, NJ 07079
201-761-9474

News-editorial, public
relations/advertising,
communication/computer graphics,
broadcast/film, theatre/speech, print
graphics

NEW MEXICO

Eastern New Mexico University
Portales, NM 88130
505-562-2130

News-editorial, radio-TV, public
relations, speech communications,
journalism

New Mexico Highlands University
Las Vegas, NM 87701
505-425-7511

Print media, broadcast production,
news-editorial

New Mexico State University
Las Cruces, NM 88003
505-426-1034

Journalism/public relations,
advertising, broadcasting

University of New Mexico*
Albuquerque, NM 87131-1171
505-277-5305

News-editorial, print media, broadcast
journalism, broadcast/cable
management, public relations

NEW YORK

Canisius College
Buffalo, NY 14208
716-883-7000

Print and broadcast journalism,
telecommunication, organizational
communication (advertising and public
relations) and
interpersonal/intercultural
communication

**College of White Plains Pace
University**
White Plains, NY 10603
914-422-4134

Print journalism, broadcast journalism,
publishing (graduate), photography

Columbia University* (graduate only)
New York, NY 10027
212-854-4150

News-editorial, broadcast

Cornell University
Ithaca, NY 14853
607-255-2111

Public communications, publications,
interpersonal communications,
communication planning/strategy

Fordham University
Bronx, NY 10458
212-579-2533

Print journalism, radio-TV (news),
media and society, communication
theory and practice

Hofstra University
Hempstead, NY 11550
516-463-5424

Print journalism, electronic journalism,
TV production, radio production,
broadcasting, film, general
communications studies

Iona College
New Rochelle, NY 10801
914-633-2230

Journalism, advertising, public
relations, film, broadcast

Ithaca College
Ithaca, NY 14850
609-274-3895

TV-radio, journalism, media studies,
corporate communications,
telecommunication, management,
cinema and photography

**Long Island University—Brooklyn
Campus**
University Plaza, Brooklyn, NY
11201-9926
718-403-1053

News-editorial (magazine journalism,
advertising, public relations, mass
media emphasis), radio/TV

Marist College
Poughkeepsie, NY 12601
914-575-3650

New York University*
10 Washington Place
New York, NY 10003
212-998-7980

News-editorial, broadcast news,
magazine journalism, public relations,
media criticism

Niagara University
Niagara University, NY 14109
716-286-8576

Print journalism, radio/TV,
communication studies,

photography/filmmaking, art and
history of cinema

Street Bonaventure University
Street Bonaventure, NY 14778
716-375-2520

News-editorial

Street John Fisher College
Rochester, NY 14618
716-385-8191

Print journalism, advertising/public
relations, broadcasting,
communications

State University College at Buffalo
Buffalo, NY 14222
716-878-6008

News-editorial, public relations,
broadcasting (general), advertising
Courses in publishing

SUNY College at New Paltz
New Paltz, NY 12561
914-257-2743

News writing, public affairs, feature
writing, copyediting, photojournalism,
mass media law, ethics, press history,
literary journalism

Syracuse University
Syracuse, NY 13244-2100
315-443-2301

Newspaper, advertising, broadcast
journalism, magazine journalism,
public relations, photojournalism,
TV-radio-film management,
TV-radio-film writing, TV-radio-film
production, illustration, photography
Courses in publishing

Utica College of Syracuse University
Utica, NY 13502
315-792-3093

Journalism public relations,
journalism/public relations

NORTH CAROLINA

Johnson C. Smith University
Charlotte, NC 28216
704-378-1062

Publishing and graphic arts (print),
public relations and organizational
communications, telecommunications,
journalism

University of North Carolina
Asheville, NC 28804
704-251-6227

Mass communications (general),
broadcasting, print journalism
Courses in publishing

University of North Carolina*
Chapel Hill, NC 27599-3365
919-962-1204

News-editorial, advertising, broadcast journalism, public relations, visual communications, graduate news-editorial

NORTH DAKOTA

North Dakota State University
Fargo, ND 58105-5075
701-237-7784

Print, broadcast, public relations

University of North Dakota
Grand Forks, ND 58202
701-777-2159

Journalism, advertising, public relations, broadcasting, speech

OHIO

Bowling Green State University*
Bowling Green, OH 43403
419-372-2076

News-editorial, public relations, magazine journalism, photojournalism, broadcast journalism

Kent State University*
Kent, OH 44242
216-672-2572

News-editorial, broadcast news, advertising, public relations, photo journalism, radio/TV
Courses in publishing

Ohio State University*
Columbus, OH 43210-1107
614-292-6291

Advertising, broadcasting, news-editorial, public relations

Ohio University*
Athens, OH 45701
614-593-2590

Advertising, magazine, newswriting and editing, public relations, broadcast news

University of Toledo
Toledo, OH 43606
419-537-2005

Broadcasting, print media, public relations

OKLAHOMA

Central State University
Edmond, OK 73034
405-341-2980 ext. 5122

Newspaper, photographic arts, public relations, education, professional writing, magazines, advertising, journalism (general), business journalism

East Central University
Ada, OK 74820-6899
405-332-8000 ext. 482

News-editorial, radio-TV, advertising/public relations, electronic and print media

Northeastern Oklahoma State University
Tahlequah, OK 74464
918-456-5511 ext. 2891

News-editorial, broadcasting, advertising-public relations, photojournalism, education (teaching)

Oklahoma Baptist University
Shawnee, OK 74801
405-275-2850

News-editorial, public relations, broadcast news

Oklahoma City University
Oklahoma City, OK 73116
405-521-5252

News-editorial, advertising-public relations, radio-TV, magazine journalism, media management

Oklahoma State University*
Stillwater, OK 74078
405-744-7936

News-editorial, photojournalism, radio-TV advertising, public relations, advertising broadcasting, agricultural communications, teacher certification

University of Oklahoma*
Norman, OK 73019
405-325-2721

Advertising, news-communication, professional writing, public relations, broadcasting, and electronic media

OREGON

Southern Oregon State College
Ashland, OR 97520
503-552-6674

Print journalism, broadcasting, public relations, photojournalism, sports information, secondary teaching

University of Oregon*
Eugene, OR 97403-1275
503-346-0895

News-editorial, advertising, radio-TV news, public relations, magazine

journalism, communications studies, electronic media
Courses in publishing

PENNSYLVANIA

Bloomsburg University of Pennsylvania
Bloomsburg, PA 17815
717-389-4633

News-editorial, broadcast production, magazine journalism, public relations, advertising, telecommunications

Duquesne University
Pittsburgh, PA 15282
412-396-6460

News-editorial, broadcast news, advertising, public relations, magazine, photojournalism, communications, corporate communications, media studies, organizational communication, print journalism

Indiana University of Pennsylvania
Indiana, PA 15705
412-357-4411

News-editorial, public relations

Lehigh University
Bethlehem, PA 18015
215-758-4180

News-editorial, science writing, public relations

Pennsylvania State University*
201 Carnegie Bldg.
University Park, PA 16802
814-863-1484

Journalism, advertising, broadcast/cable, film and video, mass communications

Point Park College
Pittsburgh, PA 15222
412-392-4730

News-editorial, broadcast media, advertising, public relations, photojournalism, journalism and communications/secondary education (undergraduate), journalism and communication news—editorial, public relations, advertising (graduate)

Shippensburg University
Shippensburg, PA 17257
717-532-1521

News-editorial, radio/TV, public relations

Temple University*
Philadelphia, PA 19122
215-204-7433

News-editorial, advertising, public relations, magazine journalism, photography, mass media
Courses in publishing

RHODE ISLAND

University of Rhode Island
Kingston, R.I. 02881
401-792-2195/792-2196

News-editorial, radio-TV, journalism, public relations

SOUTH CAROLINA

Benedict College
Columbia, SC 29204
803-256-4220

News-editorial, broadcasting, public communications/marketing

University of South Carolina*
Columbia, SC 29208
803-777-4102

News-editorial (newspaper, photojournalism), advertising/public relations (management, creative advertising), broadcasting (radio-TV), electronic and print journalism

SOUTH DAKOTA

Black Hills State University
Spearfish, SD 57783
605-642-6861/642-6420

Journalism (general), broadcasting

South Dakota State University*
Brookings, SD 57007
605-688-4171

News-editorial, broadcast journalism, advertising, science and technical writing, agricultural journalism, journalism

TENNESSEE

East Tennessee State University*
Johnson City, TN 37614
615-929-4308

Journalism, public relations/advertising, broadcasting

Memphis State University*
Memphis, TN 38152
901-678-2401

News-editorial (magazine, newspaper and photojournalism), advertising, public relations, broadcast news

Middle Tennessee State University*
Murfreesboro, TN 37132
615-898-2813

Advertising/public relations, journalism, graphic communications, radio/TV, photography, recording industry management

Tennessee Technological University
Cookeville, TN 38505
615-372-3060

News-editorial, technical communications, radio/TV

University of Tennessee
Chattanooga, TN 37403
615-755-4400

News-editorial, broadcast journalism, broadcasting and electronic media, advertising, public relations

University of Tennessee*
Knoxville, TN 37996
615-974-3031

News-editorial, broadcast journalism, advertising, public relations, graduate professional program

University of Tennessee
Martin, TN 38238
901-587-7550

News-editorial, broadcasting (radio, broadcast news, TV production), public relations

TEXAS

Abilene Christian University
Abilene, TX 79699
915-674-2298

News-editorial, telecommunications, advertising, public relations, photojournalism, corporate video, religious journalism, broadcasting

Angelo State University
San Angelo, TX 76909
915-942-2031

News-editorial, advertising/public relations, broadcasting

Baylor University
Waco, TX 76798
817-755-3261

News-editorial, public relations, masters in international journalism

East Texas State University
Commerce, TX 75429
214-886-5239

News-editorial, photojournalism, advertising-public relations, secondary school, photography, printing

Hardin-Simmons University
Abilene, TX 79698
915-670-1409

Journalism, public relations

Midwestern State University
Wichita Falls, TX 76308-2099
817-689-4243

Journalism (print, advertising, public relations, radio-TV news, radio-TV production, photojournalism)

Prairie View A&M University
Prairie View, TX 77446-0156
409-857-2229

Journalism, radio-TV, speech communications, general communications

Sam Houston State University
Huntsville, TX 77341
409-294-1497

News-editorial, advertising, public relations.

Southern Methodist University
Dallas, TX 75275
214-768-3607

News-editorial, advertising management, public relations, broadcast news, TV-radio

Southwest Texas State University
San Marcos, TX 78666
512-245-2656

News-editorial, advertising, public relations, secondary school, broadcasting, magazine journalism, agriculture-journalism

Stephen F. Austin State University
Nacogdoches, TX 75962
409-568-4001

Photojournalism, public relations, speech, broadcasting, reporting and writing

Texas A&I University
Kingsville, TX 78363
512-595-3499

News-editorial, radio/TV

Texas A&M University*
College Station, TX 77843-4111
409-845-4611

Journalism, agricultural journalism

Texas Christian University*
Ft. Worth, TX 76129
817-921-7425

News-editorial, broadcast journalism, advertising/public relations, photojournalism, teaching certification, media studies

Texas Southern University
Houston, TX 77004
713-527-7360

News-editorial, advertising-public relations, broadcast journalism

Texas Tech University[*]
Lubbock, TX 79409
806-742-3385

News-editorial, advertising, telecommunications, public relations, photocommunications, broadcast journalism, corporate telecommunications, graduate professional program

Texas Wesleyan University
Ft. Worth, TX 76105-1536
817-531-4927

News-editorial, broadcasting, advertising-public relations

Texas Woman's University
Denton, TX 76204
817-898-2181

News-editorial, advertising, broadcast news, secondary education

Trinity University
San Antonio, TX 78212
210-736-8113

Communications (news-editorial, broadcasting)

University of Houston
Houston, TX 77204-3786
713-743-2867, 3002

News-editorial, radio-TV (general), advertising, corporate communications, organizational communication, editorial, media production, public relations, telecommunications

University of North Texas[*]
Denton, TX 76203-5278
917-565-2205

News-editorial, advertising, public relations, business journalism, photojournalism, teaching journalism, broadcast news

University of Texas-Arlington
Arlington, TX 76019
817-273-2163

News-editorial, advertising, public relations, photojournalism, radio-TV news, news and public affairs, communication theory

University of Texas-Austin[*]
Austin, TX 78712
512-471-1845

News-editorial, magazine journalism, public relations, photojournalism, radio-TV news

University of Texas-El Paso
El Paso, TX 79968-0639
925-747-5129

News-editorial, advertising, broadcast journalism, communication

University of Texas-Pan American
Edinburg, TX 78539
512-381-3583

Journalism (print, advertising, public relations, broadcasting)

West Texas State University
Canyon, TX 79017
806-656-2410

News-editorial, radio-TV news, journalism education, photojournalism, agricultural communications, advertising/public relations, electronic media

UTAH

Brigham Young University[*]
Room E509

Harris Fine Arts Center
Provo, UT 84602
801-378-2997
Journalism (print, advertising, public relations, radio-TV news, broadcast production), communications studies

University of Utah[*]
Salt Lake City, UT 84112
801-581-6888

News-editorial, public relations, broadcast journalism, telecommunications and film
Courses in publishing

Utah State University
Logan, UT 84322
801-750-3292

New-editorial, public relations, secondary school, broadcast journalism, photography, media management, radio/TV news

Weber State College
Ogden, UT 84408-1903
801-626-6426

News-editorial, broadcast, public relations

VERMONT

Street Michael's College
Colchester, VT 05439
802-654-2206, 2257

News-editorial, broadcast news, public relations/advertising

VIRGINIA

Emory & Henry College
Emory, VA 24327
703-944-4121

News-editorial, mass communications (general), journalism, public relations, advertising, broadcasting

Hampton University
Hampton, VA 23668
804-727-5405

News-editorial, broadcast, advertising-public relations, mass media comprehensive, cinema studies

James Madison University
Harrisonburg, VA 22807
703-568-7007

Journalism (news-editorial, magazine journalism, public information), public relations, telecommunications (production, management, electronic journalism, media studies), media production, corporate media, visval communications

Liberty University
Lynchburg, VA 24506
804-582-2128

News-editorial, advertising, public relations, magazine journalism, journalism graphics

Norfolk State University
Norfolk, VA 23504
804-683-8330

News-editorial, photojournalism, public relations, advertising

Radford University
Radford, VA 24142
703-831-5282

Journalism (news-editorial, public relations)

University of Richmond
Richmond, VA 23173
804-289-8324

News-editorial

Virginia Commonwealth University[*]
Richmond, VA 23284-2034
804-367-1260

News-editorial, broadcast news, advertising/public relations

Virginia Polytechnic Institute and State University
Blacksburg, VA 24061
703-231-7136

Journalism, broadcasting, public relations, speech communications, film

Virginia Union University
Richmond, VA 23220
804-257-5655

Journalism

Washington & Lee University*
Lexington, VA 24450
703-463-8432

News-editorial, radio-TV news, communications

WASHINGTON

Central Washington University
Ellensburg, WA 98926
509-963-1066

News-editorial, radio-TV, public relations

Gonzaga University
Spokane, WA 99258
509-328-4220 ext. 3253

News-editorial, broadcast studies, public relations
Specialties include reporting on religion, sports, and environmental, moral, and ethical topics.

Pacific Lutheran University
Tacoma, WA 98447
206-535-7762

Journalism, broadcast journalism, public relations, communications theory

Seattle University
Seattle, WA 98122
206-296-5340

News-editorial, public relations, communications studies, broadcast

University of Washington*
Seattle, WA 98195
206-543-2660

News-editorial, advertising, broadcast journalism, media studies, public relations

Walla Walla College
College Place, WA 99324
509-527-2832

Journalism, mass communications, broadcast/film

Washington State University
Pullman, WA 99164-2520
509-335-1556

Broadcasting, journalism, advertising, general communications, public relations, speech communication

WEST VIRGINIA

Bethany College
Bethany, WV 26032
304-829-7000

General mass communications (news-editorial, advertising, public relations, radio-TV)

Marshall University*
Huntington, WV 25755
304-696-2360

News-editorial, advertising, public relations, broadcast journalism, magazine journalism, journalism education

West Virginia University*
Morgantown, WV 26505-6010
304-293-3505

News-editorial, advertising, public relations, broadcast news

WISCONSIN

Marquette University*
Milwaukee, WI 53233
414-288-7133

News-editorial, advertising, broadcast and electronic communication, public relations, film

University of Wisconsin-Eau Claire*
Eau Claire, WI 54702-4004
715-836-2528

News-editorial, advertising, radio-TV, public relations

University of Wisconsin
La Crosse, WI 54601
608-785-8368

Mass communications

University of Wisconsin—Madison*
Madison, WI 53706
608-262-3690

Advertising, broadcast news, news editorial, public relations, mass communications
608-262-1464
Agricultural journalism, family and consumer communications, science reporting, natural resources/environment

University of Wisconsin—Milwaukee
Milwaukee, WI 53201
414-229-4436

Print journalism, broadcast journalism, telecommunications, public relations

University of Wisconsin*
Oshkosh, WI 54901
414-424-1042

News-editorial, advertising-public relations

University of Wisconsin*
River Falls, WI 54022
715-425-3169

News-editorial, broadcast journalism, agricultural journalism, secondary journalism education

University of Wisconsin
Whitewater, WI 53190
414-472-1634

News-editorial, broadcast journalism

WYOMING
University of Wyoming
Laramie, WY 82071
307-766-3122/6277

Print journalism, general communications, advertising, broadcasting, public relations

APPENDIX II
PROFESSIONAL, INDUSTRY, AND TRADE ASSOCIATIONS AND UNIONS

Note: Since many of these organizations operate on limited funds, please enclose a self-addressed, stamped envelope when querying for information.

Academic Collective Bargaining Information Service
1321 H Street NW, Suite MI
Washington, DC 20005
202-727-2326

The Academy of American Poets
584 Broadway
Suite 1208
New York, NY 10012
212-274-0343

Academy of Television Arts and Sciences
5220 Lankershim Boulevard
North Hollywood, CA 91601
818-754-2800

Advertising Club of New York
235 Park Avenue South, 6th floor
New York, NY 10003
212-533-8080

Advertising Women of New York
153 E. 57th Street
New York, NY 10022
212-593-1950

American Advertising Federation (AAF)
1101 Vermont Avenue NW, Suite 500
Washington, DC 20005
202-898-0089

American Association of Advertising Agencies
666 Third Avenue, 13th floor
New York, NY 10017
212-682-2500

American Association of Sunday and Feature Editors
11600 Sunrise Valley Drive
Reston, VA 22090
703-648-1286

American Association of University Professors
1012 14th Street, Suite 500
Washington, DC 20005
202-737-5900

American Black Book Writers Association
P.O. Box 10548
Marina del Rey, CA 90295
310-822-5195

American Book Producers Association
160 5th Avenue
Suite 604
New York, NY 10010-7000
212-645-2368

American Business Women's Association
Box 8728
9100 Ward Parkway
Kansas City, MO 64114
816-361-6621

American Federation of Government Employees (AFGE)
80 F Street NW
Washington, DC 20001
202-737-8700

American Federation of State, County and Municipal Employees (AFL-CIO)
1625 L Street NW
Washington, DC 20036
202-429-1000

American Federation of Teachers (AFL-CIO)
555 New Jersey Avenue NW
Washington, DC 20001
202-879-4400

American Federation of Television and Radio Artists (AFTRA)
260 Madison Avenue
New York, NY 10016
212-532-0800

American Guild of Authors and Composers
See Songwriters Guild of America

American Historical Association
400 A Street SE
Washington, DC 20003
202-544-2422

American Jewish Press Association
c/o Malcolm Rodman
11312 Old Club Road
Rockville, MD 20852

American Library Association (ALA)
50 East Huron Street
Chicago, IL 60611
312-944-6780

American Management Association
135 West 50th Street
New York, NY 10020
212-586-8100

American Medical Writers' Association
9650 Rockville Pike
Bethesda, MD 20814
301-493-0003

American Newspaper Publishers Association (ANPA)
See Newspaper
Association of America

American News Women's Club
1607 22nd Street NW
Washington, DC 20008
202-332-6770

American Society for Information Science
8720 Georgia Avenue
Suite 501
Silver Spring, MD 20910
301 495-0900

American Society of Business Press Editors
Box 390653
Cambridge, MA
02139-0008
508-528-6930

American Society of Composers, Authors and Publishers
1 Lincoln Plaza
New York, NY 10023
212-595-3050

American Society of Indexers
PO Box 386
Port Arkansas, TX 78373
512-997-0947

American Society of Journalists and Authors, Inc.
1501 Broadway
Suite 302
New York, NY 10036
212-997-0947

American Society of Magazine Editors
919 Third Avenue
New York, NY 10022
212-752-0055

American Society of Newspaper Editors (ASNE)
P.O. Box 4090
Reston, VA 22090-1700
703-648-1144

American Theatre Critics Association
c/o Clara Hieronymus
The Tennesean
2200 Hemingway Drive
Nashville, TN 37215
615-665-0595

American Women in Radio and Television, Inc. (AWRT)
1650 Tyson's Boulevard
Suite 200
McLean, VA 22102-3915
703-506-3290

American Writers Theatre Foundation
See Writers Theatre

Asian American Journalists Association
1765 Sutter Street
Suite 1000
San Francisco, CA 94115
415-346-2051

Associated Business Writers of America, Inc.
1450 South Havana Street
Suite 620
Aurora, CO 88012
303-751-7844

Associated Writing Programs
Old Dominion University
1411 W. 49th Street
Norfolk, VA 23508
804-683-3839

Association for Business Communication
College of Business
Department of Management
University of North Texas
Denton, TX 76203
817-565-4423

Association of American Advertising Agencies (AAAA)
666 Third Avenue
New York, NY 10017
212-682-2500

Association of American Publishers
71 Fifth Avenue
New York, NY 10003
212-255-0200

Association of Earth Science Editors
c/o Marla Adkins-Heljeson
Kansas Geological Survey
1930 Constant Avenue
Lawrence, KS 66047
913-864-3965

Association of Petroleum Writers
c/o Katherine Reese
Oil & Gas Journal
P.O. Box 1260
Tulsa, OK 74101
918-835-3161

The Authors Guild
See The Authors League of America, Inc.

The Authors League of America, Inc. (Includes The Authors Guild, Inc., and The Dramatists Guild, Inc.)
330 West 42nd Street
29th Floor
New York, NY 10036
212-564-8350

Aviation/Space Writers' Association
17 South High Street
Suite 1200
Columbus, OH 43215
614-221-1900

Broadcast Music, Inc. (BMI)
320 West 57th Street
New York, NY 10019
212-586-2000

Broadcast Promotion and Marketing Executives
6255 Sunset Boulevard #624
Los Angeles, CA 90028
213-465-3777

Business/Professional Advertising Association (BPAA)
100 Metroplex Drive
Edison, NJ 08817
201-985-4441

Committee of Small Magazine Editors & Publishers
See COSMEP

Computer Press Association
7000 Bianca Avenue
Van Nuys, CA 91406
818-996-1000

Construction Writers Association
c/o Marla McIntyre
P.O. Box 30
Aldie, VA 22001
703-771-4133

COSMEP, the International Association of Independent Publishers
Box 42073
San Francisco, CA 94101
415-922-9490

Council of Authors and Journalists
c/o Uncle Remus Regional System
1131 East Avenue
Madison, GA 30650
404-320-1076

Council of Biology Editors
1 Illinois Center, No. 200
111 East Wacker Drive
Chicago, IL 60601-4298
312-616-0800

Council of Writers Organizations
c/o WIW
220 Woodward Building
733 15th Street NW
Washington, DC 20005
202-347-4973

Dance Critics Association
PO Box 1882
Old Chelsea Station
New York, NY 10011
212-477-5457

The Dramatists Guild
See The Authors League of America, Inc.

Editorial Freelancers Association
P.O. Box 2050
Madison Square Station
New York, NY 10159
212-677-3357

Education Writers Association
1001 Connecticut Avenue W, Suite 310
Washington DC 20036
202-429-9680

Garden Writers Association of America
c/o Robert C. LaGasse
13542 Union Village Center
Clifton, VA 22024
703-222-2191

Greeting Card Association
1200 G Street NW
Suite 760
Washington, DC 20005
202-393-1778

Information Industry Association
559 New Jersey Avenue
Suite 800
Washington, DC 20001
(202) 629-8262

International Association of Business Communicators (IABC)
One Hallidie Plaza
Suite 600
San Francisco, CA 94102
415-433-3400

International Black Writers
P.O. Box 1030
Chicago, IL 60690
312-924-3818

International Newspaper Advertising and Marketing Executives
See Newspaper
Association of America

International Newspaper Marketing Association
12770 Merit Drive
Suite 330
Dallas, TX 75251
214-991-5900

International Newspaper Promotion Association
See International Newspaper Marketing Association

International Radio and Television Society (IRTS)
420 Lexington Avenue
New York, NY 10170
212-867-6650

International Society of Weekly Newspaper Editors
Department of Journalism
South Dakota
State University
Brookings, SD 57007-0596
605-688-4171

International Women's Writing Guild
Box 810
Gracie Station
New York, NY 10028
212-737-7536

Investigative Reporters and Editors University of Missouri
100 Neff Hall
Columbia, MO 65211
314-882-2042

Journalism Education Association
Kedzie Hall 104
Kansas State U.
Manhattan, KS 66506
913-532-5532

Kappa Tau Alpha
c/o Drive Keith P. Sanders
Box 838
School of Journalism
University of Missouri
Columbia, MO 65205
314-882-7685

Magazine Publishers Association
See Magazine Publishers of America

Magazine Publishers of America
919 Third Avenue
New York, NY 10022
212-752-0055

Manhattan Publishing Group
c/o Cheryl Joan Jenkins
842 Blake Avenue
Brooklyn, NY 11207
718-385-4945

Music Critics Association
7 Pine Court
Westfield, NJ 07090
908-233-8468

Mystery Writers of America, Inc.
17 East 47th Street, 6th Floor
New York, NY 10017
212-888-8171

National Academy of Songwriters
6381 Hollywood Boulevard, Suite 810
Hollywood, CA 90028
213-463-7178

National Academy of Television Arts and Sciences
110 West 57th Street, Suite 1020
New York, NY 10019
212-586-8424

National Association of Black Journalists
Box 4222
Reston, VA 22090
703-648-1270

National Association of Black Professors
Box 526
Chrisfield, MD 21817
410-968-2393

National Association of Broadcast Employees and Technicians (NABET)
501 Third Street NW Suite 880
Washington D.C. 20001
202-434-1254

National Association of Broadcasters (NAB)
1771 N Street NW
Washington, DC 20036
202-429-5300

National Association of Composers, USA
Box 49652, Barnington Station
Los Angeles CA 90049
213-541-8213

National Association of Farm Broadcasters (NAFB)
26 East Exchange Street No. 307
Street Paul MN 55101
612-224-0508

National Association of Government Communicators (NAGC)
669 South Washington Street
Alexandria, VA 22314
703-519-3902

National Association of Government Employees (NAGE)
2011 Crystal Drive, Suite 206
Arlington, VA 22202
703-979-0290

National Association of Hispanic Journalists
1193 National Press Building
Washington, DC 20045
202-662-7145

National Association of Media Women
1185 Niskey Lake Road SW
Atlanta, GA 30331
404-344-5862

National Association of Science Writers, Inc.
Box 294
Greenlawn, NY 11740
516-757-5664

National Black Public Relations Society
Address Unknown

National Book Critics Circle
Address Unknown

The National Broadcasting Society/Alpha Epsilon Rho
c/o Drive John Lopiccolo
College of Journalism
University of South Carolina
Columbia, SC 29208
803-777-3324

National Conference of Editorial Writers
6223 Executive Boulevard
Rockville, MD 20852
301-984-3015

National Education Association
1201 16th Street NW
Washington, DC 20036
202-833-4000

National Federation of Federal Employees
1016 16th Street NW
Washington, DC 20036
202-862-4400

National Federation of Press Women, Inc.
Box 99
Blue Springs, MO 64013
816-466-7200

National Newspaper Association
1525 Wilson Boulevard
Suite 550
Arlington, VA 22209
703-907-7900

National Newspaper Publishers Association
3200 13th Street NW
Washington, DC 20010
202-588-8764

National Press Club
National Press Building
529 14th Street NW
Washington, DC 20045
202-662-7500

National School of Public Relations Association
1501 Lee Highway
Arlington, VA 22209
703-528-5840

National Sportscasters and Sportswriters Association
Box 559
Salisbury, NC 28144
704-633-4275

National Turf Writers Association
1314 Bentwood Way
Louisville, KY 40223
502-245-3809

National Writers Club, Inc.
1450 South Havana
Suite 620
Aurora, CO 80012
303-751-7844

National Writers Union
873 Broadway, Suite 203
New York, NY 10003
212-254-0279

Newspaper Association of America
The Newspaper Center
11600 Sunrise Valley Drive
Reston, VA 22091
703-648-1000

The Newspaper Guild (AFL-CIO)
8611 Second Avenue
Silver Spring, MD 20910
301-585-2990

Organization of American Historians
Indiana University
112 North Bryan Street
Bloomington, IN 47401
812-855-7311

Outdoor Writers Association of America
2017 Cato Avenue
South College, PA 16801
814-234-1011

P.E.N. American Center
568 Broadway
New York, NY 10012
212-334-1660

The Poetry Society of America
15 Gramercy Park South
New York, NY 10003
212-254-9628

Poets & Writers, Inc.
72 Spring Street
New York, NY 10012
212-266-3586

The Public Relations Society of America, Inc. (PRSA)
33 Irving Place
New York, NY 10003-2376
212-460-1466

Public Relations Student Society of America
See PRSA above.

Publishers' Ad Club
See Publishers' Advertising and Marketing Association

Publishers' Advertising and Marketing Association
c/o Judy Polvay
The New Yorker
20 West 43rd Street
New York, NY 10036
212-536-5460

Publishers' Publicity Association
c/o Helene Atwan
Farrar, Straus and Giroux
19 Union Square West
New York, NY 10003

Quill and Scroll Society School of Journalism
University of Iowa
Iowa City, IA 52242
319-335-5795

Radio and Television Correspondents Association (RTCA)
Senate Radio-Television Gallery
U.S. Capitol
Room S-325
Washington, DC 20510
202-224-6421

Radio-Television News Directors Association (RTNDA)
1000 Connecticut Avenue NW
Suite 615
Washington, DC 20036
202-659-6510

Religion Newswriters Association
c/o Jim Jones
Fort Worth Star-Telegram
400 West 7th Street
Fort Worth, TX 76102

Romance Writers of America
13700 Veterans Memorial Drive
Suite 315
Houston, TX 77014
713-440-6885

Science Fiction Writers of America
See Science Fiction and Fantasy
Writers of America

Science Fiction and Fantasy Writers of America
5 Winding Brook Drive, No. 1B
Guilderland, NY
12084-9719

Small Press Writers and Artists Organization
c/o Audrey Parente
167 Fox Glen Court
Ormond Beach, FL 32174
904-672-3085

Society for Collegiate Journalists
1000 Turnpike
School of Journalism
Regent University
Virginia Beach, VA 23464
804-523-7091

Society for Scholarly Publishing
10200 West 44th Avenue, No. 304
Wheat Ridge, CO 80033
303-422-3914

Society for Technical Communication
901 North Stuart Street
Suite 904
Arlington, VA 22203-1854
703-522-4114

Society of American Archivists
600 S. Federal Street
Suite 504
Chicago, IL 60605
312-922-0140

Society of American Business Editors and Writers
100 Neff Hall
Univ. of Missouri
Columbia, MO 65211-0838
314-882-7862

Society of Architectural Historians
1232 Pine Street
Philadelphia, PA 19107
215-735-0224

Society of American Travel Writers
1155 Connecticut Avenue NW
Suite 500
Washington, DC 20036
202-429-6639

Society of Children's Book Writers
Box 66296
Los Angeles, CA 90066
818-347-2849

Society of Professional Journalists
16 South Jackson
Greeneastle, IN 46135
312-653-3333

Songwriters Guild of America
276 Fifth Avenue
New York, NY 10001
212-686-6820

Special Libraries Association
1700 18th Street NW
Washington, D.C. 20009
202-234-4700

Television Critics Association
c/o Art Chapman
Ft. Worth Star Telegram
400 W. 7th Street
Ft. Worth, TX 76102
817-390-7400

Textbook Authors Association
Box 535
Orange Springs, FL 32182-0535
904-546-5419

Western Writers of America
c/o Francis Fulgate
2800 North Campbell
El Paso, TX 79902

Women Executives in Public Relations
Box 609
Westport, CT 06881
203-226-4917

Women In Cable
c/o P.M. Haeger & Assocs.
500 N. Michigan Avenue
Suite 1400
Chicago, IL 60611
312-661-1700

Women In Communications, Inc. (WICI)
2101 Wilson Boulevard
Suite 417
Arlington, VA 22201
703-920-5555

Women In Scholarly Publishing
c/o Susan Schott
Univessity Press of Kansas
2501 West 15th Street
Lawreace, KS 66049-8350
913-864-4155

Women's National Book Association, Inc.
160 Fifth Avenue Room 604
New York, NY 10010
212-737-2934

Writers Alliance
Box 2014
Setauket, NY 11733
516-751-7080

Writers Guild of America, East, Inc.
555 West 57th Street
New York, NY 10019
212-767-7800

Writers Guild of America, West, Inc.
8955 Beverly Boulevard
Los Angeles, CA 90048
215-550-1000

Writers Theatre
145 West 46th Street
New York, NY 10036
212-869-9770

Writers Workshop
Box 69799
Los Angeles, CA 90069
213-933-9232

APPENDIX III
MAJOR TRADE PERIODICALS

The following are some of the principal trade publications serving writers in various fields. For information on additional publications, consult these reference books at your public library: *Directory of Publications* *and Broadcast Media, Literary Market Place, and Writer's Market*. In addition, most trade and professional associations and unions publish periodicals for their membership.

ACADEMIC, INSTITUTIONAL

The American Historical Review
American Historical Assn.
Indiana University
914 Atwater
Bloomington, IN 47405
812-855-7609

American Libraries
50 East Huron Street
Chicago, IL 60611
312-280-4216

School Library Journal
249 W. 17th Street
New York, NY 10017
212-463-6759

ADVERTISING, PUBLIC RELATIONS

Advertising Age
Crain Communications
220 E. 42nd Street
New York, NY 10017
212-210-0168

Adweek/East
BPI Communications, Inc.
1515 Broadway
New York, NY 14th Floor
10036
212-536-5336

American Advertising
American Advertising Federation
1400 K Street NW, Suite 1000
Washington, DC 20005
202-898-0089

The National Business Wire Newsletter
Business Wire
44 Montgomery Street
San Francisco, CA 94104
415-986-4422

Public Relations Journal
Public Relations Society of America
33 Irving Place

New York, NY 10003
212-460-1413

ENTERTAINMENT

Billboard
BPI Communications Inc.
1515 Broadway
New York, NY 10036
212-764-7300

Hollywood Reporter
5055 Wilshire Boulevard
6th Floor
Los Angeles, CA 90036-7171
213-525-2000

Show Biz News
The King Network
150 5th Avenue Suite 831
New York, NY 10011
212-645-8400

Variety
475 Park Avenue South
New York, NY 10016-6902
212-779-1100

JOURNALISM

American Journalism Review
4716 Pontiac Street, Suite 310
College Park, MD 20740-2493
301-513-0001

Columbia Journalism Review
700 Journalism Building
Columbia University
New York, NY 10027
212-854-1881

Editor & Publisher
11 West 19th Street
New York, NY 10011
212-675-4380

Presstime
Newspaper Association of America
The Newspaper Center
11600 Sunrise Valley Drive
Reston, VA 22091-1412
703-648-1000

Quill & Scroll
School of Journalism
University of Iowa
Iowa City, IA 52242
319-335-5795

Washington Journalism Review
See American Journalism Review

World Press Review
200 Madison Avenue
New York, NY 10016
212-889-5155

MAGAZINE AND BOOK PUBLISHING

Folio: The Magazine for Magazine Management
Cowles Business Media
911 Hope Street
P.O. Box 4949
Stamford, CT 06907-0949
203-358-9900

Magazine & Bookseller
North American Publishing Co.
322 8th Avenue, 18th Floor
New York, NY 10001
212-620-7330

Magazine Week
49 East 21st Street
New York, NY 10010
212-979-4600

Publishers Weekly
249 W. 17th Street
New York, NY 10011
212-463-6758

Small Press
Moyer Bell Ltd.
Kynbolde Way
Wakefield, RI 02879-1915
401-789-0074

Small Press Book Review
Box 176
Southport, CT 06490
203-268-4878

TECHNICAL WRITING

Technical Communication
Society for Technical Communication
901 North Stuart Street Suite 904
Arlington, VA 22203-1854
703-522-4114

Small Press Review
Box 100
Paradise, CA 95967
916-877-6110

WRITING, POETRY, DRAMA

The Drama Review
55 Hayward Street
Cambridge, MA 02142
617-253-2889

Poets & Writers Magazine
Poets & Writers Inc.
72 Spring Street
New York, NY 10012
212-226-3586

The Writer
120 Boylston Street
Boston, MA 02116
617-423-3157

Writer's Digest
1507 Dana Avenue
Cincinnati, OH 45207
513-531-2222

APPENDIX IV
BIBLIOGRAPHY

Accredited Journalism and Mass Communications Education 1993–94. Accrediting Council on Education in Journalism and Mass Communications.

Angelo, Jean Marie and Rachel Drucker. "Editors Report Stalled Earnings." *Folio,* Aug. 1, 1993, pp. 41–46.

Becker, Lee B. and Thomas E. Engelman. "Survey of Journalism and Mass Communications Graduates 1988: Summary Report July 1989" Columbus, Ohio: Ohio State University, and Princeton, NJ: Dow Jones Newspaper Fund. (For a copy, send $3.00 to the School of Journalism, The Ohio State University, 242 W. 18th Ave., Columbus, OH 43210.)

Becker, Lee B. and Gerald M. Kosicki. "Summary Results from the 1992 Annual Graduate Survey." Columbus, OH: Ohio State University.

Bly, Robert W. and Blake, Gary. *Dream Jobs: A Guide to Tomorrow's Top Careers.* New York: Wiley & Sons, 1983.

Bone, Jan. *Opportunities in Cable Television Careers.* Lincolnwood, IL: VGM Career Horizons, NTC Publishing Group, 1993.

Busnar, Gene. *Careers in Music.* New York: Julian Messmer, 1982.

Butler, Susan Lowell. "What's Ahead for Communicators in the 90s." *The Professional Communicator,* Spring 1990. pp. 16–17+.

Cassill, Kay. *The Complete Handbook for Freelance Writers.* Cincinnati, OH; Writer's Digest Books, 1981.

Changery, Christopher M. "Newspapers March to New Beats." *Presstime,* Sept. 1989, pp. 24–26.

Chepesiuk, Ron. "The CNN Library." *Library Journal,* Sept. 15, 1992, pp. 31–33.

Click. J.W. and Baird, Russell N. *Magazine Editing and Production.* Dubuque, IA: Wm. C. Brown, 1974.

Coleman, Lillian S. and Jennifer H. McGill. *Journalism and Mass Communication Directory,* Volume 11, 1993–1994. Columbia, SC: Association for Education in Journalism and Mass Communication.

Dodds, Robert H. *Writing for Technical and Business Magazines.* New York: John Wiley & Sons, Inc., 1969.

The Dow Jones Newspaper Fund, Inc. *1990 Journalism Career and Scholarship Guide.* Princeton, NJ: 1989.

Editors of Federal Jobs Digest. *Working for Your Uncle.* Ossining, NY: Breakthrough Publications, 1993.

Ferguson, Donald L. and Patten, Jim. *Opportunities in Journalism Careers.* Lincolnwood, IL: VGM Career Horizons, NTC Publishing Group, 1993.

Field, Shelly. *Career Opportunities in the Music Industry, 3rd ed.* New York: Facts On File, 1995.

Field. Syd. *The Screenwriter's Workbook.* New York: Dell, 1984.

Gerardi, Robert. *Opportunities in Music Careers.* Lincolnwood, IL: VGM Career Horizons, NTC Publishing Group, 1991.

Goeller, Carl. *Writing and Selling Greeting Cards.* Boston: The Writer, Inc., 1980.

Gould, Jay and Losano, Wayne. *Opportunities in Technical Communications.* Skokie, IL: VGM Career Horizons. National Textbook Co., 1980.

Groome, Harry C. Jr., *Opportunities in Advertising Careers.* Louisville, KY: Vocational Guidance Manuals, 1976.

Haas, Ken. *How to Get a Job in Advertising.* New York: Art Direction Book Co., 1979.

Haubenstock, Susan H. and David Joselit. *Career Oportunities in Art.* New York: Facts On File, 1988.

Heim, Kathleen and Myers, Margaret. *Opportunities in Library and Information Science Careers.* Lincolnwood, IL: VGM Career Horizons, NTC Publishing Group, 1992.

Heim, Kathleen and Peggy Sullivan. *Opportunities in Library and Information Science.* Skokie, IL: VGM Career Horizons, National Textbook Co., 1982.

Jerome, Judson. *The Poet's Handbook.* Cincinnati, OH: Writer's Digest Books, 1980.

Kissling, Mark. *1993 Writer's Market.* Cincinnati, OH; Writer's Digest Books, F & W Publications, 1992.

Krantz, Les. *The Jobs Rated Almanac.* New York, NY; World Almanac, Fharos Books, 1992.

Krefetz, Gerald and Philip Gittelman. *The Book of Incomes.* New York: Holt, Rinehart & Winston, 1981.

Johnson, Betty and Mary Esther Bullard Johnson. "Getting Ahead: A Profile of Black Media Managers." Published by the National Association of Black Journalists, Jan. 13, 1989.

Kamerman, *Book Reviewing.* Boston: The Writer, Inc., 1978.

Lafky, Sue A. "Economic Equity and the Journalistic Work Force." Talk given for the Association for Education in Journalism and Mass Communication at Portland, OR, July 2–5, 1988; published in Sept. 1988 *Presstime.*

Lane, Susan. *How to Make Money in Newspaper Syndication.* Irvine, CA; Newspaper Syndication Specialists, 1985. `

Lloyd, Wanda. "Newsroom Salaries." American Society of Newspaper Editors Bulletin, Nov. 1993, pp. 14–15.

Mainstream Access, Inc. *The Public Relations Job Finder.* Englewood Cliffs, NJ: Prentice-Hall, Inc., 1981.

Mainstream Access, Inc. *The Publishing Job Finder.* Englewood Cliffs, NJ: Prentice-Hall, Inc., 1981.

Mogel, Leonard. *Making It in the Media Professions.* Chester, CT: *The Globe Pequot Press,* 1988.

Morgan, Bradley J. *Advertising Career Directory.* Detroit, MI: Gale Research, Inc., 1993.

———. *Book Publishing Career Directory.* Detroit, MI: Visible Ink Press, Gale Research, Inc., 1993.

———. *Magazines Career Directory.* Detroit, MI: Visible Ink Press, Gale Research Inc., 1993.

———. *Newspapers Career Directory.* Detroit, MI: Visible Ink Press, Gale Research, Inc., 1993.

Public Relations Career Directory. Detroit, MI: Visible Ink Press, Gale Research, Inc. 1993.

Ostmann, Sharon. "Facts For Sale." *APME,* Aug. /Sept. 1992, pp. 3–5.

Pattis, S. William. *Opportunities in Magazine Publishing Careers.* Lincolnwood, IL: VGM Career Horizons, NTC Publishing Group, 1992.

"Publishers Weekly Salary Survey." *Publishers Weekly,* April 25, 1994, pp. 36–38.

"PRJ's Fourth Annual Salary Survey." *Public Relations Journal,* June 1989, pp. 17–21.

Psivack, Jane F., ed. *Careers in Information.* White Plains, NY: Knowledge Industry Publications, Inc., 1982.

Reed, Robert M. and Maxine K. *Career Opportunities in Television, Cable and Video.* 3rd ed. New York: Facts On File, 1986.

Ross, Tom and Marilyn. *The Complete Guide to Self-Publishing.* Cincinatti: Writer's Digest Books, 1985.

Russman, Linda deLaubensfels. "WICI Job & Salary Survey Results." *The Professional Communicator,* Spring 1990. pp. 18–22.

Scherman, William H. *How to Get the Right Job in Publishing.* Chicago: Contemporary Books. Inc., 1983.

Shaffer, Susan E. *Guide to Book Publishing Courses.* Princeton, NJ: Peterson's Guides, 1979.

Stone, Vernon A. "Pay Gains Top Cost Of Living." *The Professional Communicator,* Feb. 1994, pp. 68–70.

Tebbel, John. *Opportunities in Journalism.* Skokie, IL: VGM Career Horizons, National Textbook Co., 1977.

Tortorello, Nicholas J. and Eliabeth Wilhelm. "Eighth Annual Salary Survey." *Public Relations Journal,* July 1993, pp. 10–19.

U.S. Department of Labor, Bureau of Labor Statistics. *Occupational Outlook Handbook 1982–83.* Washington, DC: U.S. Government Printing Office, 1982.

U.S. Department of Labor, Bureau of Labor Statistics. *Occupational Outlook Handbook 1994–95.* Washington, DC. U.S. Government Printing Office, 1994.

Weaver, David and Wilhoit, G. Cleveland. "Who Are We? " *Quill,* Jan./Feb. 1993, pp. 45–47.

"Where the Money Is: *PW's* Second Annual Publishing Salary Survey." Survey conducted by Mary Connors, commentary by John F. Baker. *Publisher's Weekly,* Sept. 29, 1989, pp. 17–21.

Williams, Gurney III. *Writing Careers.* New York: Franklin Watts, Inc., 1976.

Wilson, Jean Gaddy. "Special Report." *Presstime,* Oct. 1986, pp. 31–37.

Wright, John W. *American Almanac of Jobs and Salaries,* 3rd ed. New York: Avon Books, 1987.

Zeller, Susan L. *Your Career in Radio and Television Broadcasting.* New York: Arco Publishing, Inc., 1982.

Zipkowitz, Fay. "Fewer Graduates But Salaries Climb." *Library Journal,* Oct. 15, 1993, pp. 30–36.

INDEX